AINSLEY GOTTO

Ian Hancock

Published in 2020 by Connor Court Publishing Pty Ltd

ISBN 9781925826555

Connor Court Publishing Pty Ltd
PO Box 7257
Redland Bay QLD 4165

sales@connorcourt.com
www.connorcourtpublishing.com.au

Printed in Australia

Front Cover Image: Gotto Papers

Front Cover Design: Maria Giordano

AINSLEY GOTTO

Ian Hancock

Connor Court Publishing

Contents

ABBREVIATIONS

AG	Ainsley Gotto
AGI	Ainsley Gotto International
APEC	Asia-Pacific Economic Cooperation
ABC	Australian Broadcasting Commission
ACT	Australian Capital Territory
ACTU	Australian Council of Trade Unions
AFR	*Australian Financial Review*
AIDC	Australian Industry Development Corporation
ANU	Australian National University
ANIB	Australian News and Information Bureau
CPD	*Commonwealth Parliamentary Debates*
DT	*Daily Telegraph*
DLP	Democratic Labor Party
DT	*Daily Telegraph*
FCEM	*Femmes Chefs d'Enterprises Mondiales*
ITV	Independent Television
ITN	Independent Television News
JGG	John Grey Gorton
LC	Lee Carroll
LWT	London Weekend Television
Mac. Rob.	Mac. Robertson Girls' High School
NAA	National Archives of Australia
NLA	National Library of Australia
NIBMAR	No Independence Before Majority African Rule
PM	Prime Minister
PM&C	Prime Minister & Cabinet
PPS	Principal Private Secretary
RAF	Royal Air Force
RAAF	Royal Australian Air Force
SMH	*Sydney Morning Herald*
UDI	Unilateral Declaration of Independence
VIP	Very Important Person
WCEI	Women Chiefs of Enterprise International

Preface

In October 2013, one month after the Abbott Government took office, I sat on a plane across the aisle from a senior Federal Liberal of my acquaintance. I remarked that the new Prime Minister seemed to have made a fair start. Smiling enigmatically, the former Howard minister replied: 'Yes, she is doing OK.' It took a second or two to appreciate that he was talking about Tony Abbott's Chief of Staff, Peta Credlin.

I was already thinking about writing a biography of Ainsley Gotto who preceded Credlin by nearly half a century. In February 1968 the new Australian Prime Minister, John Gorton, appointed Ainsley, his personal secretary, to be Principal Private Secretary (PPS) – equivalent to a chief of staff in the late 1960s – to head a work force of 13 in his personal office. Whereas Credlin oversaw a staff four times that size, of whom many were highly skilled in fields critical to governance, Ainsley's office was notably devoid of well-credentialed specialists. Whereas Credlin's bailiwick appeared to extend across the government, Ainsley's field of operations was mainly restricted to Gorton's office. There were other important differences. Credlin in 2013 was just over 40 years of age and married to the Federal Director of the Liberal Party and she had a law degree and a graduate diploma in legal practice. Ainsley in 1968 had just turned 22, was single and held a Victorian Intermediate Certificate and a typing and shorthand certificate awarded by the Canberra Technical College. Credlin had spent three years as public relations manager for Racing

Victoria in between working as a political adviser and a chief of staff to ministers and shadow ministers. Prior to her three-week employment as Gorton's personal secretary, Ainsley was a clerical assistant in the government Whips' office, seconded from the Prime Minister's Department where she worked mainly as a typist for senior officers.

Ainsley's appointment as Gorton's PPS was at the very least unusual. Previous occupants of the position in the Prime Minister's personal office had all been male public servants of mature years. Ainsley's predecessor was a former Rhodes Scholar and a First Assistant Secretary in the Prime Minister's Department. Prime Ministers and ministers had habitually employed middle-aged or older women as personal secretaries who managed diaries, typed correspondence and provided a soothing presence. Two of them, Eileen ('Lennie') Lenihan and Hazel Craig, who had both worked for Menzies, became legends around Parliament House and both in their way were redoubtable. Unlike Ainsley Gotto, however, they were not political advisers or forerunners of the modern chiefs of staff.

From the outset, senior public servants and conservative Liberal politicians considered it inappropriate that 'a mere girl' should be placed in a position where she might exercise 'power and influence'. Their criticisms multiplied as Ainsley, with Gorton's collusion, became the Prime Minister's closest confidant. She was privy to virtually all his important decisions and directly or indirectly influenced a few of them. Gorton's opponents in the Liberal Party seized on Ainsley's role and actions as a weapon to attack his leadership, much as Tony Abbott's opponents, with considerably more evidence in front of them, did in relation to Peta Credlin. Some of the charges in 1968-71 were eerily like those aired in 2013-15. In addition to exercising 'undue influence' on the Prime Minister, Ainsley was accused of being abrupt, rude and disrespectful, of addressing important men by their first names, of controlling who could see the Prime Minister and sidelining the Prime Minister's wife. There were also rumours about her having an affair with John Gorton who liked the company of women, the more so if, like Ainsley, they were attractive and upfront.

Criticisms of Ainsley came to a head in November 1969 when Dudley Erwin was dumped from the Gorton ministry. Answering a journalist's call at 2.00 am, Erwin explained his removal: 'It wiggles, it's shapely, . . . and its name is Ainsley Gotto.' Erwin admitted much later that this 'explanation' for his sacking was 'a fabrication'. Nevertheless, he had contributed to Ainsley's emergence as a celebrity. For more than two decades, newspaper headlines and magazine articles in Australia and especially in London would refer to her as 'Miss Wiggle' or 'The Wiggle'. Despite fiercely protecting her privacy, Ainsley herself became a story in Australian politics: how much influence and power did she wield and, equally important, in the eyes of tabloid journalism and the women's magazines, what was she wearing and when or if did she plan to marry?

Many young women saw Ainsley's appointment as trail blazing. Ainsley, however, refused to regard herself as a role model, let alone as a champion of women's liberation. She clashed with Germaine Greer at a dinner party in 1972, telling the author of *The Female Eunuch* that she did not understand what the Women's Liberation Movement was all about; after all, she was already 'liberated'. In 1968 there was a long way to go. It took a quarter of a century before another Prime Minister (John Howard) would appoint a woman to be his chief of staff. Just one woman, a Liberal, held a seat in the House of Representatives. Three women, all Liberals, sat in the Senate and one was a member of the outer ministry, ranked 20th out of 25 in order of seniority. There were no women within sight of the First Division of the Commonwealth Public Service and very few were to be found in the upper reaches of the universities, let alone in law and in business.

Ainsley's advice to other secretaries was simple and limited: 'work hard and get lucky.' That advice reflected her experience. Ainsley had grown up in a dysfunctional family of competing egos. Having forsaken possible careers in ballet and the theatre she had secured her position as Gorton's PPS through a combination of good fortune, excellent timing, the knowledge and understanding she acquired in the Whips' office and the part she played in Gorton's succession to the Liberal leadership after Harold Holt's death in December 1967. Her loyalty, her willingness to work horrendous hours, her innate intelligence and a ready grasp of opportunities enabled her to turn the office of PPS into one recognisable, allowing for its then narrower scope, as the position Peta Credlin occupied in 2013.

The first half of this book focuses on Ainsley's rise to prominence and on her developing role in the Gorton Government. It shows how she took over a position which was already evolving into something more substantial and gave it an even stronger political emphasis. In the process, she out-manoeuvred Lenox (later Sir Lenox) Hewitt, the Secretary of the Prime Minister's Department. Yet Ainsley never wanted to be open to inspection, her every move provoking comment. As Gorton's PPS she could be the subject of speculation but was safe from dissection because she could not and would not let herself be known. If she said anything at all to a media she distrusted, Ainsley downplayed her role in the Gorton Government. The downside of spending years understating her role or refusing to answer questions was that few people recognised that 'I did once exercise a degree of power and influence'.

Two decades after Ainsley joined the international employment agency, Drake International, in 1972, journalists and gossip writers were still asking, 'what has happened to Miss Wiggle?' The second half of this book examines what Ainsley called her 'after-life'. Part of it involved holding a torch for John Gorton, and maintaining her rage against those, principally Malcolm Fraser, who brought him down. Ainsley also pursued careers and opportunities in national and international business, in the media and interior design, in Liberal Party politics and as a 60-something chief of staff to a shadow minister and, ironically, in promoting the profile of women in Australia and abroad.

There were two striking aspects of this 'after-life'. First, Ainsley never found anything to replicate, either professionally or personally, the excitement and satisfaction she found in working for John Gorton. Indeed, several friends thought her 'after-life' unhappy, damaged further by three failed longer-term relationships which ended in hurt and acrimony. Secondly, the Gorton years proved to be a mixed blessing. They provided Ainsley with opportunities and connections and the networks she inherited or created gave her access in both hemispheres to the rich, the powerful, the titled and the very interesting. The Gorton experience developed her taste for politicking, her gift for organisation and her ability to charm and convince the leaders of politics, business, the Services and the entertainment industry (all of them male). The pitfall was that Gorton had let Ainsley assume that, for her, anything and everything was possible. Ainsley believed her 'unique qualifications' were sufficient to secure and sustain employment in every field she attempted to enter. Ainsley had an opinion for every situation and, in Gorton's company, never held back, but she lacked a disciplined mind to match her sharp tongue as well as a solid background of knowledge and experience in the areas to which she was attracted. Moreover, having sacrificed a 'normal' life by working for Gorton and, later, for Drake, Ainsley was unwilling to spend the time acquiring the skills needed for the positions she sought.

Ainsley's 'after-life' was in many ways an unfulfilled life; flying so high when so young led to expectations of her and by her which could not be met without some disengagement from that experience.

In researching and writing this book I have acquired several debts, beginning with the staff in Special Collections and in the Special Collections Reading Room of the National Library who were, as always, very efficient and immensely helpful.

I have talked about Ainsley with many people over two decades and, from 2017, formally interviewed or communicated with the following: Don Cameron, Helen Coonan, Jane Dawson, Sabina Donnelly, Tony Eggleton, Rea Francis, Glen-Marie Frost, Robin Gorton, Alan Henderson, Katie Holmes, Stephen Holt, John Howard, Tom and Chrissie Hughes, Pru Goward, Jaqui Lane, Race Mathews, Laurie Oakes, Allan Pidgeon, Bill Pollock, Chris Puplick, Ron and Mavis Unwin and Michael Yabsley.

Andrew Clark, Sebastian Hancock, Clare Hanley, Race Mathews and Sophie Torney made valuable comments on parts of the manuscript and John Nethercote, Joan Ritchie and Susan Sharpe contributed in so many ways by reading the whole book. John Nethercote also gave me the benefit of his knowledge and understanding of Australian politics and government, assisted me in securing a publisher and lent his editorial experience and skills throughout the publication process.

My greatest debt is to Ainsley herself. We first met in 1999 when she was looking for someone to write a biography of John Gorton. I worked with her on that book and she helped me with three others. Still obsessed with maintaining her privacy she nonetheless agreed that I should write her story. In addition to a multitude of conversations over the years, I formally interviewed Ainsley for a total of 34 hours in 2017 and early 2018, sometimes in circumstances of extreme difficulty because of her final illness. She talked openly to me about subjects hitherto closed totally to all save a handful of friends, and even their access was often restricted to specific times of her life. Interviewing Ainsley helped me to make the best use of my exclusive access to the 97 boxes and folios of her diaries and personal and family papers held in the National Library which formed my principal and substantial source, supplemented by other material she gave me.

This book might not have progressed very far in its present form had Ainsley lived to see the manuscript. We had many hours of sharp exchanges over the Gorton biography while Ailsa Craig, who worked with Ainsley on a four-part series published by *Woman's Day* in 1971 on her Gorton years, noted how she contested almost every sentence. We would have had a vigorous debate, but it would have been worth the tension to have spent more time with a remarkable friend who came to mean a lot to me.

The responsibility for what follows is mine alone.

Note: I prefer to retain the spelling of names etc. used in quoted sources, and to indicate where that spelling is not 'correct'. Following this practice here would mean littering the text with the Latin adverb *sic* to deal with all the instances where Ainsley's name was spelt 'Ainslie', perhaps in some cases reflecting a familiarity with an older Canberra suburb and its neighbouring Mount Ainslie. Where appropriate I have replaced 'Ainslie' with 'Ainsley'.

1

The Inheritance

Ainsley Gotto was born in Brisbane on 14 February (Valentine's Day) 1946, the second daughter of Sidney and Lesley Gotto. Her older sister, Kerrie, was born on 4 May 1944 and her younger sister, Deborah, on 25 October 1949.[1]

It is generally agreed among the family descendants that the Gotto line originated in northern Italy.[2] Some Gottos left the region to live in what became Germany and from there several Gotto families migrated to the United Kingdom as converted Protestants, arriving during the latter part of the 18th century. Ainsley's direct line can be traced to John Gotto (1787-1835), a successful braid maker in London's West End. One of his descendants founded a fashionable stationery enterprise, Parkins & Gotto, located in Oxford Street, London. Ainsley's great grandfather, Henry Gaisford Gotto, a partner in that firm, married Mary Robinson, the daughter of another and better-known Regent Street retailer. Their son, Sidney Gotto, Ainsley's grandfather, was born on 31 March 1873. In 1896, Sidney married Gladys Price Williams from the west coast of Wales. They had two children: Renfrew Gotto, who rose to the rank of Captain in the Royal Navy during the Second World War; and Mary, who married into the family of A.P. Watt, the founder of the world's first literary agency. According to an obituarist,[3] the novelist John Galsworthy drew upon his experience of sitting at the Watt table for Sunday lunches when drafting the memorable opening sentence of *The Man of Property*, the first book of the *Forsyte Saga*: 'Those privileged to be present at a family festival of the Forsytes have seen that charming and instructive sight — an upper middle-class family in full plumage.'

Sidney Gotto, like one or two of the rakish, albeit fictional, Forsytes, rebelled against middle-class respectability. He abandoned Gladys and his two small children to live with Jessie Geddes, the Aberdeen-born daughter of a Scottish iron worker. Sidney's mother expressed disapproval by banishing her son to the 'colonies' as a 'remittance man'. A 'Mr. and Mrs. S. Gotto' (Sidney and Jessie) sailed from London on 17 February 1909 on board RMS *Omrah*. Arriving at Fremantle on 25 March, they were listed as transit passengers bound for Melbourne. In the following months, Sidney Gotto received several notices in the Melbourne press. Blessed with a fine singing voice, he reportedly sang two solo tenors at a fruit and vegetable auction held at Frankston at the end of April. Late in July he had a small part in the musical comedy, *Havana*, playing at Her Majesty's Theatre in Exhibition Street, Melbourne. A critic suggested that, as Don Alfonso, Sidney sounded more London than Cuban, while another critic wrote that Sidney and another member of the cast 'were distinctive after their own fashion'.

A birth certificate records that on 27 September 1909 a boy named 'Sidney Gotto' was born in Paddington, NSW.[4] His parents were registered as Sidney Gotto, theatrical actor aged 35 (he was 36), and the 24-year old Jessie Annie Geddes (she was 25). According to the certificate, Sidney and Jessie were married in London on 12 June 1907. Yet, as Sidney and Gladys never divorced, Sidney could not legally have remarried until after Gladys died in 1927. If in 1907 he had gone through a form of marriage, Ainsley's grandfather was a bigamist and, on any reckoning, her father was born illegitimate. Ainsley's grandfather bore false witness on at least one other count. He declared on his son's birth certificate that he had no other issue, either living or deceased. Renfrew, the 'disowned' son, regarded his father's actions as 'beneath contempt' and regarded him as a 'non-person'.[5]

Ainsley's paternal grandfather had a habit of telling stories that enhanced his appeal in the colonies. The Australian end of the family believed he had attended Harrow School in England. If true, he was the right age to have been a contemporary of Winston Churchill. The Harrow School register, which noted the enrolment of six Gottos, did not record a Sidney Gotto among them. Sidney told his Australian family that as a young man he gave recitals in London's concert halls but there is no available record to verify this claim. Nor is there anything to substantiate his assertion that he left England with the D'Oyly Carte Company as the principal understudy for George Goldsmith who had roles in Gilbert and Sullivan operas. Oddly enough, Sidney did not boast of once being a gold and silver assayer, his occupation listed on Renfrew's birth certificate. If true, he would have added to his standing in the colonies.

It is not known why Sidney and Jessie went to Sydney for the birth of their son. After all, the theatrical actor had found employment as a clerk in the Chief Secretary's Department of the Victorian State Government, possibly assisted in obtaining this position through his Masonic connections. Sidney's duties included being secretary of a committee which managed a training ship, *John Murray*, named after the then State Premier. The project was designed to prepare juvenile offenders for the navy and the merchant service but fewer than one boy in five completed his training and joined other ships. *John Murray* became a financial embarrassment while allegations of 'unnatural practices' brought an odium on the ship which a Police Magistrate's inquiry in 1911 and a royal commission in 1915 were unable to dispel. At least, the Victorian Public Service Commissioner completely exonerated Gotto and the committee members of neglect of duty or of condoning fraudulent practices.

The relationship between Sidney and Jessie did not survive, although they did later have a daughter, Jean. Leaving the Victorian Public Service, Sidney managed a ginger-processing factory in Carlton and then became a travelling salesman selling coke to foundries. He was a member of the Victorian Operatic Society and for decades sang with the choir of St Paul's Church of England Cathedral in Melbourne. After Gladys died in 1927 Sidney married Charlotte Millicent Ryan. They lived together in Hampton and Sidney spent much of his spare time fishing on the nearby Port Phillip Bay. Charlotte had a daughter, and an adopted son, Phillip; he took the Gotto surname. Phillip enlisted in the Royal Australian Air Force (RAAF) in the Second World War, trained as a navigator and served in Bomber Command of the Royal Air Force (RAF). He was killed along with the entire crew in March 1944 when his Lancaster was shot down after a raid on Stuttgart. Sidney and Charlotte eventually moved to the outer Melbourne suburb of Ferntree Gully. Ainsley remembered occasional visits to her grandfather's house in the late 1950s when her family lived in Melbourne. She had grown up believing him to be 'an Edwardian rake and a remittance man'. Sidney died in 1964.[6]

His Australian-born son inherited two of his father's interests and abilities: a fine singing voice and a love of the theatre. Both came to the fore when Sid was about 30 years of age. In Melbourne, he attended Toorak Higher Elementary School which was renamed Toorak Central by the time Ainsley was enrolled there. Sid then went to Scotch College where he obtained his Intermediate in 1925, having passed seven subjects but failing in French and Latin. On leaving school, he took a multitude of jobs, some in Melbourne and others in Sydney. He was in turn a storekeeper, accounting clerk, reformatory instructor, hotel manager, dry cleaner, factory department manager and an assistant company secretary. Living in Hampton, Sid and his sister, Jean, were active in the mid-1930s with the Younger Set of the Women's Auxiliary Hospital. Sid married and divorced within a short time. An entry in the Melbourne *Argus* for 21 July 1939 reported that Lauris Estelle Gotto, aged 24, of Mills Street, Hampton, had obtained a divorce on grounds of desertion from 'Sydney Gotto', a dry cleaner aged 29, formerly of Grenville Street, Hampton. The decree was made absolute on 20 January 1940. By then, Sid was living in Sydney where he had joined the Independent Theatre and was studying at the Conservatorium of Music. The Theatre had a special night to celebrate its tenth anniversary, during which 'Mr Sidney Gotto' sang 'negro spirituals'.[7]

Sid enlisted in the RAAF on 24 August 1940. He was almost 31 years of age and stood at 162 cm or slightly over 5'3" tall. He declared he was not married, which was true; Sid was not required to acknowledge a previous marriage. On his application form, where Sid listed all his activities in civilian employment, an official remarked that the applicant's multitude of jobs suggested he had not established himself in employment. Sid described himself in his application as an 'average' player of cricket, tennis, squash and golf while highlighting his considerable experience in amateur theatre and in singing. Assigned to the Equipment Branch, Sid was regularly promoted, reaching the rank of Sergeant in January 1942. He was in Townsville in the following July when the Japanese bombed the wharves. Sid helped to organise the operation to fight the fires and to protect vital supplies destined for New Guinea. After Townsville, he served in New Guinea in 1942-3 and was posted to the island of Morotai of the then Dutch East Indies where the Allies were constructing a major base. He was present during the intermittent fighting against an under-manned Japanese force, and for the 'Morotai Mutiny' when senior RAAF fighter pilots tendered their resignations because of what they considered were high losses sustained in militarily unjustifiable operations. Sid remained on Morotai until the end of the War in the Pacific.

He had been commissioned in September 1942. A report recommending his appointment assessed his conduct as 'very good'. As a storekeeper, he was marked 'Superior' in trade, and 'Superior' as a supervisor and administrator. In 1945 another report described Sid as industrious and said he had shown great enthusiasm in supervising his section and had a good bearing as an officer. At the end of the War, when Sid applied for a permanent commission, the interviewing officer recommended his appointment, with qualifications. The officer thought Gotto would fit in and get along with others 'within limits', and considered that, though 'intense and highly strung', he had a well-balanced personality. On a general note, the report reads: 'unimpressive appearance but displays an energetic personality – very keen, conscientious Intelligent [*sic*].' In 1946, Sid Gotto was a commissioned officer in the RAAF with the rank of Flight Lieutenant.[8]

By that time, he was married with two children. Early in 1942 Sergeant Gotto had met Lesley Eve Webster in Brisbane, probably at a Mess function. Born in Sydney on 12 February 1923, Lesley had just turned 19 years of age.

Like the Gottos, the male line of the Websters could claim, and sometimes boasted of possessing, a respectable pedigree. The family had links to Derbyshire, England, where they owned a grand house built in 1685 and which was later altered in the mid-18th century when it was known as 'The Mansion'. Ainsley's maternal great grandfather – Thomas Brown Webster – was born in Leicestershire and arrived in Australia in 1855 and became a mining manager in the Maldon District of Victoria. In 1874 he stood for the Victorian Legislative Assembly but was beaten by James Service, a future Premier. A Mason, he fathered three daughters and six sons, one of whom was Lesley's grandfather who went to live in Charters Towers. Lesley's father – Thomas or Tom Webster – was born in Charters Towers in 1891 and completed his schooling at Townsville Grammar School. Tom began his working life as a messenger at Charters Towers.[9] He rose to the position of Local Government Clerk by the time he enlisted in the AIF in June 1916, having previously served for four years in the Militia. After attending an officer training school at Duntroon, he was promoted to Acting Sergeant and, in May 1917, embarked at Sydney for the Western Front as Second Lieutenant Webster with the 25th Reinforcements, 13th Battalion. In France, he took a course of instruction in Signals and in March 1918 'Passed with Distinction' in achieving his Special Instructor's Certificate. Tom's older brother, Robert, was killed at Pozières in August 1916.

Returning to Australia, Tom resumed his civilian occupation

and, moving up the scale, was appointed Town Clerk of the Lane Cove Municipal Council on Sydney's Lower North Shore. In his other life Tom Webster was an unsuccessful gambler. Like so many before and after him, he sought to recoup his losses by robbing his employer. He stole £4230 worth of the Council's Commonwealth Treasury Bonds over a period of three months at the end of 1928.[10] When arrested, he said: 'I lost it all at the races. I was hoping for a win in order to restore it.' Initially bailed after posting a personal bond of £500 and a further surety of £500, he entered a guilty plea when appearing before Judge Curlewis at the Darlinghurst Quarter Sessions in February 1929. The Court heard he was a man of good character and that his superior officers in France thought highly of him, promoting him to adjutant of the battalion. Sentencing Webster to one year and 11 months in jail, His Honour used the case to urge supporters of the racing industry to attend court and observe the tears and misery caused when reputations were shattered by gambling.[11] The case was widely reported throughout Australia.

Ainsley never met her maternal grandfather but, from the stories she heard and the photos she saw, concluded he was 'very good looking, charming, feckless and a scallywag'. Clearly, Tom Webster had prospects, helped by his father possessing the means to send him to a good private school. According to family legend, one of the Websters was sufficiently well-off to buy and run a string of race horses in the United Kingdom. His story did not end well. When roaring drunk, this Webster rode one of his horses up the stairs of a country house, and then rode it down again, breaking his neck in a fall. It is not yet clear where and how Tom Webster's story ended. His name appeared in family notices announcing the engagement and marriage of his only daughter to Sid Gotto.

His long-suffering wife finally 'kicked him out', probably around the time Ainsley was in her late teens.[12] Tom Webster's name was not included in the obituary notices Ainsley posted after Lesley's death in 2017.

Lesley was identified in the obituary as the daughter of 'Violet Cecilia Webster (nee Ashworth)'.[13] Violet grew up on a farm outside Roma, Queensland, where she had a hard life. There was little money in the family, and her father absconded when she was young. But there were horses to ride. Violet's own mother, at the age of 90, rode side-saddle at the local show, and Violet always rode a pony to school. Ainsley never heard her grandmother complain about anything. She told funny stories, was a brilliant cook and, freed of her husband, grew vegetables, kept chooks and sold men's shirts and women's clothes in Brisbane. Ainsley regarded 'Nan' as 'one of the most beautiful women I've ever met'.[14]

She described her own mother as largely self-educated. Lesley had in fact attended the Randwick School of Domestic Science, a contributing factor in her appointment to run a cooking show on television in Melbourne at the end of the 1950s. After her family, which included her brother Robert, moved from Sydney to Annerley, a suburb of Brisbane, in the late 1930s, Lesley trained on the piano at Peter Brier's classical musical school. In 1938, she acquired formal, high-level qualifications through the Royal College of Music in London. In December 1940, Brier's better students performed a two-hour piano recital and Lesley's contribution, along with others, was described as 'outstanding'.[15] In 1941-2, Lesley was often mentioned or photographed in the Brisbane press when working for charities or playing the piano.

The Gotto-Webster engagement is intriguing for what Sid was prepared to acknowledge about his past. The engagement was first reported by the Brisbane *Truth* on 12 April 1942. According to a later notice published in the Brisbane *Sunday Mail* of 19 April, Sid was 'the second son of Mr and Mrs Sidney Gotto (Sandringham, Victoria). Sgt. Gotto has two brothers who also are on active service – one is a commander in the R.A.N. and the other is in the R.A.A.F.' Just what Sid told his fiancée and his prospective in-laws is unknown, so whether he chose the path of simplicity or respectability, or both, remains unclear. He was, certainly, the second son of Mr Sidney Gotto, but his mother was Jessie Geddes; the Mrs Gotto of Sandringham was his stepmother. Unlike his father, Sid was at least prepared to acknowledge Renfrew's existence, though it is unlikely that he was being 'progressive' in referring to Renfrew as a brother and not a half-brother. It is possible that it was a newspaper error to refer to Renfrew as a commander in the Royal Australian Navy instead of the Royal Navy.

Sid Gotto and Lesley Webster were married at St Andrew's Presbyterian Church, Brisbane, just two weeks after the *Truth* reported their engagement. Oscar Wilde's Lady Bracknell may have advised against long engagements because they gave couples 'the opportunity of finding out each other's character before marriage'. In this case, closer knowledge and understanding might have forestalled what Ainsley called a 'mis-marriage'. What the *Truth* of 12 April 1942 had innocently referred to as a 'wartime romance' did not advance much beyond that.

The three daughters would pay a price for growing up in a family where the parents drifted apart from each other and failed to stay close to their offspring. The daughters did, however, inherit one lasting benefit of the Gotto-Webster union – they all, in their different ways, developed a love of the arts. Ainsley, for example, might well have taken this inheritance further and had a career in ballet or the theatre. Aware of what she had inherited from both her parents, Ainsley was always more conscious of being a Gotto than a Webster, despite having more of a relationship with her mother than her father and adoring her 'Nan'. She also retained an attachment to her mother's cousin, a connection which introduced her to the Webster-Ashworth history[16] and which may have helped her get a better job in the Commonwealth Public Service. On the Gotto side, Ainsley never seriously connected with her mysterious paternal grandfather, and was estranged from her father between the mid-1960s and the late-1980s. Perhaps it was a case of the Gotto name standing out and having clear and desirable European associations. Perhaps it was also a matter of the Gotto 'clan' in England embracing Ainsley when she became 'a name'. Twice in her life she seriously contemplated accepting a man's surname and, on the second occasion, did so, but not for long. For most of her life and for most of those who knew her, or knew of her, she was always 'Ainsley Gotto'.

---

[1]   A family tree and other documents attest to the birth and death of an unnamed male child at an undeclared place and date. Ainsley grew up not knowing anything about him.

[2]   Two English Gottos compiled a family tree which they completed in December 1972, with Ainsley assisting from the Australian end. They consulted Somerset House, the Public Record Office, the Society of Genealogists, parish registers, wills, a family tree drawn up by Captain Renfrew Gotto RN and personal recollections. They were unable to trace substantial results before 1837. Gotto Papers, MS Acc07/127, Box 4. All the Gotto Papers quoted in this book are held in the National Library of Australia (NLA).

[3]   *The Times* (London), 14 February 2014.

[4]   For the purposes of this book 'Sidney' will refer to the father (Ainsley's grandfather) and 'Sid' to the son (Ainsley's father).

[5]   For Renfrew Gotto, see Brian Gotto, *Renfrew: A Short Biography of Captain Renfrew Gotto CBE DSO*, privately published, Haslingfield, 2009. p. 2.

[6]   The above three paragraphs draw upon a not always reliable source, Frank Purcell, *The Prison on the Bay: The Story of the Victorian Training Ship John Murray*, Frank Purcell, Frankston, 1997, esp. pp. 19 and 22, and on an interview with Ainsley Gotto (AG): 7 February 2017.

[7]   *Sydney Morning Herald (SMH)*, 25 June 1940.

[8]   National Archives of Australia (NAA): A12572, R/2162/P.

[9]   For the Webster and Ashworth family histories, see Gotto Papers, MS Acc15.206, Box 8.

[10]   According to the Reserve Bank pre-decimal inflation calculator, that sum would be the equivalent of $342,495 in 2018. The average annual pay of an Australian male worker in 1928 was about £180.

[11]   *Evening News* (Sydney), 12 December 1928 and 9 February 1929.

[12]   Interview: AG, 19 November 2017.

[13]   *Canberra Times* and *SMH*, 9-10 October 2017. The notice had to be re-issued because in the first version Lesley was said to be the mother of 'Ainsley Grotto'.

[14]   Interview: AG, 9 February 2017.

[15]   *Courier-Mail* (Brisbane), 12 December 1940. A young Ron Grainer was the star performer. He later achieved fame by composing music for film and television in the UK, including the theme music for *Doctor Who*.

[16]   Leslie Moore, *Not Like Ghosts at Cockrow: An Australian Family Story 1849-1998*, privately published, Canberra, 1998.

2

'a highly competent stenographer and secretary'

Ainsley's early years in Brisbane were comfortable and generally happy. Sid had charge of RAAF stores in Cannon Hill and the family lived on the base where Ainsley first attended school. Childhood photographs include one of her sitting with other children but seemingly separate and with a determined look on her face. There is also a very promising school report of Ainsley's record in Grade II. In six of the eight assessed subjects she received a maximum of ten marks, and nine each in Reading and Arithmetic. Evidently there was a question of whether she was too young to go up a Grade. The teacher sent a note to her mother: 'Can you tell me, Mrs Gotto, how we are going to hold back for twelve months a little girl who gets this result?'[1]

In the short term, Ainsley's educational future was affected not by considerations of age and ability, but by her father's career. Promoted Squadron Leader in 1950, Sid was assigned to the Suez Canal Zone as equipment staff officer for the RAF in the Middle East. In the following year he was posted to London for three years. The family joined him in England and lived in Wallington, Surrey, where Kerrie and Ainsley went to school. Living so close to Europe meant that Lesley and her daughters could travel around the Continent. There are photographs of them in Venice and there is one in England of a happy Lesley sitting next to 'Johnnie' Johnson, the RAF fighter pilot credited with 34 individual victories during the Second World War. Lesley in fact came into her own in England. She took a position with BBC television to create the live program, the very popular *Saturday Night Out* which had a six-year run. Lesley liked having a career and a life outside of the family home and she threw herself into television, the theatre and, more generally, into the arts. Ainsley became very aware later in her life that her mother, like her father, was largely absent when she was growing up.[2]

The Gottos lived in a big old house opposite the school, and Sid and the girls played cricket and other games in the garden. School became a problem for Kerrie and Ainsley because they were considered 'strange, untouchable colonials'. Their spoken English was nothing like that of the other children. Ainsley recalled that 'we played rough. If other children hit us, we hit back.' They were told that the 'good and nourishing' hot meals they were required to eat at lunch time had to be finished before leaving the table. Ainsley came from a household where both parents were good cooks and she could not abide liver, brussel sprouts and treacle pudding and had a recurring battle with authority as she sometimes sat unmoved in front of her unfinished plate. She and Kerrie 'were both lonely and unhappy for a long time at school'.[3]

Lesley introduced her second daughter to what, for the next seven years, promised to be Ainsley's own career. Her mother decided it would assist her daughters' deportment if they learnt ballet. Inadvertently, she provided Ainsley with the means to compete successfully with Kerrie. In everything else – appearance, singing, music, acting – Ainsley believed or was told that her sister was superior. Ainsley received two certificates from the Royal Academy of Dancing, of which the Queen was Patron and Miss Margot Fonteyn was President. In November 1954 she was awarded a Pass Plus, the second bottom of five Pass grades in Grade One. In December 1955 she completed Grade Two and was awarded Honours, the highest possible grade out of five. The one critical comment of the nine-year old was that she lacked spring in elevation and was advised to make better use of her spine. In the same year Ainsley was examined twice by the Associated Board of the Royal Schools of Music. In December she achieved a Pass in Grade II (Elementary) and was variously judged to be quite fluent, occasionally unsteady and hesitant but generally moving comfortably with 'a pleasant tone and touch' and 'a bright feeling'.

Sid was receiving his own good reports from the RAF which was anxious to keep him. The RAAF, however, posted him, now a Wing Commander, to Melbourne in 1956 as Director of Movements. He was later appointed Director of Equipment Distribution and, later still, was posted to the Staff College at Point Cook. The family moved with him at the end of 1956, and the Gottos took up residence in the respectable suburb of East Malvern. Ainsley was enrolled at the Central School in Lloyd Street and joined Form 1D in 1957. Ainsley received three successive grades of 'Excellent' for conduct, her results were considered 'very pleasing' and she was described as a 'keen, co-operative pupil and a very active vice-captain of the form'. A report at the end of the year recorded that Ainsley's consistently keen approach to her studies 'has made her an outstanding member of the form'. In her final test, she bettered the class average in all subjects. There was a slight dip in the first half of 1958; her work was 'marred by too much talking and inattention in class. Her results are good but she is capable of better work.' There had been a marked improvement by the end of that year. A male teacher noted how Ainsley, now enrolled from mid-year at Toorak Central School, Sid's former school, had made 'a quick adjustment' and had completed 'some pleasing work' in all subjects other than Arithmetic. Her conduct was always 'of a high standard'.

The central schools in Melbourne, selective academically, provided primary and secondary education to Year 8, and were designated as 'feeders' for the three selective-entry high schools: Mac. Robertson Girls' High School (Mac. Rob.), Melbourne High School for boys and University High School which was co-educational. These schools were described as 'the flagships of public secondary education in Victoria'. They mainly drew their students from the middle class eastern and south-eastern suburbs of Melbourne. Girls needed a principal's recommendation to enter Mac. Rob., and the general assumption was that the recommendation would focus on a student's academic ability or potential.[4] Miss Barrett, the Principal of Mac. Rob., added another requirement. She was a stickler for the girls being 'ladylike', requiring hats and gloves to be worn on public transport.

Kerrie was already enrolled at Mac. Rob. when her sister joined her in 1959. Ainsley's form teacher in IIID noted in first term that she was 'a pleasant, helpful and co-operative member of the form' and 'works consistently and well'. The same teacher noted how a prolonged absence affected her marks in the following Term but, with continued effort, expected Ainsley to recover her good marks. In Third Term the form teacher observed: 'We feel that Ainsley is capable of greater effort in her schoolwork, and that her rather disappointing results show that her schoolwork is not her first interest.' Ainsley's record improved in her second year at Mac. Rob. Like her father when he attended Scotch College, she passed her Intermediate Certificate with seven subjects. Whereas he failed in languages, she missed out in maths and science. The form teacher was generally pleased: Ainsley had completed a successful year and 'has shown keen interest in all school activities, and has been an excellent form representative on the School Council'.

Schoolwork was certainly not Ainsley's 'first interest'. On four days after classes she took the tram from Albert Park into the City to attend lessons at the Borovansky Ballet School in Elizabeth Street. Edouard and Xenia Borovansky had established their Melbourne Academy of Russian Ballet to teach 'Classical and Character Dancing, Mime and Make Up'. 'Madame Boro', as Xenia was known, came from a Russian aristocratic family who had fled their homeland before the October Revolution. While her Czech husband was the producer and entrepreneur of the Australian Ballet Company, Madame Boro schooled and formed the dancers of his corps in the early years and then trained the soloists and principals who came through the academy under her direction. She was 'a hard taskmaster' and a formidable figure who kept telling her pupils that ballet was not about playing; work hard until you are exhausted and then work harder. Ainsley never returned home before 9.00 pm, often thoroughly drained, but Madame Boro made ballet and movement 'come alive for me'. To an extent, Ainsley, as a young teenager, looked upon ballet as 'a means of escape' although she remained unsure from what she was escaping. Ballet also promised so much. Madame Boro told Lesley that her daughter had the potential to be a *prima ballerina*, even a *prima ballerina assoluta*.[5] Decades later one of the first things to notice on meeting Ainsley was her excellent posture, her very straight back, graceful movements and flexibility.

Soon after the family settled in Melbourne, Lesley approached Channel Nine with the idea of resuming her career in television. The response was enthusiastic. Lesley was invited to present *Fun with Food*, a program for housewives around the middle of the day. As 'Lesley Webster', she was also the creator, script writer, co-producer and compere for a weekly Channel Nine women's program and appeared with other hosts who were established or rising stars such as Eric Pearce, Evie Hayes, Frank Thring and Bert Newton. Lesley became such a popular presenter that Channel Nine decided to show off her two older children to Melbourne's housewives. Kerrie and Ainsley were invited to appear live before a studio audience early in 1960. Kerrie sang, and Ainsley danced. Unfortunately, Ainsley slipped doing the first pirouette and fell flat on her face. 'I picked myself up and went on dancing. It seemed the only thing I could do.'[6] Lesley found other work for her two older daughters who both related well to the camera. Kerrie and Ainsley were soon appearing in Melbourne newspapers advertising clothing for young teenage girls.

Towards the end of 1960, when Ainsley was completing the Intermediate Certificate year, her father received what would be his final posting in the RAAF. He was transferred to Canberra where he would represent the Air Member for the supply of equipment. The family stayed behind for the completion of the school year and, after years of living in RAAF and rental accommodation, the Gottos took a mortgage on a house in Getting Crescent, Campbell, a better suburb situated near the War Memorial.

Ainsley would have been happy staying at Mac. Rob. Although she considered herself 'terribly shy' and felt overwhelmed growing up between 'two strong sisters', Ainsley had made some friends at school. She lost touch with them after leaving Melbourne though two made contact when they heard she was working for the Prime Minister. Ainsley threw herself into school sports and played basketball and hurdled 'reasonably well'. While Kerrie took up hockey, Ainsley did not; injury could have affected her career in ballet. Both girls proved to be good at debating. Ainsley would almost certainly have matriculated had she stayed at Mac. Rob. and would probably have gone to university. If she had taken that route, she may have stopped doing ballet. The move to Canberra certainly had that effect. In 1971 Ainsley spoke of having 'a marvellous teacher' in Canberra who had danced in Europe; in 2017 she recalled feeling more advanced than the only available teacher, leaving her no opportunity to learn something new. Nonetheless, Ainsley continued to practise and, in April 1963, she and her much older male partner came first in the National Eisteddfod in the *Pas de Deux*. In her view, this feat was not a major triumph: 'we were competing against children.'[7]

The plan in Canberra was for Ainsley to go to high school. Under the system then operating in the Australian Capital Territory (ACT), it took five years of secondary school to matriculate and not six as in Victoria. Either Ainsley had to undertake another fourth year or take courses in the final year she had never studied or had proved too difficult for her at Mac. Rob. She could return to Melbourne and board with family friends, an option that did not appeal to Ainsley or her parents. While Ainsley was still thinking of a career in ballet, her father entered a caveat. Suppose she experienced a career-ending injury, what job qualifications would she have? It was a prescient intervention. Ainsley had inherited the weak bone structure of other Gottos; she broke an ankle on six occasions in her lifetime. With her parents' support, she enrolled in a secretarial course at the Canberra Technical College. Ainsley graduated at the end of 1961, finishing top in typing, gaining a high pass in English and achieving good results in shorthand and office practice.

One day in the summer of 1961-2 the 15-year old joined friends at a watering hole just out of Canberra. George Lazenby, a future 'James Bond', was among them. Sitting by herself and watching the others at sport, Ainsley decided she wanted 'to make a difference'. She was not thinking about having her name in lights, but was determined to make a mark, even if the way ahead was not at all clear. At best, she knew that leaving Melbourne represented a fork in the road; the path towards matriculation, university and Madame Boro appeared to be closed.[8]

By now, Ainsley was conscious of being on her own in a family whose members went their separate ways. Her parents had little time for each other, and not enough time for their daughters, though Lesley did try. For much of her early life Ainsley had followed Kerrie's lead. As a teenager she became aware of dissimilarities. The pair drew apart and Ainsley never again felt comfortable with her older sister. Her younger sister seemed very different, albeit that the nature and extent of the difference did not become fully apparent until after 'Debs' or 'Debbie' completed her secondary education. Ainsley had entered puberty without any maternal or sisterly guidance but had learnt what to expect and how to deal with it by reading books and articles. The camera continued to like her, as evidenced in the photo which appeared in the *Canberra Times* on 1 September 1962 with Ainsley framed by prunus blooms in Wakefield Gardens, Ainslie. She could also ask awkward questions. Ainsley was confirmed at St John the Baptist Church in Canberra on 24 November 1962 by Bishop Clements of the Church of England in the Diocese of Canberra-Goulburn. She was older than most members of her confirmation class, and much bolder. The classes Ainsley attended were not held to answer searching questions about the Virgin Birth, the Resurrection or the Trinity. Told not to raise questions, she began to have doubts and would soon abandon her inherited faith.[9]

After leaving Technical College, Ainsley applied for jobs in business and received several offers, all of which were withdrawn when potential employers realised how young she was. Instead, at aged 15, she joined the Department of Immigration to work in the typing pool, 'which I loathed'. Ainsley left the Department after about six months to take a position as private secretary to the manager of a furniture removals and storage company that had just started operations in Canberra. She worked in the light industrial suburb of Fyshwick, where most of the employees were 'pretty rough' but they 'put up with me'. The manager clearly approved. In a reference, he explained that, because he was frequently working outside Canberra, Ainsley 'virtually ran the office for the company including the accounting and the control of staff'. Further, 'she has shown her potential to develop into a sound stenographer/secretary', adding that 'Miss Gotto is pleasant in appearance and has always been found to be completely trustworthy'.

Ainsley stayed with the company for six months, after which she secured a position as private secretary to K. Le Rossignol, Director of the Trade Commissioner Service in the Department of

Trade. She enjoyed the work 'enormously' and was exceptionally happy there; he was 'a very civilised man'. In February 1965, Le Rossignol, then Trade Commissioner-Designate, Kuala Lumpur, wrote a *To Whom It May Concern* reference. Pointing out that Ainsley had worked for him from November 1962 to February 1964, he described her as 'a highly competent stenographer and secretary', 'diligent, discreet, very intelligent, trustworthy, and co-operative'. Ainsley had 'displayed an unusually high degree of responsibility and flair for managing affairs, dealing without direction with a multitude of minor matters, and keeping me informed of all developments of consequence wherever I happened to be.' He 'would welcome her assistance again in this capacity.' Le Rossignol had observed the qualities in Ainsley which would later appeal to John Gorton, and which marked her out as someone who would never be satisfied with just performing 'normal' secretarial tasks.[10]

There was a momentary interruption in her progression. The re-named Department of Trade and Industry closed the offices it occupied in Canberra City and placed the Department's secretarial staff in huts in the suburb of Barton on the south side of Lake Burley Griffin. Ainsley was assigned to a typing pool where some 15-20 'girls' were brow-beaten by two older women managers. One of the young typists remembers Ainsley's first day. She arrived wearing a pillbox hat (no one else wore a hat) and looked 'very trim' and 'the height of sophistication' as she smoked Black Russian cigarettes. Ainsley sat in the front of the pool. The girl sitting behind her could see she did not want to be there, noting she did not join the other typists at tea breaks.[11]

Although Ainsley could not recall exactly when she came to the typing pool, she has a clear recollection of her departure date. It coincided with the arrival of the Beatles in Australia in June 1964. She left the pool to join the Prime Minister's Department and work for a Senior Policy Officer, Don Munro, a First Assistant Secretary in charge of the Economic Division. Ainsley believes that Canberra's small and interconnected world of the mid-1960s worked to her advantage. Les Moore, a senior official in the Prime Minister's Department and Menzies' former Private Secretary (1960-2), was the husband of Lesley's cousin, Dorothy Moore. Ainsley believed that Moore was probably responsible for getting her into a position which offered more than routine work. Within a few days she was reading and typing papers which were then forwarded to the Prime Minister and to Cabinet.

Ainsley rapidly acquired a social life. Canberra, with a population of 60,000 in 1960 and 96,000 by 1966, had several circles accessible to a teenage daughter of a senior RAAF officer. Ainsley's files include a clipping from the *Canberra Times* of 10 January 1962 containing the names and photos of Canberra students who had obtained top passes in the recent Leaving Certificate examinations. Alongside the photo of ('Tira') Vokariat Charuvastra, a student from Thailand, Ainsley had written 'AG's 1st boyfriend'.[12] She made friends with the daughters of several diplomats and was frequently invited to receptions at embassies in Canberra. She attended a reception at the Pakistan High Commission for Pakistan Day in March 1963, went to the Indian High Commission for cocktails in July in 1964 and in May of the following year was invited to the 21st birthday of the daughter of the Minister [ambassador] of Peru.

On one occasion, Ainsley was invited to a New Year's Eve

party at the Embassy of The Philippines. She protested when her mother said she had to be home by 10.00 pm. Her father smacked her hard across the face, telling her that she should not talk to her mother like that. Sid was not normally violent, but he could be, and the blow left Ainsley severely bruised. She rang the Embassy to present her apologies. The Ambassador's two daughters told her to come anyway, and they spent time with make-up for her to look presentable. Ainsley could not recall what time she got home that night, but it was later than the stipulated hour.[13]

In 1963 Kerrie, who had passed her Leaving Certificate in 1961, married John Smith, an English-born geologist. Ainsley remained convinced that Kerrie's early marriage released her from an unhappy home. She thought, very briefly, of taking the same path. During 1963 Ainsley became attached to an officer in Trade who was about ten years older than herself. He proposed they marry in Lima, Peru, where he was stationed, but Ainsley's parents had no intention of giving their approval, considering her far too young at 17. Sid, who probably disliked him, simply did not reply to his letter seeking permission to marry. While Ainsley was habitually slow in responding to letters, even when in full romantic mode, the fact that by November 1964 Ainsley had not replied to eight letters should have told her erstwhile lover that interest was waning.[14]

Ainsley as a teenager dreaded the thought of marriage, of sitting at home as a housewife and mother. When Kerrie was about to marry, friends visiting the Gotto household in Campbell asked Ainsley if she had a boyfriend. The answer was 'No' and, further, she was not looking for one. The reaction was one of 'shock, horror – but don't you want to get married and have children?'.

The answer to that question was even firmer: 'No!'[15] Perhaps there was an underlying qualification in the form of 'not yet'. Certainly, the jobs Ainsley took with John Gorton and then with Drake International extended any 'not yet' for another decade.

In 1965, Ainsley formed a relationship with another, even older, man. Kerrie's friend, Basil Dean, was a sculptor and an artist who lived in Sydney and was altogether more exciting. His one surviving letter explains some of the attraction. Dated 4 June 1965 and headed, 'Darling', it began: 'Come and join me for God's sake – I am tired of you buzzing around that cold hole of a place – doing what you don't really want to do anyway.' Dean confessed his own desire for a dramatic change. He loved and needed her but, if he could not have her, then he must re-direct his life. He suggested that Ainsley should take 'a long contemplative look'. If she was doing what she wanted, she should continue to do it. He refused, however, to believe that she wished to remain in the Public Service and, if he was right, Dean was going to pluck her out it, if only to save her from self-destruction. 'Our relationship has been studded with stupidity and doubts – out of this interminable struggle one word is the saviour – the truth.' His truth was that he loved her, he was alone out of choice but wanted to move on, and with 'that little girl with the big temper & the deplorable lack of understanding'.

The offer was tempting, and the relationship up to late 1967 was not casual. In between seeing Dean and receiving letters from Peru, Ainsley met John Hartley not long before he graduated from the Royal Military College, Duntroon, in December 1965. They were always likely to meet; Hartley's mother and Lesley Gotto were good friends. Hartley invited Ainsley to attend the graduation ceremony after which the young officer went to South Vietnam where he commanded a platoon in 5 Royal Australian Regiment (RAR). Ainsley recognised that he was 'a high-flyer' and he saw her as 'a rather gifted girl'. Both accepted that their relationship was what he called 'a brief interlude in life'. They corresponded during 1966 but, as Ainsley saw it, 'I let him go'.[16]

Four of the five Gottos of Getting Crescent did have one common interest and activity: the theatre. Sid returned to the boards, taking parts where he could display feelings he declined to show his family. He also put in many hours helping with the productions of the Canberra Repertory Society. Lesley worked in administration and Kerrie and Ainsley played prominent parts in several plays. It was an opportune time to engage with the theatre in Canberra. It was the era of Peter Batey, and when Alan Harvey and Ric Throssell, the son of a VC winner in the First World War and of Katharine Susannah Prichard, were deeply involved.[17] Ainsley's credits included *A School for Scandal*, *Charley's Aunt* and *The Moon is Blue*. Some of the contacts she made became personal friends who provided emotional support during the Gorton years. Grant MacIntyre, who acted with Ainsley in *Charley's Aunt*, was one who stood up for her. An officer with the Department of Immigration and a friend of Harold and Zara Holt, MacIntyre was a noted Canberra figure on several counts, one of which was the flamboyant and unusual décor of his house in the suburb of Deakin.

Ainsley was interviewed by the *Australian* on 4 May 1965 during rehearsals for *The Moon is Blue*. She was playing Patty O'Neill, aged 21, who is 'picked up' or 'picks up' on the top of the Empire State Building, and whom Ainsley described as 'a naïve and innocent girl who cannot understand the implications of any of the situations she becomes involved in'. Ainsley confessed that it was 'very hard to maintain a wide-eyed, innocent stare when you can hardly stop yourself laughing'. She found it a physically tiring role, being on stage with just one little break and talking non-stop but she preferred the big parts because it was possible to get more out of them. This play was 'particularly rewarding for it is a comedy, and is great fun to act in'. Comic roles may have been her special gift. A French diplomat based in Canberra offered to help her try out for the prestigious Comédie-Française in Paris, but Ainsley felt she was too young for such a venture.[18]

Hope Hewitt reviewed *The Moon is Blue* for the *Canberra Times* on 14 May. Hewitt lectured in English at the Australian National University (ANU) and was a regular theatre reviewer. She was also the wife of Lenox Hewitt, who became the Secretary of the Prime Minister's Department under John Gorton, and the mother of Patricia Hewitt, a Cabinet Minister in the Blair Labour Government in the UK. Hewitt described Ainsley's part as that of 'an engaging little nitwit' in 'an unsubstantial plot'; it was 'a light confection' needing 'careful handling'. Ainsley Gotto 'was not only pretty and wholesome and scatter-brained as the part required; she showed a command of timing and facial expression which successfully carried the play over some potentially sticky patches'.

Not surprisingly, the *Canberra Times* in 1965 looked upon Ainsley as a 'promising young Repertory actress'. Yet while enjoying the challenges of taking on different parts, and feeling assured on stage, Ainsley never saw acting as a career. Although she knew for certain she did not want to be a housewife or a public servant, Ainsley never advanced any further in the mid-1960s than the vague thought of qualifying for entering a university. She did have the portable skills of typing and shorthand, some useful connections in Canberra, the ambition to make a difference and a lot of natural charm and practical intelligence. As it turned out, someone who was not heading anywhere in particular needed outside intervention to provide direction.

[1]   Gotto Papers, MS 9895, Folio Box 5.
[2]   Interview: AG, 22 February 2017.
[3]   Ainsley Take One, Gotto Papers, MS 9895, 2/12, held in Folio Box 1, pp. 17-18.
[4]   Pauline Parker, *The Making of Women: A History of Mac. Robertson Girls' High School*, Australian Scholarly Publishing, North Melbourne, 2006, pp. 158-9; Richard Teese, *For the Common Weal: the Public High Schools in Victoria, 1910-2010*, Australian Scholarly Publishing, North Melbourne, 2014, pp. 58-9, 89.
[5]   Interview: AG, 13 July 2017. See also, Robin Grove, 'Edouard Borovansky (1902-1959)', *Australian Dictionary of Biography*, vol. 13, MUP, Carlton, 1993.
[6]   *Woman's Day*, 25 October 1971.
[7]   *Ibid.*, and interview: AG, 7 February 2017.
[8]   Interview: AG, 7 February 2017.
[9]   The above two paragraphs draw upon an interview with AG, *ibid.*
[10]   *Ibid.* For the two references, see Gotto Papers, MS 9895/2/8.
[11]   Interview: Hilary Merritt, 17 July 2017.
[12]   Gotto Papers, MS 9895/2/2.
[13]   Interview: AG. 22 February 2017.
[14]   For the correspondence, see Gotto Papers, MS Acc07.127, Box 4.
[15]   Interviews. AG, 7 and 22 February 2017.
[16]   The above two paragraphs draw upon an interview with AG, 22 February 2017 and Gotto Papers, MS Acc07.127, Box 4. Major-General Hartley AO (Retd) was twice deployed in South Vietnam and wounded three times, received several awards for valour, became Deputy Chief of the Army and since his retirement has published extensively, been a public commentator and is now the Institute Director and CEO at Future Directions International.
[17]   For Canberra Repertory, and references to the Gotto family involvement, see Anne Edgeworth, *The Cost of Jazz Garters: A history of the Canberra Repertory Society 1932-1982*, Canberra Repertory Society, Kingston, 1992, see esp. ch. 13 and Appendix.
[18]   Interview: AG, 29 June 2017.

3

'that remarkable little thing called the mini-whip'

Early in 1966, Ainsley received a phone call from 'Bill' (later, Sir William) Aston, the Chief Government Whip. Aston asked Ainsley to join the Whips' office as a clerical assistant. She was not enthusiastic, telling Aston she did not have a high opinion of politicians. Aston kept ringing her and, in April, Ainsley eventually accepted a trial secondment from the Prime Minister's Department.[1] She had no idea who recommended her for the post, but Aston's persistence suggests that there were strong references in the offing.

While attached to the Whips' office, Ainsley remained available for secretarial duties in the Prime Minister's Department. At times, she returned to work for Sir John Bunting, the Secretary of the Department, and for his deputy, Peter (later Sir Peter) Lawler. There was one such occasion when Air Vice-Marshal Ky, the Prime Minister of South Vietnam, made his controversial Australian visit early in 1967. Ainsley worked through most of the night with Ky's speechwriter and with Richard Woolcott, an experienced and talented Australian diplomat, preparing Ky's well-received address to the National Press Club in Canberra on 19 January.[2]

Following Prime Minister Harold Holt's landslide election victory in November 1966, Aston was elected Speaker of the House of Representatives. Holt appointed Dudley Erwin, the assistant Liberal Whip, to succeed him. First elected in 1955, Erwin had, with the aid of Democratic Labor Party (DLP) preferences, converted the marginal Victorian seat of Ballaarat[3] into a relatively safe Liberal one. Liked rather than respected by his parliamentary colleagues and overshadowed by other members of the 1955 Liberal intake such as Malcolm Fraser, Jim Killen and Billy Snedden, Erwin looked and sounded too pedestrian to have a political career to match his ambitions, let alone those of his forceful American-born second wife, Joan.

As Chief Whip, Erwin received limited help from the man originally appointed to assist him. Killen believed Holt gave him the job to silence a noisy and maverick right-winger. Killen could not take 'the dizzy position of Assistant Whip' at all seriously, sending telegrams from his home city of Brisbane declaring he was 'coming' to Canberra, without specifying when.[4] Ainsley Gotto seized the opportunity of Killen's absence to become, in effect, the assistant Whip. Although Holt eventually replaced Killen with Kevin Cairns, a Brisbane dentist with close ties to the DLP, Cairns' arrival did not greatly diminish Ainsley's activities.

Erwin came to rely on her because she was a quick learner, alert to problems and adept at dealing with them. Not that he was prepared, even near the end of his life in 1984, to acknowledge the full extent of Ainsley's contribution. 'She was an able little girl (who) wasn't a high-class stenographer but she could type and she was good at administration.' Killen's absence meant that Erwin had to spend more time in the House, leaving Ainsley in charge of the office. 'She took up that responsibility and did it wonderfully well . . . administration didn't worry her at all and she was good... I enjoyed working with her and I think she enjoyed working with me.' Ainsley, he added, liked acting and 'was tremendous on the stage' and she applied that ability in Parliament where 'it also worked'.[5] The Chief Whip and his young assistant established a friendship outside of Parliament House. 'Dudley' would 'ring Mummy up from the airport when he'd land in Canberra from Ballarat and say, "look have you got any food, or can I bring out some Chinese food"? He was in and out [of] my mother's house in Campbell as a very close family friend.'[6] Friendship aside, Ainsley thought Erwin was 'hopeless': 'I wouldn't say he was stupid, but he was not very bright, and didn't know how anything worked.'[7]

Sitting alone in the Whips' office, Ainsley had the job of recording, sorting out and dealing with backbench concerns and problems. She talked easily with backbenchers who often approached her first about speaking on legislation. Some would just drift in and out of 'our frantically busy office' seeking company or conversation. Ainsley also had to make sure that ministers were in the House when it was their turn to sit at the main table during a debate, that MPs were available for debates and divisions, and that 'pairs' were arranged when needed and leave of absence applications were considered. Ainsley did not have the authority to make decisions but could assess situations and advise Erwin or Kevin Cairns. Importantly, throughout a long day in the Parliament, Ainsley's keen and alert mind was absorbing information and learning about political and personal likes and dislikes. She also learnt something about the other side of politics. Her job involved many discussions with the Opposition Whips' office. She formed a warm relationship with the gentlemanly Gil

Duthie, an ordained Methodist minister who held the Tasmanian seat of Wilmot (1946-75) and was Opposition Whip from 1956 to 1972. Duthie recalled that he and his secretary came to know Ainsley 'very well' as she came to their office several times a day with information, lists and timetables. 'We liked her. [Ainsley] was a vivacious, talented, hardworking pleasant person and a first-class secretary.'[8]

The job occasionally required her to be forceful with her own side. Some backbenchers objected to being 'managed'. Don Jessop, a South Australian Liberal, said that sometimes at a diplomatic event Ainsley would 'bustle around' at about 7.30-7.45 pm saying, 'You've got to get back to the House'. Jessop would argue with her: 'Look, I'll go back when I'm ready and I'm not going to have you tell me.' He 'had to stand over her a little bit', but thought his actions did her some good, and Jessop did get a Christmas card after one exchange 'so it couldn't have done any harm'.[9] Don Cameron, aged 26 when first elected in 1966, became a long-time friend. He accepted that Ainsley had a duty to perform but wrote a mock 'letter of protest' after she insisted he be 'home' by midnight. While appreciating her 'motherly interest', 'I am a big boy now'. He had planned to meet a girl, and there was the possibility of a marriage proposal. Cameron accepted Ainsley's ruling but feared remaining forever 'lonely, frustrated and worst of all unwanted'.[10]

Ainsley established many friendships in the Liberal Party Room. Gordon Freeth, a West Australian ex-serviceman who was elected for Forrest in 1949 and had been a junior minister since 1958, often dropped into the Whips' office for a chat. Ainsley also got on well with Don Chipp, the future leader of the Australian Democrats, who, in 1967, held the Navy portfolio when the Government was under pressure to hold a second Royal Commission into the sinking of HMAS *Voyager* in 1964. Ainsley met Andrew Peacock, the young rising star of the Liberal Party, who had replaced Menzies in the seat of Kooyong in April 1966. The irrepressible Killen became another great mate and so, over time, did Tom Hughes, the Sydney QC who would deliver eulogies at the Gorton and Gotto memorial services.

Of all the contacts Ainsley made in the Whips' office, two caused her discomfort. She found Malcolm Fraser, the Minister for the Army, 'aloof', 'imperious' and 'unlikeable'. William ('Bill' or 'Billy') McMahon, the Treasurer and Deputy Leader of the Liberal Party, was at best 'strange' and at worst 'repellent'. After totally ignoring her, he would suddenly put his arm around her and insist on a kiss. On one occasion, he came into the Whips' office to see Erwin and barked an order to Ainsley: 'Stand up, stand up! Let me look at that dress.' She jumped up. 'Turn round, turn round, marvellous!'[11] When Fraser and McMahon became prominent figures in Gorton's political downfall in March 1971 Ainsley's uneasiness transmuted into a bitter and enduring loathing.

Ainsley was not a passive listener and observer. She had opinions and was not afraid to express them. Throughout 1967 Ainsley consumed books and articles covering history and politics, particularly of Britain and the United States. Apart from the press, she did not read much about Australian politics, relying on her experience in the Whips' office to advance her understanding. Erwin occasionally prevailed upon his 'able little girl' to research and write speeches for him. Her output included a speech on the Commonwealth's increased role in scientific and technical education, one on Apex for a convention in Ballarat, one on the grant for Research and Development in the 1966-7 budget, and another for the opening of a new science block at a Catholic school in Western Australia.[12]

Speaking on 9 November 1967 at the traditional end-of-session pleasantries and expressions of gratitude, Billy Snedden, the Leader of the House and another of Ainsley's good friends, thanked Erwin, the Chief Whip, Winton Turnbull (Country Party), the Deputy Whip, and Kevin Cairns, the Assistant Whip, 'and that remarkable little thing called the mini-whip'.[13] Jim Killen had already organised the presentation of a small riding crop which lay on a shelf in Ainsley's apartment at the time of her death. On 11 November, Max Beattie in the *Weekend News* of Western Australia expanded on Snedden's comment. Beattie wrote that a parliamentary whip had 'a tough job, one generally reserved for a man either blunt or persuasive, or both'. In an 'unexpectedly ferocious parliamentary year ... Ainsley has had to be a Girl Friday in this notoriously thankless task'. Beattie, like Dudley Erwin, had mis-applied a commonly-used descriptor in 1967. Ainsley had fashioned a role for herself that went beyond the notion of 'a girl' who was 'a jack of all trades' who could be counted upon to help a boss deal with all his chores.

Her higher role became more obvious in the final months of 1967 and in the opening days of 1968 when Ainsley became involved in events affecting the leadership and future direction of the Liberal Party. Once again, she was fortunate. Just as Erwin's promotion to Chief Whip and Killen's many absences had given her greater notability, three occurrences – the damaging 'VIP affair', the death of Harold Holt and John Gorton's pitch for the

Liberal leadership – thrust her into the centre of Liberal Party politics.

Ainsley played a significant, albeit last minute, role in rescuing the Government from its self-inflicted wounds emanating from Harold Holt's determination not to release details on the use of VIP (Very Important Person) flights.[14] In May 1966 the Prime Minister's Department and Peter Howson, the Minister for Air, provided Holt with answers to parliamentary questions stating that records of VIP flights were not kept for long, and that there were no available records of flight destinations or of the passengers carried. Those answers were incorrect on all counts. RAAF regulations required the permanent retention of flight authorisation books while manifests recording the names of passengers had to be kept for 12 months. When they knew – or should have known – that Holt's replies were false, neither Bunting nor Howson attempted to correct them. From March 1967, when further questions were raised in the Senate, Howson and senior public servants adopted delaying tactics, quibbled over words, and engaged in obfuscation. By October, suspicions about misuse of VIP flights had escalated into accusations that the Prime Minister and the Minister for Air had misled Parliament. As the Senate called for all relevant papers to be tabled, Ainsley Gotto in the Whips' office saw that the mood inside the Government parties had travelled from apprehensive to downright alarmist.[15]

On 24 October, Ainsley received a phone call from her father, with whom she was not on good terms. Sid Gotto told his daughter about regulations for the retention of passenger manifests. Ainsley passed this information to Erwin who suggested they both go to see John Gorton, Holt's newly-appointed Leader of the Government in the Senate.[16] The three met in Gorton's office at Parliament House on the afternoon of 25 October, just after Gorton had made a ministerial statement in the Senate.

Gorton already knew that some records were available[17] and, with Holt's approval, used his statement to present a set of papers to the Senate, giving details of flights and including passenger numbers. Gorton promised to provide more information. After meeting Erwin and Gotto, he now understood the full extent of what could be produced. He called the Secretary of the Department of Air to his office. A. B. ('Tich') McFarlane, the Secretary of Air, previously obliged to observe a cover-up, arrived bearing samples of the flight authorisation books and of the passenger manifests.[18] On the evening of 25 October, Gorton tabled three flight authorisation books and thirteen sets of passenger manifests and, at a stroke, defused the VIP affair. Ainsley observed 'a collective sigh of relief' in the ministry and on the backbench.[19]

Gotto and Gorton had different recollections of just when Gorton learnt about the passenger manifests. Gorton was emphatic; he knew of their existence before he made his ministerial statement. Ainsley was equally emphatic: Gorton first heard of the *requirement* to retain the manifests when she and Erwin saw him on 25 October.[20] Importantly, Gorton had become a hero within the Liberal Party for rescuing the Government. Without his intervention in the VIP affair it is inconceivable he would have become Prime Minister after Holt's death; Gorton was largely unknown outside the Senate and had only recently joined Cabinet from the outer ministry. Ainsley Gotto's information had another outcome. Gorton had received further evidence that Bunting and Howson had misled Holt and thereby damaged him politically.

When he became Prime Minister, Gorton sidelined the former and dumped the latter.

Gorton was now a frequent visitor to the Whips' office and especially enjoyed talking to a bright and attractive young woman who liked to speak her mind. Ainsley, in turn, shared Erwin's view that Gorton was like a 'breath of fresh air'. She was captivated by his fervent Australian nationalism and his vision of a country being proud of itself and united in purpose. Ainsley had for some time thought that the Liberal Party's concern for 'States' rights' inhibited progress and she had experienced at first hand the problems created by the different education systems between the States. Here was a politician near the top who asked many of the same questions which had bothered her, and who wanted to find answers and to implement change.

The Senate election of 25 November delivered a sharp rebuff to the Holt Government. The Coalition share of the primary vote fell to 42.8 per cent, compared with just under 50 per cent for the House of Representatives in 1966 and 45.7 per cent in the 1964 Senate election. This result increased the chatter about Holt's eventual successor first prompted in mid-1967 when Erwin and Gotto witnessed Holt's sudden stagger in the Whips' office. It transpired that Holt had been affected by a vitamin deficiency and had not experienced a heart attack. Nevertheless, discussions continued in the wake of the Government's deteriorating standing and Malcolm Scott from Western Australia, the Liberal whip in the Senate, joined in. Erwin approached Gorton three times in December, bringing copies of letters he proposed to give Holt urging him to improve his performance. Ainsley was fully aware of what was afoot; she typed the letters. She also typed

Erwin's proposed solutions which included his appointment as Leader of the House and Minister without Portfolio entitled to all the privileges and allowances enjoyed by members of the outer ministry.[21] Ainsley's stupefied reaction to the Chief Whip's delusions was well controlled.

Gorton told Erwin he would do his best to defeat any move against Holt and described Erwin's first letter as 'far too abrasive and hurtful'. Gorton thought the second draft more acceptable. On a third draft Ainsley handwrote in pencil: 'John: See what you think of this – Dudley would like to know.' Erwin accepted all the Gorton amendments and, so what began as a very long letter, ended up as a brief note. Dated 12 December 1967, it referred to 'various members' of the Party at all levels expressing 'feelings of disquiet' to him. These feelings had permeated the electorate and reached the press. Erwin asked Holt if he saw 'some reason' for this attitude, and if he wanted Erwin to probe further.

The mini-whip was privy to many conversations about the Party leadership in the second half of 1967. Many MPs told her it was 'awful' that 'such a nice man' was not getting anywhere against Gough Whitlam, the Leader of the Opposition since Labor's electoral debacle of November 1966. Bill Bridges-Maxwell, who held the north-central seat of Robertson (NSW), sent Ainsley some handwritten notes calling for the jettisoning of some out-of-date policies of the 1950s and for Holt to demonstrate 'he is made of steel'. No one talked about removing Holt; they just wanted him to 'lift his game'. Yet ministers, in the words of one, who described Holt to Ainsley as 'a good chairman of Cabinet but not a Leader', sounded pessimistic about the prospects of Holt re-inventing himself as commanding and ruthless.[22] Tony

Eggleton, Holt's press secretary, became involved. Ainsley made a record of the conversation of 14 December where Eggleton revealed to Erwin that he had written to the Prime Minister 'along the lines of the Whips' thinking'. He told Erwin it was 'vital' for Holt's reaction to be favourable.[23]

At some stage just before 12 December Ainsley presented Erwin with her handwritten report of a conversation she had with Allen Fairhall, the Minister for Defence.[24] The exchange began with Ainsley telling Fairhall about Erwin's 'thinking' and his plan to meet the Prime Minister. Fairhall asked if Erwin proposed 'going it alone'; should he wish, Fairhall would accompany him. Ainsley mentioned Senator Gorton's 'involvement'. She had previously raised the subject with Erwin, and Gorton had raised it with her. Would Holt trust Gorton in view of talk he might seek a House of Representatives seat with the object of eventually becoming Prime Minister? She asked a fair question, having accepted as common knowledge around Parliament House that Gorton had leadership ambitions either inspired or strengthened by his handling of the VIP affair. Gorton rightly insisted he was not part of any plot to remove Holt but was ready to lead in the event of a Holt resignation. Erwin, Scott and Gotto already constituted the nucleus of a campaign team should one be needed. Fairhall did not express an opinion on the subject.

Ainsley told Fairhall she was not too optimistic about his succeeding in an approach to Holt – 'at least you'll have tried'. It appears that Fairhall and Ainsley agreed that Holt was the only person who could lead the Government at the time. The minister added that if Holt did not learn from his recent experiences, the Government would lose the next election. Fairhall cited three instances of failure or embarrassment: the handling of the *Voyager* disaster; the VIP affair; and the complications and delays in receiving the ordered 24 F-111C aircraft from the United States. He thought the answer lay with Holt himself. He did not foresee a double dissolution (the results of the recent half-Senate election indicated that the Government could not win control of the Senate where the DLP presently held the balance of power). In response to Ainsley's question about which course to take, Fairhall said it was important to be blunt and honest, and not to mince words; the 'PM is not so much stubborn as sometimes unintelligent'.[25] The pair then discussed whether Fairhall and/or Gorton should join Erwin in seeing Holt, and whether the delegation should claim it had been authorised by the Party. Ainsley advised Fairhall it would be better to 'keep it close' and say only that a fair cross section had spoken to Erwin. Fairhall evidently agreed, saying he would be talking to the Prime Minister about these matters anyway.

As the conversation proceeded, Fairhall gave Ainsley several scraps of information she could store for future use. The most valuable piece, as will be seen, was that in any future leadership contest Fairhall was 'not for McMahon at all'. Ainsley might have found Fairhall's further comment disturbing: for the first time, he was not 'completely negative' about standing for the prime ministership. Ainsley's further note was ambiguous: '[Fairhall] Expressed thought re Gorton – PM job.' Fairhall told Ainsley which ministers were performing well in Cabinet (Snedden and the Country Party's Ian Sinclair). On the other hand, David Fairbairn, the Minister for National Development, kept getting knocked back and two other ministers – Jim Forbes (Health) and Alan Hulme (Postmaster-General) – had recently suffered the same fate.

Fairhall reported that the Holt twins were now living separately from their wives. He thought the filing of divorce papers might lead to the revival of the VIP issue, presumably because of the question of entitlement to join a VIP flight. Fairhall also referred to a fight over a woman at a drunken party in South Yarra that caused a man to lose the sight of an eye; he now threatened to sue. The Holts had talked him out of it 'but only so far'. The Minister for Defence returned to the subject of the F-111C aircraft, saying they would not fly because of engine design problems. Ainsley promised to obtain some more information for him. He wanted the facts by the following week. Ainsley did not think she could have them by then, possibly because her father would need time to follow up on his sources.

It may be wondered why Allen Fairhall, fifth in seniority in the Government, a Cabinet minister since 1963, able and highly regarded by nearly all his colleagues, talked so freely and frankly with Erwin's 'little girl'. The short answer is that, like anyone who spent time in the Whips' office, Fairhall realised that Ainsley was no ordinary clerical assistant. Her comments to Fairhall, as she recorded them, were acute and reflected a shrewd understanding of political strategy and tactics. Fairhall had been indiscreet, but obviously felt he could trust her. Reading Ainsley's record of the conversation suggests something else: it could be construed as an exchange between two wise old political heads thinking they were on the same level.

Just after midday on Sunday 17 December 1967, Ainsley Gotto heard a newsflash on the radio that a prominent person had disappeared in the sea at Portsea. She immediately concluded that Harold Holt was the missing person and had almost certainly drowned. The mini-whip acted swiftly and with considerable acumen. She rang Dudley Erwin in Ballarat, telling him he must come to Canberra immediately and should contact John McEwen, the Deputy Prime Minister. Ainsley saw the need to forestall any move by McMahon, as Deputy Leader of the Liberal Party, to get himself installed as Holt's successor. Stopping McMahon was the essential first step for securing Gorton's election to the leadership. Ainsley understood that Erwin, as the secretary of the Parliamentary Liberal Party, had the authority to call a Party Room meeting. She correctly surmised that McMahon would bring pressure on Erwin for an early meeting as his best chance of winning the coveted leadership. She knew that Erwin and McEwen were close and that neither would want McMahon to succeed Holt. Ainsley did not foresee, however, that Lord Casey, the Governor-General, would intervene to swear in McEwen as Prime Minister pending the election of a new leader of the Liberal Party. Nor was she aware that McMahon dithered on the Sunday about whether he should fly to Canberra on that day.[26]

The Chief Whip did as the mini-whip 'instructed'; he abandoned his holiday plans for Victoria's south-west coast, contacted McEwen and both men arrived in Canberra on the Sunday afternoon. Erwin and Gotto went to John Gorton's house in Narrabundah to tell him he must stand for the leadership. The three of them started making up lists of the Liberals who were to be lobbied, placing the names under three headings: 'impossible', 'difficult' and 'possible'.[27]

Ainsley, like Gorton and Erwin, was unaware at this stage of exactly what position McEwen would take in relation to McMahon. On the Sunday evening, and with the agreement of his 'young

Turks' in the Country Party – Doug Anthony, Ian Sinclair and Peter Nixon – McEwen resolved not to serve in a McMahon-led government. Later in the same evening, Anthony arrived at Narrabundah to tell Gorton that the Country Party preferred him over the other obvious contender, Paul Hasluck, the Minister for External Affairs. Gorton told Ainsley about the McEwen 'blackball' on McMahon and about the Country Party's preference for himself when he phoned her well into Sunday night.

Erwin was busy on several fronts. McMahon spoke to him on the Sunday and several times on Monday pressuring him to call an early Party Room meeting. Erwin was also involved in the discussions preceding Lord Casey's decision as Governor-General to swear in McEwen as Prime Minister. On the Monday morning, Erwin was one of four people involved in discussions in the Chief Whip's office. The journalist, Alan Reid, noted that the other three were Malcolm Scott, Malcolm Fraser and 'Miss Ainsley Gotto, Erwin's young, intelligent and attractive secretary'.[28] Although Reid wanted to argue that the process of making Gorton Prime Minister had its origins in the McEwen-McMahon feud, he liked the idea of the meeting in the Whips' office as the superficial starting point. Reid believed that the four people present resolved to make Gorton their candidate for the leadership. Evidently, he did not know Gorton had already decided to nominate and that Erwin and Ainsley were already members of his team. According to Ainsley, the first and main business of the morning meeting was to stop McMahon from building a case for holding a Party meeting on the following Wednesday.[29]

Ainsley continued to play a part in this exercise. Acting on her knowledge that Fairhall would not want McMahon to lead the

Party, she had telephoned him at his home in Newcastle on the Sunday to alert him to McMahon's likely activities and to enlist his support for delaying a leadership vote. On the Monday, when she knew of the McEwen 'blackball', Ainsley wanted to ensure that McMahon would not complicate matters. Erwin was in a state of panic as McMahon kept pestering him about holding a Party Room meeting. She rang Fairhall again and spoke to him 'at some length'. Ainsley recalled being 'quite strong' as she argued that McMahon might listen to someone of Fairhall's standing. She told him to come to Canberra 'right now'.[30]

When ministers, including Fairhall, assembled in Canberra they decided it was inappropriate to hold an early Party meeting. McMahon announced on Wednesday 20 December that the Liberal Party would elect a new leader on Tuesday 9 January 1968. On the same day as McMahon's announcement, McEwen issued a public statement confirming the Country Party's refusal to serve in a government led by McMahon. Inevitably, a few Liberals resented what they saw as interference in their Party's affairs. Others wanted McEwen to remain as Prime Minister. Importantly, from Ainsley's viewpoint, McEwen had destroyed McMahon's hopes of taking the Liberal leadership in January 1968.

On the Monday afternoon, after leaving the meeting in the Whips' office, Ainsley was fully employed in the Prime Minister's Department, working with Deputy Secretary Peter Lawler on preparations for Holt's Memorial Service which was to take place in Melbourne on Friday 22 December. There was much to be done in bringing VIPs to Melbourne, accommodating them and dealing with various bottlenecks. Ainsley was directly involved in making decisions, amid taking phone calls from an agitated

Dudley Erwin. One of her contributions was the idea of using the RAAF base at Richmond to relieve the pressure on Sydney airport. In meetings she worked closely with Wing Commander (later, Air Commodore) Ray Drury, the Commanding Officer of No. 34 Squadron responsible for transporting VIPs. Ainsley was in frequent telephone contact with Kim Jones of the Department of External Affairs. He would provide her with the names of international VIPs and she would pass on the details to those dealing with transport and accommodation. Jones met her for the first time in 1970 but in telephone contact found her to be 'really good to deal with', 'very clear, very crisp and very constructive', 'a willing worker' who did not resist anything External Affairs passed on to her. He especially liked her approach of 'let's get on with it'.[31]

It was a hectic week. For Ainsley, it was the first time she had seen the Public Service act as one, overcoming their jealousies and rivalries and working together: 'Everyone should have got gold stars . . . there was angst (but) no bitchiness'. She also learnt how to look after herself; Ainsley hitched a ride to Melbourne on the plane of the President of The Philippines.[32]

Lobbying for the leadership began in earnest on the steps of St Paul's Cathedral as the congregation filed out of the Memorial Service. Ainsley was not part of that tasteless exercise, but she did spend the next two days with Gorton and Erwin in Gorton's Melbourne office re-working the lists they had first prepared on the day Holt disappeared. Malcolm Scott was also involved though the Senate numbers for Gorton were known to be overwhelming. Seventeen of the 22 Liberal Senators were considered certain supporters. Ivy Wedgwood had a definite set against Gorton, possibly dating from the 1949 election when Gorton, a newcomer to Liberal politics, was placed ahead of her in the Senate team. Hasluck believed that Sir Alister McMullin, the President of the Senate, and Senators Sim (WA) and Cotton (NSW) were 'strongly' for him.[33] On the assumption that most ministers could be expected to support Hasluck, the key was to win over 20 or more backbenchers in the House. Few of them knew very much about Gorton other than his role in the VIP affair. It helped that Hasluck had left it to others, including Sir Robert Menzies, to engage in the mundane and demeaning business of soliciting support on his behalf. There was also the factor of two more nominations for the leadership: Les Bury, the Minister for Labour, and Billy Snedden, the Minister for Immigration. They were rank outsiders, but where would their votes go after they were eliminated from the exhaustive ballot?

Ainsley recalled that her list was the shortest and consisted mainly of the newer and younger Liberals in Parliament. Some on her list asked how senators would vote. She replied that Gorton had their overwhelming support. Edward St John was on her list. He was elected in 1966 for the safe North Sydney seat of Warringah. A lawyer who had taken a stand against white minority rule in southern Africa, and who had used his maiden speech to call for the re-opening of the *Voyager* case, St John was sanctimonious and self-important, prim and ascetic, and hardly a 'natural' Gorton supporter. Whether Ainsley influenced his decision is unknown, but she talked with him 'at quite some length'. She used the arguments that Gorton had been an outstanding Leader of the Senate and was highly respected there as a Leader and as a Minister. He had chaired difficult committees, was an

Oxford graduate, very well read and not afraid to say what he thought. Above all, John Gorton wanted change, he looked at policy issues from an Australian and not a State perspective and was an unashamed Australian nationalist.[34] St John did vote for Gorton and soon regretted doing so.

Ainsley joined Erwin in Ballarat in the week preceding the vote on 9 January. They worked the telephones on Gorton's behalf, and spent a day in Gorton's office in Melbourne comparing notes and making final preparations. At some point, Erwin suggested to Gorton that he might think of employing Ainsley: 'She's really pretty good.' Gorton turned to her and said that, although he had not made any promises to anyone, if he did become Prime Minister would she come and work for him. 'I said yes, I would.'[35] The Chief Whip and the Senate Leader were at cross-purposes. Erwin thought of Ainsley as an extremely efficient secretary and a very good typist. Gorton wanted a secretary who understood what he wanted to do and had the determination and skills to help him do it.

The mini-whip was confident that Gorton would win the ballot on 9 January, expecting him to secure a clear majority of seven or nine votes. Erwin and Ainsley worked out, and Ainsley typed, a meeting program which kept McMahon to making a brief statement stressing that the Party was 'basically here to elect a leader'.[36] Wedgwood, Max Fox (a future Chief Whip) and the anti-communist Bill Wentworth (openly pro-Gorton) were appointed scrutineers. Erwin was the returning officer. Bury and Snedden were both eliminated after the first ballot and Gorton defeated Hasluck in the second by a reputed 43 votes to 38: Erwin later claimed the result was 42-39.[37] Apparently, two of

Ainsley's presumed Gorton supporters changed sides on, or just before, the day. Ironically, McMahon and his NSW supporters took Gorton up to and over the line. They were among the first to begin plotting his removal. Proposals on the agenda to retain McEwen as Prime Minister, to reconsider aspects of the Coalition and introduce elected ministries were quietly passed over, and the meeting concluded.

How important was Ainsley Gotto in the leadership outcome? In 1979, Sir Nicholas Parkinson, the Secretary of Foreign Affairs, asked Sir Gordon Freeth, the Australian High Commissioner in London, if there was any possibility of employing Ainsley in a public relations role on behalf of the High Commission. Although in 1968 Freeth had voted for Hasluck, his fellow West Australian, he and Ainsley had established a friendship from the time she joined the Whips' office.

> I agree that she is a remarkable person and undoubtedly a public relations expert – after all, it was probably due more to her efforts than most others that John Gorton [became] Prime Minister.[38]

Clyde Cameron, a Labor front bencher in 1968, told Gorton in 1984 that Ainsley was very active in supporting his candidature and 'it's accepted by all of those who saw what was happening that she had just as much influence, perhaps more than some, in canvassing or winning support for your prime ministership'. Gorton was more circumspect. He did not think Ainsley had secured a lot of support, but she certainly secured some in places around Australia besides Victoria.[39] At the very least, it was obvious to anyone observing Liberal Party politics late in 1967 and early in 1968 that Erwin's 'little girl', in her words, 'wasn't just a secretary'.[40]

1   Interview: AG, 22 February 2017.

2   Richard Woolcott, *The Hot Seat: Reflections on Diplomacy from Stalin's Death to the Bali Bombings*, HarperCollins, Sydney, 2003, pp. 78-80.

3   'Ballaarat' was the name of the Federal seat from 1901-1977. The seat is now spelt in the same way as the city of Ballarat.

4   *Killen: Inside Australian Politics*, 1989 ed., Mandarin Australia, Port Melbourne, 1989, pp. 109 and 116.

5   Interview (Robert Linford): Dudley Erwin, 29 November-1 December 1984, NLA, TRC 4900/7, 3:18-19, and *Woman's Day*, 25 October 1971.

6   *Woman's Day*, 25 October 1971.

7   Interview: AG, 13 September 2017.

8   Gil Duthie, *I had 50,000 Bosses: Memoirs of a Labor Backbencher 1946-1975*, Angus & Robertson, Sydney, 1984, p. 234.

9   Interview, Bruce Edwards, 1990 and 1991: Don Jessop, NLA, ORAL TRC 4900/91, 1:13.

10   Gotto Papers, MS 9895, Folio Box 5.

11   Interview: AG, 22 February 2017; *Woman's Day*, 18 October 1971.

12   Gotto Papers, MS 9895/5/1.

13   *Commonwealth Parliamentary Debates* (*CPD*), House of Representatives (H/R), vol 57, p. 2849.

14   Ian Hancock, 'The VIP Affair 1966-67: The Causes, Course and Consequences of a Ministerial and Public Service Cover-Up', *Australian Parliamentary Review*, vol 18, no. 2, 2004, pp. vi-xiii + 1-106.

15   Interview: AG, 11 April 2017.

16   Interview: AG, 17 February 2017.

17   See Gorton's article on the VIP affair in *Sunday Australian*, 9 August. 1971.

18   Interview: A.B. McFarlane, 7 September. 2000.

19   Interview: AG, 11 April 2017.

20   Interview: AG, 22 February 2017.

21   Gotto Papers, MS 9895/5/2.

22   Interview: AG, 22 February 2017.

23   Gotto Papers, MS 9895/5/2.

24   *Ibid.*

25   Fairhall believed that Holt was 'never really . . . an adequate Prime Minister'. Interview: Sir Allen Fairhall, 3 March 2000.

26   For a full account of McMahon's actions and those of senior figures between Holt's death and in the lead-up to the leadership vote, see Patrick Mullins, *Tiberius with a Telephone: The life and stories of William McMahon*, Scribe, Melbourne, 2018, pp. 235-52. For Erwin's error-ridden account of the events

of 17-18 December, important for air-brushing the 'little girl' out of the story, see Ballarat *Courier*, 6 May 1968.

[27] The lists are supposed to be in the Gotto Papers but appear to have been mislaid.

[28] Alan Reid, *The Power Struggle*, Shakespeare Head Publishing, Sydney, 1969, pp. 7-8. See also, Ross Fitzgerald and Stephen Holt, *Alan "The Red Fox" Reid: Pressman Par Excellence*, New South, Sydney, pp. 188-9.

[29] Interview: AG, 22 February 2017.

[30] *Ibid.*

[31] Interview: Kim Jones, 20 December 2017.

[32] Interview: AG, 22 February 2017.

[33] Paul Hasluck (Nicholas Hasluck ed.), *The Chance of Politics*, Text Publishing, Melbourne, 1997, p. 153.

[34] Interview: AG, 28 February 2017.

[35] *Woman's Day*, 25 October 1971.

[36] Gotto Papers, MS 9895/5/2.

[37] Interview (Linford): Erwin, 5:16.

[38] Freeth to Parkinson, 5 April 1979, Gotto Papers, MS 9895/6/5.

[39] Reminiscential Conversations between Clyde Cameron and Sir John Gorton, August-October 1984, NLA, ORAL TRC7 1702, vol. 2, p. 385.

[40] Interview: AG, 22 February 2017.

4

'I (am) always known as Mr. Fairbairn'

Sworn in on 10 January 1968, the new Prime Minister faced several pressing problems, including a full-scale domestic postal strike and unresolved issues relating to the Vietnam War and to the defence of Malaysia-Singapore. At the end of January, the 'Tet offensive' in South Vietnam raised the prospect of Canberra being asked to increase Australia's troop commitment. Gorton had already declared his opposition to any addition to the Task Force and was not enamoured of what was popularly called 'forward defence'. While dealing with these matters, Gorton had to win the by-election for Holt's former seat of Higgins – set down for 24 February – to move to the House of Representatives. He could then implement his planned ministerial changes, of which the most significant were the dumping of Howson and Chipp and the surprise promotion of Phillip Lynch who had won the Victorian seat of Flinders at the 1966 election.

The Prime Minister could act immediately in making administrative appointments. His first step was to retain Holt's press secretary. As Minister for the Navy in 1960, Gorton had placed Tony Eggleton in charge of the Navy's public relations. Gorton had failed to persuade Eggleton to stay with him when he moved portfolios but was delighted to take on the press secretary who had captured public attention and approval for his dignified handling of Holt's disappearance. The two men had a warm relationship even though Eggleton considered Gorton to be his most 'difficult' Prime Minister.[1] Gorton was probably not aware that Eggleton was criticised for 'destroying' Holt in the 1967 Senate election by exposing him to so many press conferences at a time when he was losing his grip.[2]

Gorton's next two appointments were controversial. He wanted to sack Bunting from the Public Service for his role in the VIP affair. Discovering he could not do this, the Prime Minister established the Department of the Cabinet Office and installed Bunting in a post for recording and disseminating Cabinet decisions. Gorton then appointed Lenox Hewitt to head the Prime Minister's Department. When Minister for Education and Science in 1967, Gorton had selected Hewitt to chair the Australian Universities Commission. Hewitt's formidable mind, his grasp of detail and ability to make quick decisions endeared him to a new Prime Minister bent on doing things in a hurry and not captivated by Public Service procedures. It never bothered Gorton that the mandarins disliked Hewitt, nor that Hewitt broke convention by occupying the room in Parliament House next to the prime ministerial suite. Hewitt wanted to be on hand to advise his chief, and he and Gorton ignored Public Service criticism of Hewitt becoming more of a political adviser than a departmental head.[3]

Gorton's second controversial decision was to appoint Ainsley Gotto as his Principal Private Secretary. Senior public servants and some conservative Liberals strongly disapproved. Whereas they might have accepted a much older woman, they considered a 22-year old female a totally inappropriate choice for a Prime Minister's PPS. In 1959 Menzies told Bunting he wanted 'a man of mature years' and eventually appointed Ainsley's relative by marriage, Les Moore, as his PPS (1960-2). Bunting added his own prerequisite. When Holt as Prime Minister wanted to appoint a favoured Treasury official as his PPS, Bunting advised him to choose someone from the Prime Minister's Department. A Treasury official might be inclined to apprise Treasury of information ahead of the Prime Minister's Department. Moreover, a Treasury official would not have the broader connections necessary for the smooth management of prime ministerial business. That said, Bunting did not have in mind just *anybody* from his department. Les Moore was a senior officer when he joined Menzies' private office and Frank Jennings who served both Menzies and Holt as PPS was an experienced officer in the Department he had joined in 1951. Ainsley was merely a clerical-assistant with good typing skills. Worse, as Bunting saw it, the man she replaced as PPS met all the essential criteria.

Son of the former Solicitor-General, Sir Kenneth Bailey, Peter Bailey was aged 39 when he succeeded Jennings as Holt's PPS. A Rhodes Scholar, an Oxford graduate and a First Assistant Secretary in the Prime Minister's Department, Bailey was bound to progress further in the Public Service. Bunting almost pleaded with Gorton to retain him. He argued that a Prime Minister needed 'a person who is seasoned and resourceful – the channel for papers and other official business into you and your normal channel for them out to the Department and beyond'. Bunting accepted that a Prime Minister must have people on his staff able to work to his 'methods and idiom', but he also needed at his elbow 'an official of experience, of grasp of the machine, and of all-round quality'.[4] It was a good argument but the wrong one to use with Gorton. The Prime Minister preferred compatibility over experience and did not want public servants who appeared to be for, by and of the system. He sent Bunting, through Ainsley Gotto, a curt response. He was not prepared to retain Bailey 'at this time'.[5]

Bunting was also troubled because he was aware of the changes in job description. A PPS had acquired greater responsibilities. Frank Jennings had seen his position as one of looking after parliamentary, cabinet and general departmental matters. 'I saw my role was basically to keep the paper flying, get the urgent material signed and through, and make sure that the PM had available to him anything necessary for his decision-making . . .'. Jennings' remit was 'strictly . . . paper management' for the Prime Minister; 'feeding him ideas wasn't our plot, it wasn't our job.'[6] Bailey took the role of PPS to another level. With Holt's approval, Bailey advised the Prime Minister on policy and political issues. For example, when the VIP affair was coming to a head, Bailey drew up 'debating points' as he and Holt mapped out a response to insistent Senate questioning. Based on a report he had commissioned into the VIP affair, Gorton was convinced that Bailey's advice exposed Holt to further political damage. His determination to appoint Gotto was backed by a determination to remove Bailey.

On 22 January, the Prime Minister initially appointed Ainsley Gotto to his staff as a personal secretary. She was just over two weeks shy of turning 22. Interviewed at Getting Crescent and photographed with one of the family's five Siamese cats, she described herself as 'a career girl' who loved her job, liked her boss and was adaptable. She described her new employer as 'different, a direct person, almost a visionary'. Ainsley was uncertain about what the job entailed and was 'a bit worried about my age, although I believe age is immaterial'. She expected to work herself into the job as she had always done.[7]

Bunting and Sir Frederick Wheeler, the Chairman of the Public Service Board, did their best to minimise the job itself. It took some time before Ainsley was paid as a Principal Private Secretary. Bunting informed her that she was fortunate to be appointed to the Prime Minister's office and wondered whether she realised what an honour it was to work there. She assured 'Sir John' she was aware of the privilege. Ainsley knew that Bunting and Wheeler were 'offended' that someone so young should hold such a position. She also knew that Bunting was 'pretty shattered' at losing his job to Hewitt.[8]

Despite objections from the most senior levels of the Public Service, the immediate reactions to Ainsley's appointment were mostly very favourable. She received scores of telegrams, letters and other messages of congratulation.[9] Richard Woolcott, the Australian High Commissioner in Ghana, sent a telegram: 'Congratulations. You have landed an exacting but fascinating job which, judging from my brief experience of the Ky visit, you will do with charm and efficiency.' Labor's Chief Whip wrote 'to say she richly deserved the appointment'. On the night of her appointment, she swept into Gil Duthie's office, came over to him, suddenly kissed him and, before he could reciprocate, she was gone. 'Just like that! No speech! But what a nice way to say cheerio.'[10] Three Liberal MPs who would become some of Gorton's fiercest critics were enthusiastic supporters. Kevin Cairns sent a message from London: 'Congratulations old girl!' He wished Ainsley well and asked her to plead with Dudley 'to get a good and understanding young lady like yourself'. A Victorian Liberal, Alex Buchanan, spoke of learning the 'Wonderful News' and said he would be 'cheering madly in the sidelines'. Don Dobie, a NSW Liberal, sent a congratulatory card while travelling on the north coast of Papua New Guinea.

Some messages spoke of the importance of a young woman taking such a position. Patricia Dobson, the Hon. Sec. of the Institute of Private Secretaries, wrote that the Institute wanted to elevate the profession of private secretaries. She considered that Ainsley's success 'will act as an inspiration and incentive to many young women anxious to enter public life in some rewarding capacity, but uncertain until now as to whether any worthwhile opportunities existed'. In reply, Ainsley said she hoped that 'the 'unwritten rule that good private secretaries must be 45 or over will now not necessarily be applied'. Kay Brownbill, who won Kingston, South Australia, for the Liberals in 1966 (she was defeated in 1969) was the third woman elected to the House of Representatives and the only woman in the House in January 1968. She was obviously happy about another woman gaining advancement. The mothers of three former boyfriends sent very warm messages. Basil Dean, in fact, had only just become a 'former'. A few days after Ainsley's appointment, he turned up at Getting Crescent in a Mercedes and proposed marriage. Ainsley told him he was 'too late'.[11]

Replying to well-wishers, Ainsley often referred to her 'chaotic first week' in the job. She described some of it to Albert Witanachchi, Private Secretary to the Leader of the House and

Chief Government Whip of Ceylon (now Sri Lanka), who had recently sat in the Whips' office in Canberra and whom she described as 'AG trained'. She told him about taking over a job which 'is a more than onerous burden and one which makes me feel rather humble when I think of the responsibility it involves'. Even so,

> it is exciting and stimulating and it is marvellous at last to feel that the capabilities I think I have are being fully extended. Quite frankly, I do not think it has been a popular appointment of mine, particularly with the public service, as I do not think there has ever been a 22 year old girl in charge of the Prime Minister's office before.

Ainsley told a friend working with the UN in Lusaka, Zambia, that she was 'going to boast a little'. Holt's staff included a First Assistant Secretary, another departmental Private Secretary and a female Personal/Private Secretary. She was first appointed as Gorton's Personal Secretary. After a couple of weeks, she took over the duties of both the departmental people while still doing some personal secretary duties, and now 'a young twit of 22 years of age has been further promoted to be in sole and complete charge of the Prime Minister's office and has been made his Personal Aide. That is not bad for a 22 year old, irresponsible female?'[12]

Although Ainsley tended to see age rather than gender as the more controversial aspect of her appointment the two were inextricably linked. Ian Fitchett, the legendary Press Gallery journalist and reputedly a misogynist, sent Ainsley a piece of what he called 'Fitchett philosophy' scrawled on a bit of paper, possibly after an indulgent lunch: 'Why doesn't [Ainsley] go home – get a good job & get off the rat race of politics – an attractive young doll shld be at home getting courted by her future bloke [sic].'[13] The 'philosophy' lacked internal consistency, but it did reflect some prevailing assumptions about the 'proper' ambitions for a young woman and helps to explain the regular questioning of Ainsley about her marriage plans.

Ainsley survived the 'chaotic first week' with the assistance of Tony Eggleton with whom she established a friendship as well as a professional relationship.[14] They often travelled together with the Prime Minister and, when overseas, Eggleton provided much-valued support. There was, indeed, a lot of travelling. On 11 March, Ainsley told one of her mother's friends that she would spend 48 hours in Canberra at a time and then dash around the country for the rest of the week, 'always running late for something or other'. Between mid-February and mid-May 1968, she travelled with the Prime Minister on 17 domestic VIP flights. Ainsley came to doubt whether she would ever find the time to 'just sit down and paint my nails'.[15]

The responsibilities of the new PPS included the supervision of a staff of 13, thus placing Tony Eggleton and the Press Office notionally under her authority. Fortunately, because Ainsley and Eggleton got on well there were few problems. The relationship with Hewitt was another matter. Hewitt sang Ainsley's praises long after she left the job, claiming that he, Gorton and Ainsley got on 'very well'.[16] Malcolm Fraser had a different view of the Hewitt-Gotto relationship. Early on, he observed a 'power-play' between the pair of them over who would exercise the greater influence on the Prime Minister.[17] The initial focus of this power-play was the control of information. Hewitt believed that all papers and letters intended for the Prime Minister should pass through his office.

Ainsley argued that, to advise the Prime Minister, to look for potential political problems and to raise 'red flags', she needed to see all Cabinet documents and have access to all communications from State Premiers. Hewitt tried to stop her but, within weeks of taking the job, Ainsley had won her battle. Gorton wanted his PPS to have access to everything directed to him.

Ainsley moved quickly into administration though not quite as swiftly as Peter Bailey remembered. Forty-five years after he was displaced, Bailey conceded that Ainsley was a devoted and very effective private secretary who generally gave good advice and 'was not unskilled'. His recall, however, was not completely accurate. Bailey mistakenly told an interviewer that Ainsley had been a private secretary to a minister. More seriously, he said that Gotto arrived at the Prime Minister's office on the afternoon of the day Gorton succeeded McEwen. There was in fact a gap of 12 days between Gorton's elevation and Ainsley's appointment as a personal secretary. According to Bailey, she said on her arrival that 'I'll be taking over your office tomorrow so can you move any papers that need moving right now?' Bailey thought her approach 'a bit summary', but decided 'if that's how it is, that's how it is'. He moved the papers on, vacated the office overnight and left her with papers that she needed to carry forward any business of government that came to the Prime Minister. Bailey also recalled how he 'tried to be kind of friendly and supportive but she was obviously not interested in taking any notice of anything I said about anything'. He decided not to butt in; he let her go ahead. Besides, Ainsley may have said critical things to Hewitt about what Bailey had done in Holt's office, and Hewitt might well have said, 'he's a hopeless guy anyway so . . . don't take any notice of him'.[18]

It is possible that Bailey had simply reproduced the received wisdom about Ainsley's brisk and business-like manner. Shown Bailey's comments in 2017, Ainsley was at once outraged and incredulous. She said it would have been totally out of character for her to address a senior public servant in that manner, and especially at a first meeting. She had been brought up to be polite, and she was polite. Besides, given that she did not know much about what her job entailed, it was inherently unlikely she would have engaged in a discussion about shifting papers.[19] Yet, clearly, something had entered and stayed in Bailey's mind and he was far from alone in finding Ainsley's manner disagreeable.

Her day began between 7.00 and 7.30 am reading the press clippings, looking especially at what the media saw as the current issues. A large part of the day's work involved the mail coming into the Prime Minister's office. One reason for standing up to Hewitt was that if the letters went straight to the Prime Minister's Department, some 'could be lost forever'. Ainsley quickly changed the system whereby Bunting had replied to letters addressed to the Prime Minister. She read 'every single piece of paper' which came into the Prime Minister's office, and would sometimes make a note such as, 'this seems unfair, can't we do something about it?' and arrange for a problem to go to the appropriate person for action. As she explained to Gorton, if someone had a problem and, not having made any progress, wrote to the Prime Minister, there must at the very least be an immediate response from the Prime Minister's office that the letter had been received. It did not matter that this response letter was signed by the PPS, so long as her signature was handwritten and not stamped.[20] One recipient of an acknowledgement from Ainsley did not understand her intention and found the procedure 'downright offensive'.[21]

If the response letters came back to Ainsley with typing errors, she would return them to whoever was responsible – her own office or another department – and insist on them being retyped (there were no word processors available to staff in her time). A perfectionist herself, she demanded high calibre work and recognised that her demands did not please those castigated. Ainsley's brusque manner, which she explained by a need to get on with a heavy workload, and her clipped – almost English upper class – voice did not endear her to subordinates or, as she became more confident in the job, to ministers and important visitors who expected the Prime Minister to be available.

The Prime Minister himself was occasionally intractable. John Gorton could be lazy, and it did not help that 'paperwork bored him'. There were times when she had to make Gorton come into her office to sign letters. He and Ainsley had some blazing rows, sometimes started by Ainsley's attempts to 'manage' him after he had been drinking. Gorton resented being prompted to do his job and he did not always want to hear her opinions. Ainsley resigned at least twice in her first year as PPS; each time she and Gorton 'made up' the next day. The saving grace, for Ainsley, was that she respected him 'utterly', saw something 'very special about him' and could 'feel the greatness of the man'.[22]

Question Time in the House could be fraught. Ainsley recalled that the deadline for preparation was an hour before a black folder would arrive from the Prime Minister's Department. Ainsley would go through all the material with the Leader of the House and the Chief Whip (respectively, Snedden and Erwin in 1968), and she would also try to induce the Prime Minister to focus on the briefs. He could be 'irascible' and ignore them. Sitting in a special seat, near the Prime Minister's place at the table, she could pass him notes or make calls on the phone linked to her office. She was close enough to feel the tension as Gorton replied to Opposition questions. It was always a relief, therefore, when Question Time was over. There were, however, moments of calm watching Whitlam, sometimes driven to distraction, observing Gorton, seemingly unbothered by what was going on around him, just writing or doodling on notepaper. There were no cameras in the Chamber to record his apparent lack of interest.

Ainsley was always noticed in Parliament House and around Canberra. She was easily spotted, arriving at work in a smart Volvo sports car, dressed in many striking and different outfits and with her small face half-hidden behind by large and round dark glasses. In the early days, however, some media outlets were more interested in Tony Eggleton. On 21 February 1968, the *Australian Women's Weekly* published two articles by Kay Keavney on 'The Prime Minister's Lieutenants'. The first, and much longer piece, told the story of Eggleton, a 'courteous modest young man' who became 'a reluctant celebrity' for standing 'like a rock in the turbulent sea' after the disappearance of Harold Holt. The second was headed 'Ainsley, aged 21, enjoys a challenge'. Two-thirds of the article consisted of a colour photo of a smiling Ainsley sitting on the grass alongside the road in front of Parliament House.

> Ainsley . . . has big, lively brown eyes, a cute nose, strong white teeth, a firm jaw, an intricate powdering of freckles, a capacity for hard work, and a salary of $5500 a year.

Jackie Leishman wrote an article for the Saturday *Age* of 17 February which reported on Ainsley's conservative taste in clothes, her views about marriage as a full-time job and her admission that she had 'a special friend' in Sydney but would say no more about him. Ainsley referred several times to her job as 'the top Government secretarial post' which she thought was as far as she could go 'in this country'. Her job, she said, entailed typing and telephoning, dealing with correspondence, making bookings for travel and accommodation and arranging appointments. In other words, she started out as a very well-paid personal secretary.

Nevertheless, Ainsley became a minor celebrity in Canberra during 1968. In March the *Canberra Times* carried a staged photograph on its front page of her packing a brief case preparatory to an official visit to New Zealand. *Woman's Day*, a magazine which in time almost adopted Ainsley, published an article in April on three young women of a similar age who were earning incomes of over $5000 a year. One worked with a Sydney computer firm and another was a model but Ainsley, identified as the Prime Minister's 'personal private secretary', received the most attention, including a full-page photograph. Ainsley said her job was to look after the personal side of the Prime Minister's job though she thought it was 'still too early to say' what her duties were. It was certainly too early to magnify her importance at a time when seen to be 'a mere girl'. In July the *Canberra Times* reported rumours that Ainsley might be the Liberal opponent for Jim Fraser, Labor's sitting member for the ACT, at the next Federal election. Ainsley was considered sufficiently important to be a target of the students' 'scavenger hunt' which formed part of the annual mid-year Bush Week events of the ANU. There were also murmurs around this time about her habit of parking illegally in reserved spaces because of a need to get into her office quickly.

Illegal parking was just one of the criticisms levelled at Ainsley during 1968. Peter Howson never forgave Gorton for dropping him from the ministry in February, and he whispered and connived against Gorton during the following three years. Howson regarded Ainsley as a convenient ancillary target; he could exploit any real or imagined misdemeanour on her part to attack the man who appointed her, while appearing concerned about her impact on the Prime Minister's standing. On 17 May Howson referred in his diary to 'a general dissatisfaction in many quarters with the performance of Miss Gotto, John Gorton's private secretary, and a feeling that her antics will bring the PM into disrepute if he keeps her there much longer'.

Ainsley's 'antics' took two principal forms. First, she addressed or referred to important people by their Christian names. David Fairbairn, the Minister for National Development, was an early and principal complainant. [23] He felt that the PPS undermined the Prime Minister's prestige by calling him 'John' in public. If an industrialist wanted contact with the Prime Minister, she would check 'if John can see you'. Fairbairn had heard that in Bali in 1968 Ainsley was wearing a bikini when she met Adam Malik, the Indonesian Foreign Minister and, either on the telephone or by calling out to him, said to the Prime Minister, 'John, Malik wants you'. McEwen was reportedly ropeable on the occasion when he went to see the Prime Minister and Ainsley opened the door saying, 'John, Jack is here to see you'. Gorton believed she might have said that and should not have done so. Ainsley had no recollection of stepping out of line.

Fairbairn thought it had reached the stage where she was calling virtually every Cabinet minister by their Christian name. Ainsley tried it with him once, and he pulled her up: 'I (am) always known as Mr. Fairbairn.' Ainsley did not recall ever addressing Fairbairn by his first name and claimed she only used Christian names when invited to do so. She also insisted she always addressed Gorton as 'Mr Gorton' or 'Prime Minister' in public. Perhaps there were occasional slip ups, or situations where the line between the public and private was blurred. And Ainsley could be perverse. Labor's Clyde Cameron claimed that Ainsley always kept her distance with him. He could never get her to address him as 'Clyde'; it was always 'Mr Cameron'.[24]

Secondly, Ainsley was accused of blocking access to the Prime Minister. The charge was accurate enough, but the job required her to stem the flow of traffic into the Prime Minister's office. Ainsley did what chief executives, bishops and vice-chancellors, among others, expected of their secretaries. Gorton was particularly anxious to see less of David Fairbairn who was forever pestering him. Apparently, the Minister for National Development needed constant reassurance. If a much older woman had told senior ministers and long-serving backbenchers that the Prime Minister was unavailable, they might have shrugged their shoulders or sat down to wait their turn. Receiving the same message from someone Fairbairn called 'a young girl', and possibly delivered in a brusque manner, would not have been received with the same equanimity or resignation.

Fairbairn said he had nothing against Ainsley personally – she was 'able and quick-witted' – but Gorton needed an older and senior male secretary. Other critics appeared to separate age and gender and saw Ainsley's age as the core of the problem, even if the form of their objection was 'sexist'. John McLeay, a South Australian conservative on the Liberal backbench, described

Ainsley as a good friend. He saw her as 'a very competent secretary who protected her boss and because he trusted her so much that created jealousies among people who couldn't get to Gorton and couldn't get his ear.' Yet McLeay thought her appointment was 'probably a mistake, perhaps Gorton should have employed some old bag with thick lenses and big hips'.[25]

John Gorton remained unrepentant. In 1968, Lord Casey, the Governor-General, told him of complaints he had received from businessmen in Sydney that they could not get through to the Prime Minister on the telephone because of Ainsley. Casey advised Gorton to 'get rid of her'. Gorton said he couldn't and wouldn't do that: 'she'd been loyal and decent . . . everything else to me, and I couldn't see why I should sack her. So I didn't.'[26]

One of the charges made against Ainsley was that she influenced ministerial appointments. There was one very early instance where she may well have swung the case against a preferred candidate. Gorton originally intended to appoint Andrew Peacock to the ministry when making changes to the cast he inherited from Harold Holt. Born in February 1939, Peacock was aged 26 when he was elected President of the Victorian Division of the Liberal Party. He arrived in Canberra with the pedigree, talent and looks to advance quickly. Peacock was stunned and hurt when the Prime Minister preferred Phillip Lynch. Peacock believed that Gorton had reneged on a promise of promotion because Lynch had actively campaigned for Gorton during the leadership election and offered him overnight accommodation at the Lynch household and a swim in the family pool.[27]

Gorton told Ainsley of his plans to promote Peacock. She quickly pointed out two good reasons for appointing Lynch instead. First, Lynch was a Roman Catholic, and no Catholic had held ministerial office since 1963. Secondly, Ainsley in the Whips' office had observed and heard about Lynch's dedication to hard work. He would give any job his undivided attention. Ainsley regarded Peacock as 'a player', and as someone who was inherently lazy. She grew closer to him in time, and to his glamorous wife Susan, but in February 1968 there was no question in her mind that Lynch would give more to a Gorton Government.[28] While there is no way of knowing how and why Gorton made his decision to appoint Lynch Minister for the Army – he did like to swim – Ainsley's arguments obliged him to reconsider the options.

Howson was unaware of the lead-up to Gorton's decision to promote Lynch, but he seemed pleased enough that Lynch's early gaffes as a minister reflected poorly on the Prime Minister who had elevated him.[29] What Howson would have known was that Gorton had introduced a practice in 1968 which attracted interest and started rumours around Parliament House. The Prime Minister liked to have a drink at the end of the day and a few friends, Ainsley among them, would gather in his office for refreshment and gossip. Outsiders saw these sessions as meetings of 'a cocktail cabinet'. During 2017 Ainsley wanted to play down the frequency and significance of these gatherings, and claimed she listened rather than contributed to the talk which flowed freely. Yet these unscripted social occasions placed her in Gorton's inner sanctum where the Prime Minister could observe her loyalty and discretion. Very occasionally the two of them might drink together without other company, further enhancing Ainsley's status as a close confidant.[30]

In January 1969 Ainsley accompanied Gorton to the

Commonwealth Prime Ministers' Conference in London. There she met Gorton's fellow Old Geelong Grammarian and former Menzies minister, Sir Alexander ('Alick') Downer, who had been Australia's High Commissioner to the UK since 1964. Downer had received warnings about Gorton's PPS, 'of her sway over him, her familiarity, proneness to addressing even senior Ministers by their Christian names and an assertiveness intolerable in a twenty-two year old'. Downer's long experience in public life had taught him to be sceptical of things said about people occupying positions of influence. Besides, reports described Ainsley as 'an attractive girl'. To his surprise, 'she seemed self-effacing, a little reserved, at first almost shy'. Gorton asked him to be kind to one of his team and spoke well of her industry and loyalty. The High Commissioner had no difficulty in carrying out the Prime Minister's wishes. He found Ainsley to be 'no ordinary person': efficient, resourceful, able to grasp problems, devoted to Gorton's welfare. These 'attributes', Downer wrote, were 'enhanced by good looks, personal charm, conversational ease and a tasteful dress sense'.[31] The High Commissioner had encountered the other Ainsley Gotto.

[1]   Interview: Eggleton, 13 April 2018.

[2]   Interview (Helen Rusden and Mungo MacCallum): Ian Fitchett, NLA ORAL TRC, 2249/10: 2/5.

[3]   Interviews: Lawler, 13 July 2000; Hewitt, 1 May 2001. Hasluck noted that two Secretaries of the Department – Sir Allen Brown and Bunting – occasionally used this office.

[4]   Bunting Papers, NAA: M319/18 (Jan. to Mar. 1968).

[5]   Some of this correspondence will be found in Sir Frederick Wheeler's Papers, NLA, MS 8096/4/4.

[6]   Interview (Barry York): Frank Jennings, 10 October 2007, Museum of Australia Democracy, OPH-OHI 141, Part 5.

[7]   *Canberra Times*, 23 January 1968.

[8]   Interview: AG, 22 February 2017.

[9]   Gotto Papers, MS 9895/2/1.

[10]   Duthie, *50,000 Bosses*, p. 234.

[11]   Interview: AG, 22 February 2017.

[12]   For the two letters, see Gotto Papers, MS 9895/2/1.

[13]   Gotto Papers, MS 9895, Folio Box 5.

[14]   Interviews: AG, 11 April 2017 and Eggleton, 13 April 2018.

[15]   AG to E. Maas, 11 March 1968, Gotto Papers, MS 9895/2/1.

[16]   Hewitt told the ABC in 1994 that she exercised the responsibilities of her 'very high office . . . with great ability and great skill'. Interview, Hewitt, ABC series 'The Liberals', 1994; *Australian*, 10 January 2018.

[17]   Philip Ayres, *Malcolm Fraser: A Biography*, William Heinemann Australia, Richmond, 1987, p. 134.

[18]   Interview (Garry Sturgess): Peter Bailey, 2013, NLA, ORAL, TRC 6552, pp. 237-8 and 246

[19]   Interview: AG, 11 April 2017.

[20]   Interview: AG, 22 February 2017.

[21]   Muriel Power to Miss Gotto, 13 November 1969, Gotto Papers, MS 9895/2/3.

[22]   *Woman's Day*, 18 October 1971.

[23]   Interview (Mel Pratt); Sir David Fairbairn, 1976, NLA, ORAL TRC, 121/74, pp. 95-6.

[24]   Reminiscential Conversations, Cameron-Gorton, vol. 2, pp. 386-7.

[25]   Interview (Bruce Edwards, 1986 and 1987): John McLeay, NLA, ORAL, TRC 4900/101, 1:13.

[26]   Reminiscential Conversations, Cameron-Gorton, vol. 2, pp. 385-6.

[27]   Interview: Peacock, 31 August 2000.

[28]   Interview: AG, 17 December 2017.

[29]   See Howson's diary entry for 28 March 1968.

[30]   Interview: AG, 11 April 2017.

[31]   Alexander Downer, *Six Prime Ministers*, Hill of Content, Melbourne, 1982, pp. 112-113.

5

'I cracked up, I was exhausted'

Ainsley joined three prime ministerial trips abroad in 1968. Two of those trips landed her in controversy while the other caused considerable angst. In addition, there was an evening spent at the American Embassy in Canberra in November 1968 where John Gorton embarrassed Ainsley and himself and which would have personal and political implications during 1969.

Two months after she was appointed PPS, Ainsley accompanied the Gortons and Lenox Hewitt on a visit to New Zealand. An official from Trade and Industry as well as Tony Eggleton and Betty's secretary, Jean Lester, made up the rest of the party who took a VIP flight to Wellington on 27 March. The New Zealand trip had been planned as a 'Goodwill Visit' by Harold Holt. Gorton happily inherited the arrangement and wanted to discuss defence, trade and foreign relations with his New Zealand counterpart, Keith (later Sir Keith) Holyoake, the National Party Prime Minister.

Holyoake had briefly held the prime ministership in 1957, losing the election in that year to the Labour Party led by Walter

Nash. He served as Leader of the Opposition for three years, won the 1960 election and remained in office until his voluntary retirement in 1972. Holyoake could fairly claim to have the edge of experience over John Gorton. His mistake, in terms of personal relationships, was to spend some time telling his Australian visitor how to be a Prime Minister. Gorton did not take kindly to Holyoake's approach, and appeared tired and distracted for much of the visit. The highlight for him, and for Ainsley, was the visit to a hot springs pool 250 miles north of Wellington. She was not present when Gorton visited Massey University on the way to the pool where the Australian Prime Minister used the letter 'X' to sign a contract with students to sell Australia to New Zealand for a leg of lamb and a pound of butter to be paid on the 'never-never'.

Gorton and Holyoake did find common ground in opposing any thought of New Zealand joining the Australian federation, in maintaining their countries' current military commitment to South Vietnam (both really wanted to reduce it which, in Holyoake's case, meant to withdraw altogether), and in being worried about the implications of Britain's proposed withdrawal from defence commitments east of Suez. They reached some agreement on trade matters, though Gorton expressly ruled out lifting the barriers on the importation of New Zealand's dairy products. It was noticeable that the opportunities for informal talks were mostly avoided. Ainsley subsequently described the 'Goodwill Visit' as a 'nightmare'. Holyoake, she thought, was 'arrogant', 'rude', 'not very bright' and 'a bastard'.[1]

More than a year later, Peter Howson visited Wellington where he talked with Sir Edwin Hicks, the former Secretary of Defence who was the Australian High Commissioner at the time of the Gorton visit. On 6 July 1969, Howson relayed Hicks' story in his diary about 'the dinner at which Ainsley Gotto placed herself next to Keith Holyoake and caused a great deal of friction between Gorton and Holyoake as a result'. Hicks may have pleased Howson with this account, but he had entirely mis-read the situation. Holyoake had insisted that Ainsley sit next to him at the dinner. She and Betty had agreed beforehand to do everything they could that evening to rescue what had been an uncomfortable visit. They did their best on the night but the flight home on 30 March was a blessed relief.[2]

On 23 May 1968 Ainsley flew with the Gortons to the United States. Hewitt and Frank Jennings – then a senior adviser in the Prime Minister's Department – as well as Eggleton joined the party but no one represented Defence or External Affairs. A pleasant part of this trip was the time taken to get to Washington. The party stopped over at Honolulu and then flew to the blissful island of Maui where they spent a couple of days relaxing in the sun by the sea. Returning to Honolulu, they boarded Air Force One especially sent by President Johnson, stopping overnight at San Francisco before arriving in Washington on Monday 27 May.

John Gorton had a specific purpose. He wanted the American President's promise to come to Australia's aid should its defence of Malaysia and Singapore come under serious threat. President Johnson, however, was in no position to make additional commitments. On 31 March, the day after Gorton arrived back in Canberra from his New Zealand visit, Johnson announced the cessation of the bombing of North Vietnam and his withdrawal from the 1968 race for the White House. Nobody had bothered to warn the Australian Government in advance of the decision to de-escalate the war in Vietnam, a tactic designed to prop up the faltering peace talks in Paris. As for Gorton's objectives, a lame-duck President who had lost confidence in his ability to 'win' the Vietnam War had no intention of making further commitments. Johnson's objective was to make sure that Gorton 'understood' his role to support the decisions of the United States.

First, however, President Johnson needed to know more about John Gorton himself. He may have been advised to approach the subject through Ainsley Gotto, following an event that occurred on the flight from Honolulu. Ainsley, as a secretary, was initially placed at the rear of the aircraft with other junior officials. Gorton would have none of it. He insisted she join him at the front. The Americans on board would have observed her superior status. Any uncertainty about her standing would have been removed on the first night in Washington. The Australian party had just arrived at Blair House and were settling in when President Johnson phoned. He invited the Gortons and two of the Prime Minister's senior staff to join himself and Lady Bird Johnson on board the Presidential yacht, the *Sequoia*, to cruise on the Potomac. Gorton selected Hewitt and Gotto and the four of them went to a party the Prime Minister was not keen to attend.

The *Sequoia* evening damaged the American visit from the start. Keith Waller, the Australian Ambassador to the United States, who was also on board, had never seen 'a more uncomfortable meeting between two men'.[3] Conversation was not easy as Johnson and Gorton sat together at the stern trying to talk above the noise of the engine and of the wind. Gorton's mood was not improved by Johnson's decision to show family movies. At one stage in the evening the President took Ainsley aside and plied her with questions about Gorton's personality, character and policy preferences. He appreciated that she was an important figure in the Gorton entourage and evidently hoped she might improve his understanding of a man who seemed resistant to Texan charm.

Ainsley had an even more important role as a go-between on the second night in Washington. The occasion was a formal White House dinner in honour of the Prime Minister's visit. After dinner, the guests were invited to watch a live ballet. Gorton had expressly eliminated ballet from the options presented to him well before he went to the dinner. He turned around in his seat to glare at his Principal Private Secretary whom he blamed, unfairly, for his discomfort.

At the end of the evening, the guests lined up in accordance with protocol to shake hands with the Johnsons and the Gortons. When it was Ainsley's turn, the President took her arm and escorted her to an adjoining room. He knew full well that Gorton had an important lunch meeting in New York on the following Friday. David Rockefeller, the brother of Governor Nelson Rockefeller, a potential Republican candidate for the Presidency, had organised a meeting between Gorton and some very important American businessmen. Whether the American President was just interested in asserting control over the Prime Minister's agenda, or also wanted to keep him from meeting Nelson Rockefeller, is unknown. But the proposition he put to Ainsley had very clear implications. He wanted Gorton to go to Texas with him on the Friday. Johnson had arranged for General Westmoreland to join them at LBJ Ranch. Westmoreland had commanded American forces in South Vietnam since 1964 and was about to be replaced.

Johnson applied another inducement. He also told Ainsley he intended to present a certificate to the 6th Battalion RAR in honour of its participation in the battle of Long Tan on 18 August 1966. Ainsley pointed out that the meeting with David Rockefeller had been long in the planning and was important for increasing American investment in Australia. Johnson gave her 15 minutes to secure Gorton's agreement to the revised plan for a day trip to Texas. In the event of a negative response, he would ensure that the Australian and American media learnt that the Australian Prime Minister had decided not to attend the presentation of a certificate for bravery to an Australian Army battalion.

Ainsley delivered the message, and its accompanying threat, to the Gortons. She knew, and John and Betty Gorton knew, there was no choice. Johnson would succeed with his 'act of bastardry'. Ainsley, as the messenger, had to put up with the combined anger of the Gortons. She had, however, extracted a promise from the President; if she did as he asked, and received the right response from Gorton, Johnson would agree to dance with her. The President prided himself on not dancing, but he did take a few steps with the Principal Private Secretary from Australia. It was a small victory, which in no way modified Ainsley's view of the American President as a 'horrible bully'.[4]

Ainsley had another role in Washington. At the end of every day Gorton would return to Blair House at once tired and frustrated. He was going from meeting to meeting without achieving very much. Once inside Blair House, and holding a drink and a cigarette, Gorton unburdened himself to Ainsley. The pair would talk late into the evening, with Gorton giving his PPS a full rundown of the day's highly confidential sessions.[5] He knew he could trust her. In time, as Betty confided to her son Robin, Ainsley would replace her as Gorton's principal confidant.[6] The exclusive 'debriefing sessions' in Blair House probably marked a stage in that process.

Gorton did go to LBJ Ranch on the Friday. His mood can be measured by his facial expression in a photograph of him sitting alongside Johnson as the President drove Gorton, Westmoreland and Hewitt in a cart around the Ranch.[7] He told Waller that the President was 'too demanding' and was attempting 'to annexe me as though I was a piece of colonial territory'. This exchange confirmed Waller's assessment; there was no rapport and no 'meeting of minds'.[8]

Many commentators were critical of Gorton's visit to the United States, principally because it appeared to achieve very little. Paul Hasluck, the Minister for External Affairs, claimed that the visit gave Sir James Plimsoll, the Secretary of the Department, and himself, as well as Waller, 'some anxiety but we worked hard at it. The Prime Minister's confidants, Tony Eggleton and Ainsley Gotto, were a perpetual nuisance but the visit did not go off as badly as represented.'[9] Hasluck did not elaborate on any of these points but it is not hard to see why he disapproved of Gotto and Eggleton. They were present in Washington and, apart from Waller, Hasluck's people were not.

The Australian Prime Minister's next scheduled trip abroad took him to South Vietnam, Singapore, Malaysia and Indonesia. Ainsley thought she would be accompanying him to all locations, but Gorton ruled out her visit to South Vietnam, explaining that Ainsley's mother would never forgive him if something happened to her daughter in the war zone. Ainsley joined the party in

Singapore. Once again, Hasluck was not happy. 'As in the United States, Gotto and Eggleton were a nuisance on the Asian tour and an impediment to Australian interests.'[10] After a strenuous few days, the party left Djakarta for a restful stopover in Bali. Soon after the Gortons returned to Australia, stories began circulating that the Prime Minister had 'gone missing' in Bali and was 'found' in Ainsley Gotto's suite.

According to Ainsley, Betty Gorton went out late one morning to visit the artist, Donald Friend, who had a house not far from the hotel. The Prime Minister did not accompany her and later went to Ainsley's suite where he, Hewitt and Gotto had a pre-lunch drink. When Mrs Gorton returned at lunch-time she asked whether her husband had gone to lunch. At this point, the security officer (Ray Whitrod) realised he did not know the whereabouts of the Prime Minister. He made some enquiries until he rang Ainsley and learnt that the Prime Minister was talking to his PPS on the balcony of her suite.[11]

Gorton's brief handwritten account of the episode had him leaving Ainsley's suite, asking Betty if she needed him for anything and, upon learning that she did not, returned to Ainsley's suite and finished the discussion. 'Somehow or other this became an "incident" – complete with highly coloured stories of an argument between the PM and Whitrod, of Mrs Gorton being disturbed, of the PM being missing for hours and hours in some other part of the Island – and so on.' Gorton called the episode his first experience of unfounded malicious rumours concerning himself.[12]

Ray Whitrod provided another and longer version of the same incident.[13] Whitrod, a career police officer and criminologist, and the first Commissioner of the Commonwealth Police, had responsibility for the Prime Minister's security for part of the East Asian trip. He explained that Gorton was 'a much more free-ranging man' than Holt and some of his 'habits . . . didn't flourish under surveillance and so he didn't like it'. Having previously checked the situation, Whitrod had warned Gorton in Singapore that 'wherever you are in Indonesia, your bedrooms will be bugged. Please don't talk there, go out on the balconies.' According to Whitrod, Ainsley spoke up: 'Who are you, Mr Whitrod, to tell our national Prime Minister where or when he's to talk.' Whitrod replied: 'I'm sorry, Miss Gotto, I'm responsible for security here. The Prime Minister is my responsibility.' Whitrod believed that Ainsley 'hated me ever since so I never got on well with her'. Ainsley did not recall this exchange, did not believe it occurred and did not accept Whitrod's versions of their subsequent relationship. Nevertheless, as in the case of Peter Bailey's recollections, it is unlikely that Whitrod invented the conversation.

Not only did Whitrod provide further evidence of the kind Howson liked to record, he also contributed to rumours about the Gorton-Gotto relationship. He told his interviewer: 'as you know, there was some relationship between Gorton and Ainsley Gotto that attracted some attention and he disappeared one day in Bali and at the Bali Beach Hotel from the wing that I'd established for him.' Whitrod was worried, and enlisted the help of a bystander he knew to be a member of the Indonesian secret service who asked: 'Have you checked Miss Gotto's bedroom?' Whitrod rang Ainsley's suite, told her that Mrs Gorton was looking for her husband, and was relieved and thanked her upon learning the Prime Minister was with her and that Ainsley would tell him that his wife was looking for him. Whitrod finished with the words, 'I wasn't sure how to make this approach, I wasn't going to go down and knock on the door, I thought a telephone was neutral'.

The sequel, from Whitrod's perspective, was a ten-minute dressing down from Betty Gorton for interfering, and the subsequent claim, which Whitrod vehemently denied, that Gorton banished him to the post of Commissioner of Police in the Territory of Papua New Guinea. For Ainsley Gotto the significance of the 'incident' was that a perfectly innocent conversation taking place on a balcony grew into gossip that the 'missing' Australian Prime Minister was alone with Ainsley in her bedroom. For this she blamed the Australian media.

On the morning of 1 November 1968, William H. Crook, the American Ambassador, arrived at the Lodge, without an appointment, to tell the Prime Minister that President Johnson had again ordered the cessation of the bombing of North Vietnam. On two counts, John Gorton was highly displeased: the Australian Government, a loyal ally, had not been informed, let alone consulted, before the order had been given; and Gorton was angry that the American Ambassador thought he could simply turn up at the doorstep and pass on the news. To ease the situation, the Ambassador invited the Prime Minister to call in at the Embassy at any time in the evening. It was the start of what Ainsley described as 'a shit of a day'.

The Prime Minister remained 'ropeable' when, as the principal guest, he arrived at the Park Royal Motel in Canberra for the annual dinner of the Parliamentary Press Gallery.[14] After the dinner concluded at about 11.00 pm, Gorton continued drinking and talking to journalists who had gathered around him. They included Geraldine Willesee, the 19-year old daughter of a senior

Labor senator, Don Willesee. Employed by Australian United Press, she was the sole female member of the Canberra Press Gallery. Although Willesee had met Gorton on previous occasions, she had attended the Gallery dinner only because Alan Reid had persuaded her to do so. Her colleagues at the dinner had urged her to join the conversation with the Prime Minister.

Meanwhile, across town at the American Embassy, Ainsley Gotto was having drinks in the company of her friend, Jeff Darmon, an aide to Ambassador Crook. Aware of John Gorton's displeasure, the Ambassador was especially anxious to apologise for what had happened earlier that morning. He prevailed upon Ainsley to contact the Prime Minister to arrange a meeting. Aware of Eggleton's presence at the Gallery dinner, she rang the Park Royal Motel to tell the Press Secretary of Ambassador Crook's invitation for Gorton to visit the Embassy after the dinner. She rang a second time because the embarrassed Ambassador was becoming agitated. Eggleton organised transport to drive Gorton to the Embassy but was startled when Gorton approached the car sometime after midnight accompanied by Geraldine Willesee. The Prime Minister later claimed she asked him for a lift home; in fact, he had suggested giving her a lift. Eggleton feared that her presence would be a cause for comment. Gorton and Willesee had already talked about the inevitable gossip if she accepted his offer.

Eggleton recalled how Gorton 'looked daggers' at him when the Press Secretary deliberately sat alongside Willesee in the back seat, leaving Gorton to sit beside the driver in the front. Gorton announced he was taking Geraldine to a 'Black and White Ball' which was being held at the Rex Hotel. When Eggleton said 'this is not a good idea', Gorton told him to 'mind your own business'.

The two men exchanged further views, with Eggleton pressing the importance of seeing the American Ambassador. Eventually, a disgruntled Prime Minister agreed to go to the American Embassy while insisting on taking Geraldine with him. Her account of these conversations is different and emphatic on one point. She made it clear before entering the car that, if there had been any question of going to the Ball, she would have called a taxi and gone straight home. She was not dressed for such an occasion and would have felt distinctly embarrassed and out of place.

Arriving at the Embassy, the Prime Minister offered Geraldine his arm as they walked towards the main entrance. Seeing them both, Ainsley realised she had made a mistake in meeting the Ambassador's wishes. She saw that Gorton was 'quite drunk', and the situation hardly improved when Gorton and Willesee went to one end of the room and engaged in close and private conversation. The Prime Minister wanted to know what the Press Gallery thought of him. He learnt of his reputation for drinking and womanising. Gorton told Geraldine that he wanted to withdraw Australian forces from South Vietnam but was prevented by party policy from doing so.[15] The story she planned to write was later spiked because Gorton's remarks were 'off the record', and Willesee was dismissed for filing the story. When Ainsley tried to join the conversation, Gorton brushed her aside. She recalled that 'he was extremely rude to me'. On reflection: 'The whole evening was a disaster'. The Ambassador had insisted she call the Prime Minister, 'he was really keen to apologise . . . I should have refused given the hour'. But Ainsley was not to know that Geraldine Willesee would be arriving with the Prime Minister, though she assumed there had been a fair amount of drinking during and after the Press Gallery dinner. Had she been aware of the full circumstances, there would have been no phone calls to the Park Royal Motel.

For all the different versions of what happened that evening, including the different recollections of the times of departure from the Embassy, it all ended without incident. Gorton, Eggleton and Willesee left together, and resumed the same seats in the Prime Minister's official car. Geraldine was taken to her home in nearby Yarralumla, where her father also resided, and Gorton returned to the Lodge. At no stage did Gorton proposition her.

A second hand and largely inaccurate version of the 'Willesee affair' is worth consideration, if only because the source became a major critic of Ainsley Gotto.[16] Dudley Erwin thought as Chief Whip he should 'carry out lots of inquiries . . . directly after it'.[17] According to the Erwin version, Ainsley was 'very jealous and protective of John Gorton, terribly protective'. She wanted to get him away from the Gallery function and used the issue of the time (Erwin could not remember what it was) and made several calls to get Gorton 'to come home via the Embassy'. Ainsley 'really set it up'. At the Embassy, she tried to intervene in the conversation with Willesee, but Gorton said, 'you are irritating me. For God's sake piss off and leave us alone.' Erwin had spoken to Geraldine Willesee, 'a very able little girl' who realised that Ainsley was jealous and had led her boss into 'that trap'. Erwin further claimed that Willesee lost her job 'because of a jealous woman'. Ainsley was furious, describing as 'absolute nonsense' the implication she had asked Gorton to have Willesee sacked: 'I didn't know she'd been sacked until she HAD been sacked.' As for jealousy, 'the only thing I have to say is, why on earth should I be jealous of Geraldine Willesee?'[18] Eggleton believed she had two reasons to be both jealous and furious: 'jealous because Gorton was with another younger woman, and furious because of the impropriety.'[19]

It was hardly surprising that, at the end of 1968. Ainsley was in a fragile state. When the House was sitting it was usual for her to leave the office near or soon after midnight at the end of a 17-hour day at work. It was never easy working with Gorton and the gossip about Ainsley was relentless. On top of everything else, Ainsley had to deal with two family crises in 1968. Her parents' marriage had long been crumbling. Ainsley felt that 12 years constituted a significant age difference between them. Her father was 'a bit of a martinet' who did not give Lesley 'an easy time'. Her mother, Ainsley believed, tried hard to be a good wife but her husband had trouble displaying emotion except when singing or acting in a play. If there was any active infidelity, none was mentioned in the divorce petition. On one occasion, Ainsley came home to find her father in the company of another, much younger woman. Both were 'fully dressed' although Ainsley thought it unlikely that this was a one-off meeting. She knew something was odd about that day; her father had given her money to go out. He was not inclined to make generous gestures.[20]

Citing mental cruelty, Lesley sued for divorce in 1967. Kerrie and Ainsley each received subpoenas to appear in court in 1968, an experience Ainsley found 'shattering'. At the end of her day in court, Ainsley had occasion to call at the Lodge. Betty Gorton took one look at her, realised Ainsley did not want to go home and set another place at the table for dinner. On 24 April, Justice Fox of the ACT Supreme Court granted a decree of judicial separation on Mrs Gotto's petition. A week later, the judge approved orders for an agreed settlement of the two parties who remained at Getting Crescent.

'Debbie' was shaping as Ainsley's second family problem. Her younger sister had a very high IQ and the Principal of Canberra High School, which she had attended for her entire secondary education, considered that her work in drama and art 'bordered on the brilliant'. He supported her application for matriculation under a rule which allowed a pass for a student who had not completed the Leaving Certificate. The Principal thought she should go to university, take an honours degree and 'make some definite contribution to the cultural life of this country'. He admired Debbie for what she had become after experiencing 'some restless and trying times mostly triggered off by domestic conditions'.[21] Those 'conditions' had already taken their toll. Ainsley was aware of her sister's intention to walk out of Getting Crescent and knew that Debbie was already something of 'a wild child'.

With so many pressures on her, Ainsley was ready to crack. In mid-1968, when in the bathroom at Getting Crescent, she suddenly she lost her sight. Ainsley called out to her mother who rang the family doctor. He told Lesley that her daughter should lie down for an hour. If her sight had not returned Lesley should ring him again. Within an hour everything was back to normal. It was a different matter in the following December. 'I cracked up, I was exhausted.' Lesley took her to the Emergency Ward in the Royal Canberra Hospital and the doctor met her there. Ainsley remained in hospital for a week of complete rest. Afterwards she learnt that Barry Everingham, a journalist, was saying she had been confined to recover from the effects of an abortion. Inevitably, the gossip included the claim that John Gorton was the father.[22]

1   Interview: AG, 19 November 2017.

2   *Ibid.*

3   James Curran, *Unholy Fury: Whitlam and Nixon at War*, Melbourne University Press Carlton, 2015, p. 91.

4   Interviews: AG, 19 and 26 November 2017. Gorton went to New York on Thursday 30 May and to Texas on Friday and returned to New York later that day to have a low-key dinner with David Rockefeller and his wife.

5   Interview: AG, 19 November 2017.

6   Interview: Robin Gorton, 5 March 2018.

7   Ian Hancock, *John Gorton: He Did It His Way*, Hodder, Sydney, 2002, between pp. 224-5.

8   Alan Fewster, *Three duties & Talleyrand's dictum: portrait of a working diplomat*, Australian Scholarly Publishing, North Melbourne, 2018, p. 169.

9   Paul Hasluck, *Light that Time has Made*, National Library of Australia, Canberra, 1995, p. 157.

10 *Ibid.*

11 Interview: AG, 18 January 2018; Gotto Papers, MS 9895/2/9.

12 Gotto Papers, MS 9895/2/9.

13 Interview (James Griffin): Raymond Whitrod, NLA, TRC 3380, pp. 38-9.

14 The account which follows draws principally upon interviews with Geraldine Willesee 18 November 2001; AG, 11 April 2017; and Tony Eggleton, 13 April 2018. There are published versions in Edward St John, *A Time To Speak*, Sun Books, Melbourne, 1969; Reid, *The Gorton Experiment*, ch. 10; the Howson *Diaries*; Hancock, *Gorton*, pp. 213-23 and Niki Savva, *The Road to Ruin*, Scribe, Melbourne, 2017, pp. 83-5. See also *SMH*, 21-2, 24-8 Mar. 1969 and Geraldine Willesee's article in *ibid.*, 22 October 2010.

15 Interview: Geraldine Willesee, 18 November 2001.

16 Interview (Robert Linford): Erwin, 5: 20-2.

17 He noted, gratuitously, that the American Ambassador was a Baptist minister who, 'by the way, turned out to be a homosexual'. Crook had brought his own personal aide (Darmon) to the Embassy, 'a very attractive boy'.

18 *Woman's Day*, 1 November 1971.

19 Savva, *Road to Ruin*, p. 84.

20 Interview: AG, 17 February 2017.

21 Gotto Papers, MS Acc07/127, Box 2.

22 Interview: AG, 17 December 2018.

6

'it is the same old problem, not free'

Ainsley needed a longer break. To that end, she left Australia on Boxing Day to spend a week in Manila with a diplomatic family she had met in Canberra. Ainsley had a wonderful time. She told her mother about eating, dancing and partying, and hardly sparing a thought for John Gorton. She signed off her 16-page letter as 'A. (the international jet-setter)'.[1] After leaving Manila Ainsley flew to Rome to meet more friends and to have lunch with Ambassador Walter Crocker before joining Gorton's official party to attend the Commonwealth Prime Ministers' Conference in London, 6-15 January 1969.

The Australian Government had taken several suites and rooms at London's Savoy Hotel – Harold Holt once called it his 'second home' – and Ainsley could enjoy the trappings of luxury. Yet she still had to undertake a heavy daily workload of managing a staff of six other secretaries, eating meals at odd hours and adjusting to a new and different atmosphere. Unlike her Washington experience, however, Ainsley was not needed as an after-hours confidant to an unhappy John Gorton. The Prime Minister of Australia, an Oxford graduate, felt comfortable in England and had four well-credentialed advisers by his side: Hewitt, Hasluck, Plimsoll and Downer.

Everything to do with the Conference was thoroughly planned and in place, and Ainsley found time to shop and to dine and visit the theatre and the galleries. Except for a brief note in *The Times* of 7 January, she passed almost unnoticed in the media. *The Times* referred to Gorton as 'the wartime fighter pilot' who 'enjoys the company of attractive, amusing, intelligent women at parties'. Describing his 'secretary, Ainsley Gotto', as 'young and attractive', *The Times* reported that it 'somehow worries people that he has taken her, with a fellow member of Parliament, into dinner in the parliamentary dining room. A more prudent man would not do this.'[2]

The Conference itself was held against the background of two matters critically important for the future of the Commonwealth: the continuing civil war in Nigeria and Southern Rhodesia's Unilateral Declaration of Independence (UDI) of 1965. The Commonwealth had barely survived the previous Conference of September 1966, which was also held in London. Several of the new African states in the Commonwealth wanted the British Government to use force to end UDI and White minority rule in Southern Rhodesia. Harold Wilson's British Labour Government rejected force in favour of a negotiated settlement, but its hand appeared tied by the African demand for NIBMAR (No Independence Before Majority African Rule). In 1968 negotiations with Ian Smith, the Prime Minister of Southern Rhodesia, Wilson had seemingly compromised the NIBMAR principle by introducing an unenforceable requirement of 'unimpeded progress towards majority rule'. Most African Commonwealth states were outraged by Wilson's concession. Although Wilson planned a two-day debate on Southern Rhodesia, he wanted to avoid the friction and threats of the previous Conference. He needed credible allies, notably the backing of two new Prime Ministers – Pierre Trudeau of Canada and John Gorton – both of whom were sceptical about the value of the Commonwealth.

Wilson first courted the charismatic and captivating French Canadian, inviting him to Chequers on the weekend before the Conference. Whereas President Johnson had engaged Ainsley in his plan to get closer to Gorton, Wilson had no need for an intermediary. The British and Australian Prime Ministers hit it off at a meeting without officials and a lunch at Downing Street. As Ainsley learnt in conversations with her boss, Gorton quickly warmed to Wilson for his intelligence and humour, just as Wilson appreciated Gorton's ability, openness and common sense. With a debate in progress in the Conference over Rhodesia, Wilson passed a note to the Australian Prime Minister which Gorton transcribed in his own hand before passing it onto Ainsley:

> I do not pretend to be an expert on blood sports such as your Australian football but I do know about Rugby and it seems to me you and I have been passing the ball to each other with real team spirit and [in] the best traditions of Anglo Australian co-operation.[3]

Gorton spoke briefly but firmly at the session on 9 January. He acknowledged that the 1968 concession and NIBMAR were incompatible but said the Australian Government believed that the responsibility for a settlement lay between the British Government and the Smith regime. He ruled out the option of force, wanted the British Government to have room for manoeuvre and said that the countries of the Commonwealth should trust the British

Government to arrive at a suitable solution. Ainsley's boss managed to oppose the African standpoint while remaining on very good personal terms with the African heads of government.

For Ainsley, the Conference was more notable for the contacts she made or resumed. Her mother's cousin, Dorothy Moore, was in London with her husband Leslie, Menzies' one-time PPS. In September 1966, Moore became the Official Secretary to the Office of the Australian High Commission in the UK. Judging by Ainsley's letter of 4 February 1969, Dorothy Moore had advised Ainsley to move on from her post as Gorton's PPS. Perhaps she raised the health issue and was worried that Ainsley was acquiring skills which were not easily transportable. Ainsley responded by saying she could not leave Gorton until after the 1969 election. 'Perhaps in some ways I am not at all sensible, but I feel I cannot walk out when, rightly or wrongly, I feel I am performing a useful function and a very much needed one.'[4]

Another contact extended Ainsley's knowledge of the Gotto family tree. Arthur Corry Gotto had read the reference to Ainsley in *The Times* of 7 January. Aged 68 and living in Esher, Surrey, Arthur Corry traced his forbears to the early 19th century and could introduce Ainsley to the Irish element in the Gotto line. Arthur Corry's great grandfather, James Corry, was the Conservative member for Belfast, 1874-85, thus serving in the House of Commons during the prime ministerships of Disraeli and Gladstone. Elevated to an hereditary baronetcy in 1885, Corry later represented the Irish Unionist Alliance as the member for Mid Armagh. Arthur himself had just missed preselection for a Northern Ireland seat in 1950. On the day Arthur wrote to Ainsley, he had lunched with Terence O'Neill, the moderate and ill-fated Prime Minister of Northern Ireland, who resigned office in April 1969 after an inconclusive election result and almost losing his seat to the Rev. Ian Paisley. Arthur correctly predicted in his letter to Ainsley that 'things could be extremely serious' if O'Neill did not win the election.

Acknowledging she was probably heavily engaged and under considerable pressure, Arthur asked if Ainsley might be free for a drink at his London club, the National Liberal Club, founded in 1882 and whose first President was William Ewart Gladstone. Ainsley subsequently had a 'delightful lunch' at the Club with Arthur's family on Friday 17 January. Presumably they sat in the magnificent dining room with its view of the Thames and beneath the portraits of the 19th century Liberal luminaries Gladstone, Bright, Cobden and Harcourt. In her letter of thanks, Ainsley said she enjoyed discovering more about the Gotto family and had passed on the information to her mother (but not, apparently, directly to her father). Arthur replied that he was 'thrilled' to meet a relative 'who is not only very able but also very attractive', hoping he could say that without causing any embarrassment. He sent her a copy of the family tree, and Ainsley had to be reminded to return it.[5]

Ainsley made another contact which, in different circumstances, might have changed her life. On Wednesday 8 January, the Queen entertained the heads of government and their senior staff for drinks at Buckingham Palace. Ainsley prepared for the occasion by taking a chauffeur-driven car to Upper Grosvenor Street W1 for a hair appointment. At the Palace she found herself in a 15-minute conversation with the Queen Mother. She also met Ivan Head, the foreign policy adviser to Pierre Trudeau. Born in 1930, an Arts and Law graduate from the University of Alberta and a Harvard Master of Laws, Ivan Head became a full Professor of

Law at Alberta in 1967. He had worked with Pierre Trudeau in 1967 when Trudeau was Minister for Justice and, in the following year, was appointed legal assistant to Prime Minister Trudeau. Head later recounted meeting Ainsley at Buckingham Palace on that Wednesday evening. He was 'confronted with a beautiful girl with fiery eyes', became defensive and talked foolishly but, as they walked out, surprised himself by asking her to the theatre.

Ainsley spent a frustrating 24 hours in Paris during the following weekend. The trip was set up by the French Embassy in Canberra. She visited Versailles, saw *Carmen* at the Opera and spent too much time with a vivacious female guide who had an interesting personal life. Ainsley had her hair trimmed at a famous salon which was a costly disaster and an Anglophobe taxi driver took her miles out of her way and used most of her remaining funds. Everything improved when she linked up with Ivan Head on Sunday evening. For the next four days they walked and talked, kissed on London Bridge, gate-crashed a party, went dancing, and saw *Fiddler on the Roof* at the theatre. Riding in a taxi on the second night, Head confessed he was married. Nevertheless, what he called 'a fairyland adventure' continued uninterrupted. There were mad as well as magical moments. One night they walked so far that they needed a taxi to take Ainsley back to her hotel. The driver looked surprised as he observed the expensively-dressed couple getting into his cab. He was even more astonished when ordered to drive to the Savoy. After all, he had picked them up in a part of London notorious for the buying and selling of cheap sex.

Ivan Head was infatuated. In the days and weeks that followed he inundated Ainsley with letters recalling their time together and fantasising about future meetings. They did plan to spend a day and a night in New York where Ainsley was stopping over on her way back to Australia. Head's aeroplane was diverted because of turbulence and the assignation never took place. There was another opportunity when the Gorton entourage arrived in Washington for a meeting with new American President, Richard Nixon. The death of the former President Dwight Eisenhower on 28 March had forced a postponement. The party moved onto Ottawa. In a letter written soon after their brief time together, Head recalled standing with Ainsley in the snow on a bright sunny day looking over a frozen lake, laughing as she parked herself outside a telephone booth and glowered at a talkative old fellow, and 'best of all' sitting close together in a ski lodge, warmed by coffee, and 'conversing in silence'.

Head's letters travelled beyond dreams and reminiscences. He touched on a sensitive issue when he advised Ainsley to cease worrying about not having a degree. She had probably told him of the letter she sent to the Academic Registrar of the ANU on 5 February 1969 applying for admission to the ANU's evening classes to obtain a matriculation pass. Ainsley acknowledged she would have difficulty attending lectures because of the limited time available but she was 'more than prepared to try and obtain a good pass in the required matriculation subjects'. Her overall objective was to start a part-time Arts degree in 1970 (she never did). On 15 February Head told Ainsley she was 'silly' to think of herself as uneducated without a degree. 'By all means go to university, but never with the thought you're incomplete without it. You're more mature, with more common sense and more basic knowledge of people than almost any professor you'll encounter.' He wished she was in his classes. They had talked a lot about politics in London and Head continued the conversation by devoting many long sections in his letters to constitutional issues, and to the political situation in Canada and to Canada-US relations. He also wondered when he would finish his current book. By mid-March he was fully occupied with a defence and foreign policy review.[6]

Ainsley's replies to Head are not available. While she did not match Ivan's letters in volume, she remained affected by their contact. She saw him as one of the most intelligent men – indeed, 'probably the most intelligent man I have ever met'. There was a further bonus. Through Head, Ainsley met the 'mesmerising' Pierre Trudeau. In a letter she wrote to her friend, Rosa Boffa, on 3 February 1969, she summed up the London experience and put it into perspective. 'I also met "P.M. Pierre" – he really is a gorgeous man Rosa. I did meet somebody in London who made the very little free time I had there absolutely wonderful, but it is the same old problem, not free.'[7]

Soon after Gorton returned to Canberra it was announced that Paul Hasluck would succeed Lord Casey as Governor-General of Australia. Ainsley Gotto's friend, Gordon Freeth, succeeded Hasluck as Minister for External Affairs and Dudley Erwin was appointed Minister for Air and succeeded Snedden as Leader of the House. Ainsley was dumbfounded by Erwin's elevation; 'it was the one appointment [Gorton] never discussed with me'. If asked, she would not have recommended him: 'anyone else would have been better. I had worked with the man for years and I saw how incompetent he was, and I wasn't shy of saying that.' At best, Erwin was 'quite competent being the Whip – sometimes, not all the time'. Yet Ainsley held a small champagne dinner at Getting Crescent to mark the elevation of her former boss. The journalist,

Alan Barnes, an after-dinner guest, recalled watching Ainsley toast Erwin's future success.[8]

Her damning assessment was broadly shared in the Party Room. Erwin's promotion was a flagrant, if belated, reward for helping Gorton win the Liberal leadership in January 1968. Menzies told his daughter that 'Dudley has no possible qualifications for Ministerial rank' and he could only guess what the better qualified backbenchers were thinking.[9] Peter Howson recorded in his diary on 11 February that, while Erwin's promotion to the ministry was expected, his appointment as Leader of the House 'flabbergasted everyone'. Howson also reported that Roger Dean, a former MP, likened Gorton's decision to make Erwin Leader of the House to Emperor Caligula's contempt for the Roman Senate signalled by appointing his horse to the chamber.

Ainsley believed that her criticisms of Erwin's appointment were soon justified. Cabinet was still trying to get some order into the rules and guidelines governing the use of VIP aircraft. Erwin as Minister for Air prepared a Cabinet submission, to which he attached a new set of rules. Ainsley, who read all submissions, considered Erwin's sub-standard; it was 'seriously appalling' for its wordiness, lack of clarity and handout approach. Her principal objection was that, at a time when it was important for the public to know that the Government was not supporting a free-for-all, Erwin was planning to expand the entitlement to use VIP aircraft. Notably, he wanted to extend the privilege to 'Leaders of other recognised political parties in the Commonwealth Parliament', giving Senator Gair of the DLP, a party without representation in the House of Representatives, access to VIP aircraft on terms equivalent to those enjoyed by the Leader of the Opposition. Erwin also wanted to extend access to the Leader of the Opposition in the Senate, as well as to senior ministers and the Deputy Leader of the Opposition should they experience problems in meeting election commitments.

Ainsley decided she needed to talk to Gorton about the submission. He asked her to present him with a summary of what Erwin had proposed. Ainsley insisted Gorton should read it himself. After he had done so Gorton asked Ainsley what she would suggest as an alternative. She said that either Gorton should ask Dudley to re-write it or invite her to do so. Gorton asked Ainsley to show him what she could do. Ainsley did re-write the submission and believed that, in its final form and with minor exceptions, it became her version.

Erwin was 'furious' about her intervention, especially because she told him it was better for the submission to be in a form that might pass through Cabinet than be knocked back.[10] Gorton then decided not to make any submission to Cabinet and instead to re-draft and tighten the existing rules, ditching all of Erwin's additions that Ainsley had strenuously opposed and reducing the number of words in Erwin's attached rules by 25 per cent. Gorton told Erwin: 'You may of course prefer to put to the Cabinet your existing submission and attachments. I would of course have no objection to this proposal although I think it is only fair to let you know that I would oppose it in the Cabinet very strongly.'[11]

Erwin continued to present Gorton with problems,[12] but they were insignificant seen next to those he created for himself. The incident in the American Embassy returned to embarrass him. After a few oblique references in January 1969 to the Embassy incident of the previous year, Max Newton on 10 February referred, in his newsletter *Insight*, to Ainsley Gotto having 'made a valiant but unconvincing attempt to hide her dissatisfaction since an uncomfortable social occasion at the United States Embassy late last year'. Just over a month later, a Labor backbencher referred to the evening at the American Embassy as well as rumours concerning an improper relationship between Gorton and Liza Minnelli, the American singer and daughter of Judy Garland. The Minnelli story was soon dispatched[13] but accounts about Gorton's behaviour at the Embassy had important ramifications for Gorton's political and personal standing. During the exchanges at the end of March over what did or did not happen that night, and about the timing of events that did or did not take place, Geraldine Willesee made a statutory declaration where she referred to Ainsley Gotto coming over to Gorton and herself 'about three times'. Gorton told her to leave as they were in the middle of a private conversation. Willesee also mentioned that Ainsley, Ambassador Crook, Jeff Damon and Tony Eggleton were talking and dancing to music at the other end of the room. It was the sort of public notice that Ainsley resented.

Gorton left for the United States on 1 May to make up for the abortive trip in March. On this occasion, in addition to Hewitt, Eggleton and Gotto, he took with him Plimsoll, the Secretary of External Affairs, and another senior official from the Prime Minister's Department. This visit to Washington was very different from the one Ainsley experienced in 1968. There were no late-night drinks and debriefing sessions at Blair House with a depressed and angry Prime Minister. Gorton liked and got on very well with President Nixon. He and Ainsley both despaired of the Australian media which equated his comment to Nixon, 'we will go Waltzing Matilda with you', with Harold Holt's embarrassing

'All the Way with LBJ'. Gorton's comment ended a long preamble in which he listed the circumstances under which Australia would act. Faced with a choice of reading and understanding a lengthy text or fastening onto a throwaway line, the fourth estate settled for the latter. Ainsley was gathering more evidence to sustain her contempt for the media. She also gathered another admirer in Washington. Henry Kissinger enjoyed meeting her, just as she admired him.[14]

It was time for publicity of a different kind. In mid-February 1969 Richard Walsh, the former co-editor of *Oz* magazine, wanted to interview Ainsley for *POL*, the national women's monthly magazine he now edited. He explained that *POL* was 'directed at intelligent women in the higher socio-economic bracket'. Walsh planned an issue devoted to women in politics and wanted an article on 'a young Australian woman who holds an important and responsible position on the Prime Minister's staff'.[15] There was another reason for meeting her; apart from John Gorton, 'probably no person is more talked about in Canberra than Ainsley Gotto'. It was Ainsley's first serious interview and she managed to give nothing away.[16] The closest she came to telling Walsh what she really thought was her answer to his questions about Erwin's recent promotion. Ainsley said she was happy for him and when Walsh asked if she would have been 'sad' if Erwin had been passed over, she replied, 'I don't know whether I'd quite say that'. She successfully downplayed her role, saying she was not 'mentally empowered' to judge government decisions and was just there to do a job. Walsh referred to her 'mystique' but added that to meet her was to dispel doubts that 'she is an incredibly capable and intelligent girl, who knows very well how to look after herself'. Walsh detected something about Ainsley that she might have acknowledged in a less private mood: she was 'not quite sure of herself as would appear'.

One welcome story could not override damaging rumours, especially when concerning Gorton's personal office. A month after returning from his Washington visit Gorton went to Bendigo to campaign for the by-election caused by the resignation of the Labor member on grounds of ill-health. Reporters accompanying him saw Gorton bawl out Ainsley on several occasions when she approached him on work matters, reportedly leaving her close to tears. Geraldine Willesee did not observe these exchanges at first hand but had seen and heard Gorton in action on a more celebrated occasion and proceeded to draw the wrong conclusions. She now worked for the Perth-based *Independent*, a weekly newspaper owned by Lang Hancock and his mining partner Peter Wright who had appointed Maxwell Newton, a Gorton hater, as their managing editor. Drawing on the reports from Bendigo, Willesee edited a column on 15 June 1969 claiming that the formerly close Gorton-Gotto relationship 'had broken down almost completely in the last six months', and Gorton was making Ainsley's glamour job 'one of the most unenvied and unglamorous in Canberra'. Willesee told her readers that Gorton 'obviously no longer even likes her'. She said it was 'a shame' Gorton could get a good relationship with his two secretaries (the other one being Eggleton); and he 'surely cannot be unaware that [Ainsley Gotto] is probably the most loyal secretary he will ever find'. The rumours received another boost with the resumption of Parliament for the Budget session. Tony Eggleton sent Ainsley a note on 13 August saying that 'the rumours about our futures have been given a new lease of life'. Barry Everingham had told him there was talk in the lobbies and the Gallery that both he and Ainsley had resigned.[17]

Ainsley's contempt for the fourth estate did have a firm basis.

By this time several Liberal backbenchers, Howson being the most prominent, were ready to believe anything detrimental to Gorton's image. The anti-Gortonites were appalled by the Prime Minister's seemingly cavalier methods of running a government and by his centralist and 'socialist' tendencies. They were also outraged by the emergence of the 'Mushroom Club'. Whereas they were honourable men selflessly working for the good of the Party and of Australia, they regarded members of the Club as ambitious politicians who had founded a bloc to support Gorton. Howson believed that the Prime Minister had handpicked the membership. In fact, Gorton neither established the Club nor determined who should belong. The 13 Liberal backbenchers formed the Club after Andrew Peacock had been gagged by his own side in a tariff debate.[18] The 'mushrooms' constituted a diverse group whose principal interest was to wine, dine and indulge in ribaldry. They held their dinners one night a week when Parliament was in session and usually invited guest speakers, one of whom was the transport officer at Parliament House. Gorton was given the title of 'Chief Spore' and attended one dinner but later asked the Club to disband because of allegations that its existence was dividing the Party Room. Apparently, someone dubbed Ainsley Gotto the 'reigning queen' though she was a guest for only two dinners. She was invited because some of her closest friends in politics – Chipp, Hughes, Killen and Peacock – were 'mushrooms'.

Bridges-Maxwell was also a member of the Club and, for a time early in 1968, his friendship with Ainsley seemed headed beyond the platonic. A married man with children, Bridges-Maxwell's letters reflected a troubled mind which was nonetheless certain of one thing: 'I believe that you believe that I love you and that you believe that I believe that you love me.' [emphases in the original][19] It is unclear who pulled back the sooner but the pair of them remained good friends in 1969. They also managed to keep their relationship out of sight.

Ainsley continued in 1969 to attract older men who, like Ivan Head, were enjoying stellar careers. An American who would become a distinguished judge in international law was enraptured by the young woman he met in Canberra. He loved Ainsley's 'pungent prose' and 'salty lingo', 'the flair of your intelligence, your remarkable maturity, your taste and style' and of 'feeling the deep, probing gaze of your marvellous, profound eyes'. After describing Ainsley as 'an exquisite creature' it was probably a mistake to add 'I want to make you my creature'. Perhaps, like others before him, he eventually grasped the significance of Ainsley not being 'the most energetic of correspondents'.[20]

She did maintain contact with a future President of Fiji she met at a diplomatic cocktail party sometime after the October 1969 election. Ainsley considered him 'a gorgeous and interesting man', and said he was 'very gentle' and possessed of 'a naughty sense of humour'. After a long lunch at a property outside of Canberra they agreed to marry but the engagement did not last 24 hours. On her side, Ainsley knew that her 'fiancé' would need the permission of his well-connected Fijian family and she had a concern about mixed marriages. As she recalled, they had a farewell lunch at The Lobby restaurant in Canberra and remained good friends thereafter.[21]

Debbie Gotto had a slightly longer first engagement. Ainsley had moved out of Getting Crescent and taken a flat in Narrabundah.

Debbie also wanted to escape home and the 'wild child' moved in with her sister. Ainsley, who saw herself as taking 'custody', had few opportunities to be a custodian. On weekdays Debbie was usually out all night until 3.00-5.00 am, and Ainsley had to leave for work while she was still asleep. In May 1969 Debbie changed her circumstances by becoming engaged to the son of a wealthy Yass family. Her parents held a celebration party at Getting Crescent. The engagement did not survive, and Debbie went to Sydney, continued to take heroin and used prostitution to pay for her habit. Senator Malcom Scott, who had been appointed Minister for Customs and Excise as a reward for his role in Gorton's election to the Liberal leadership, informed Gorton that Customs had arrested Deborah for attempting to import drugs. Gorton told Ainsley what had happened, and both agreed that the law must take its course. Customs decided not to proceed with the case. In the meantime, Ainsley had gone to Sydney to find her sister and bring her back to Canberra.[22]

By October 1969 Ainsley's boss was engaged in an election which he had originally thought would produce a substantial if slightly reduced majority for his Government. Ainsley did not have a role to play and remained in Canberra for much of the campaign. Unlike Gorton, she was not convinced that her continued employment as the Prime Minister's PPS was assured.[23]

[1] LGN Correspondence, 1960s-1970s, Gotto Papers, MS Acc15.206, Box 9.

[2] *The Times*, 7 January 1971.

[3] Gotto Papers, MS 9895/2/7.

[4] AG to the Moores, 4 February 1969, *ibid.*, 2/2.

[5] *Ibid.*

[6] For Head's letters, see Gotto Papers, MS Acc07/127, Box 4.

7   Gotto Papers, MS 9895/2/1.

8   *Age*, 14 November 1969.

9   Heather Henderson (ed.), *Letters To My Daughter: Robert Menzies, Letters, 1955-1975*, Pier 9, Millers Point, 2011, p. 207.

10 Interview: AG, 11 April 2017.

11 V.I.P. Aircraft, Gorton Papers, NLA, MS 1984, 24.

12 See, for example, Gorton's intervention on the side of the left-wing Labor MP, Tom Uren, in forcing Erwin to retract statements impugning Uren's loyalty. Hancock, *Gorton,* pp. 231-3.

13 See, David McNicoll, *Luck's a Fortune: An Autobiography*, Sun Books, Melbourne, 1979, pp. 237 and 240. Liza Minnelli herself described the story as 'a pack of lies'. For a very different version of the Minnelli incident, see, http://cometherevolution.com.au/untold-story-canberras-first-coup-political-assassination-prime-minister-john-gorton-part-3/.

14 Interview: AG, 26 November 2017.

15 Gotto Papers, MS 9895/9/3.

16 *Pol*, June 1969.

17 Gotto Papers, MS 9895, Folio Box 5.

18 For the Mushroom Club, see Ian Hancock, *Tom Hughes QC: A Cab on the Rank*, The Federation Press, Annandale, 2016, pp. 129-30 and fn 28. For Ainsley's account, see *Woman's Day*, 1 November 1971.

19 Gotto Papers, MS Acc07.127, Box 4.

20 *Ibid.*

21 Interview: AG, 6 April 2017.

22 Interview: AG, 7 February 2017.

23 Interview: AG, 20 April 2017.

7

'It wiggles, it's shapely, and its name is Ainsley Gotto'

The Government barely survived the election of 25 October 1969. The Coalition's majority of 39 seats was slashed to seven, and the Government was returned because DLP preferences saved it in four seats. The Liberal Party itself lost 14 seats to Labor. Even allowing for the expected revival in the Labor vote after the 1966 debacle, the result in 1969, on top of growing internal complaints about Gorton's habits, style and policies, meant that the recriminations focused mainly on his leadership.

David Fairbairn, the Minister for National Development, went to Canberra to discuss the results with the Prime Minister. He complained later that he was kept waiting for most of the day before being allowed into Gorton's office. Fairbairn would have been even angrier had he known that Ainsley was under strict instructions to bar his entry. Gorton had grown even more weary of Fairbairn's need for guidance and reassurance. On 30 October,

Fairbairn announced he would not serve in a Gorton-led ministry, and three days later declared his candidacy for the leadership. The Fairbairn challenge was totally unexpected. As Ainsley put it: 'We [Gorton and herself] had no idea it was happening'. Gorton had spoken to Fairbairn about succeeding Downer in London. 'We' both thought he was 'a truthful gentleman' but that notion was thrown out of the window by his leadership challenge. 'We didn't think he was very intelligent, but we had had no idea he could be so stupid.' Gorton regarded him as a friend and was hurt. 'We didn't make enough allowance for [Fairbairn's wife] Ruth. We were silly to think that someone of a similar background would behave in the same way.'[1] It is true that Gorton and Fairbairn were both Old Geelong Grammarians and had served as RAAF officers in wartime. Yet according to Ian Sinclair of the Country Party, Fairbairn the grazier and Gorton the orchardist had occupations which placed them classes apart. Fairbairn was more at home with Malcolm Fraser than he had ever been with Gorton.[2]

McMahon joined the contest on 2 November after McEwen removed his threat to withdraw from the Coalition should McMahon be elected Liberal Leader. The leadership vote was set down for 7 November. Ainsley's role in the contest was principally one of assembling lists of Gorton's known supporters and opponents and identifying the 'doubtful'. She and Tom Hughes had to spend time listening to a cantankerous retired bank manager, Les Irwin, the member for Mitchell. Irwin who described himself as 'a lone wolf', told Ainsley he deplored Fairbairn's letter and had told journalists that Australians did not have 'a pansy' for Prime Minister. As for Ruth, she 'had become ruthless'.[3] Neither Gotto nor Hughes were fooled by these remarks; they knew Irwin would be supporting McMahon.

Gorton retained the leadership on 7 November by a narrow absolute majority of three votes over McMahon and Fairbairn. McMahon retained the deputy leadership by a larger margin over two pro-Gorton contenders. Four days after the event, Gorton announced his new ministry. On the Liberal side, a retirement (Fairhall), a resignation (Fairbairn) and an electoral defeat (Freeth) had left three vacancies and Gorton created three more by dropping two of his original supporters – Erwin and Scott – as well as Bert Kelly from South Australia. The Country Party's improved numerical strength within the Coalition allowed McEwen to claim an extra ministry, as well as an additional member of Cabinet. Gorton promoted five Liberals from the backbench: Chipp, Senator Cotton, Hughes, Killen and Peacock. All save Cotton were 'mushrooms'. The anti-Gorton faction accused the Prime Minister of 'cronyism', but Gorton could fairly claim he had injected much-needed new talent into the ministry.

Within a day of the announced changes Dudley Erwin became the centre of attention. Scott accepted his demotion with good grace and Kelly remained quiet except to say his one concern was what to do with the striped trousers he wore just once – at his swearing-in. An embittered Erwin, on the other hand, sounded off on several occasions. In his first statement, made at his home in Ballarat on 12 November, Erwin explained that his original promotion was a 'payoff' for supporting the Prime Minister after the death of Harold Holt. A 'political manoeuvre' had been building over months. 'The pressures were on to get rid of me.' Erwin was said to be too close to Gorton, though the Prime Minister 'was never a close friend'. Erwin also pointed out he was not a 'mushroom'. His potentially damaging comment, however, was that Gorton was being groomed for the prime ministership six months before Holt disappeared at Portsea. The grooming started after Holt had suffered the presumed heart attack in the presence of Erwin and Gotto in the Whips' office.

Gorton replied to Erwin's initial 'charge' with a press statement on the afternoon of 12 November. He emphatically denied being involved in a plot against Holt; he had never been approached and would have reported any approaches to the Prime Minister. The suggestion he might stand for the party leadership came after Holt's death and did not emanate from Erwin (which was not quite true). Gorton's firm riposte silenced all except the malcontents and the issue was quickly overshadowed by a further Erwin statement.

Sensing he had said too much, Erwin contacted Eggleton late in the afternoon of 12 November to assure him he would now be cautious with interviews. It took just a few hours and probably as many drinks for the former minister to abandon restraint. At around 2.00 am on 13 November Erwin answered a telephone call to his Ballarat home. A young Laurie Oakes, recently appointed head of the Canberra bureau of the Melbourne *Sun*, had been trying to reach Erwin for most of the previous day. He wanted to know the source of the 'political manoeuvre' used to remove him from office. Erwin replied: 'It wiggles, it's shapely, it's cold-blooded and its name is Ainsley Gotto'.[4] Erwin did not explain how Ainsley was involved in his dumping, except to say it 'wasn't pleasant'. She had stopped him several times from speaking to the Prime Minister and had 'ruled with a ruthless authority'. Erwin said he 'took personal affront and she resented this'. Acknowledging he had recommended her to Gorton, Erwin said Ainsley had changed since then and her attitude towards him had also changed. He now believed that 'a girl so young' should not be placed in such authority because of the psychological effect on a female of her age. A Prime Minister needed a highly qualified mature male as his principal private secretary.

Laurie Oakes broke this story in the Melbourne *Sun* on the morning of 13 November. The headline – 'AXED MINISTER ERWIN BLAMES A GIRL' – captured the essence of Erwin's complaint; he had been brought down by 'a girl'. The report appeared alongside a photo of Ainsley watching the 1969 election television coverage and a story headed, 'I'm a career girl and I like my job and my boss', a quotation taken from the time of her appointment in 1968. The *Sun* also noted that Ainsley had worked in a typing pool six years earlier. To avoid legal complications, a sub-editor had removed 'it's cold-blooded' from a sentence which by the end of the day and next morning had been repeated in news stories throughout Australia. Erwin's statement also had an immediate impact in London. The afternoon tabloids of 13 November had first use of the story: 'Wiggly girl secretary got me sacked – ex-Minister' (*Evening News*); 'Lost-job Minister blames it on girl's wiggle' (*Evening Standard*). The broadsheets and the tabloids followed suit on 14 November: 'Ex-Minister puts blame on "wiggle"' (*The Times*); 'Ex-Minister Blames "Wiggly" Secretary' (*Daily Telegraph*); 'It wiggles, it's shapely, it's [*sic*] had me fired' (*Daily Mail*); 'The Girl Who Wiggled A Man Out Of Office' (*Daily Express*).

When the media sought Ainsley's response, she replied very simply: 'No comment. I've thought about it and I have no comment.'[5] Ainsley might have looked and sounded very cool but inwardly she felt demeaned and embarrassed. The word which hurt most was 'wiggles', although 'shapely' carried for her the same message: it was her body not her brain that mattered. Ainsley's 'Nan' highlighted one inaccuracy. She sniffed at the notion of her granddaughter having anything to wiggle: 'you go straight up and down'.[6] Ainsley would have liked to pursue another matter. She had no need to persuade Gorton to dump Erwin, nor did she try to do so. The Prime Minister had accumulated his own evidence to justify reversing his decision to promote Erwin in the first place. In fact, media comment focused more on Gorton's initial mistake than on his act of dumping Erwin. Gorton was not going to make another one. He told Erwin that he was not in the running for an appointment as Australian Ambassador to the United States. Erwin was angry and embarrassed when the story of his request for Washington was leaked from Gorton's office.[7]

Not that Erwin deserved much sympathy. He had publicly blamed Ainsley when he knew that she was not responsible for his dismissal from office. Erwin admitted just before his death that his one-line account of Ainsley's involvement was a 'fabrication'. There was, indeed, a 'political manoeuvre' designed to remove him from the ministry but the culprits were Snedden and Fraser. The former wanted to regain his old job as Leader of the House, and the latter wanted a place in the ministry for Tony Street[8] who could be expected to support Fraser's political advancement. Erwin never did explain how Snedden and Fraser set about achieving their alleged objectives. Nor did he ever properly apologise to Ainsley for his insulting and hurtful accusation. Instead, he claimed credit for her fame and notoriety: 'She would have been an unknown quantity if it hadn't been for the statement I made.'[9]

Ainsley's papers contain some of the encouraging and sympathetic letters she received in the wake of Erwin's remarks.

Much older men and women offered lessons drawn from their own lives on how to deal with problems and crises. Tony Street admired her for the way she handled 'a difficult & unpleasant situation' and reminded her that she had 'many friends in this place'.[10] A public servant from Western Australia commended her for taking the correct position of 'no comment'. An RAAF officer based in Townsville was one of two correspondents who sent original poems. Grant MacIntyre, her friend from Canberra Repertory, sent her his love and best wishes. As a former Private Secretary, he understood the 'stupidities' that inflict themselves. He wished Ainsley good luck in her 'terrific job;' and assured her of 'the sympathy of everyone in politics'. A different kind of mail was also welcome. A young man of 22 from California described her as 'breathtakingly beautiful and intoxicatingly scrumptious', and another from Warrnambool offered to take her out to dinner.

Erwin's comments unleashed a media focus on Ainsley, and she was glad to accept an offer from Athol Guy of *The Seekers* for the use of his house at Mount Martha in Victoria to escape the attention. Unidentified sources looked at her time as the 'mini-whip' where Ainsley was accused of dressing down Liberals who missed a division and of having ideas above her station. Male secretaries were said to dislike her brusque manner and one who complained to his minister was told she had 'too much influence for me to interfere'. A 'Liberal MP' declared there was 'no doubt Ainsley ruled the roost down there'. Ministers and members were told that when Gorton was in Brisbane during the 1969 election campaign they could not contact him until Ainsley returned from the hairdressers.[11]

In the absence of proper documentation, the above 'evidence' falls short of finality. There is, however, one source lending weight to an argument that Ainsley's behaviour was in some respects a precursor of Peta Credlin's actions in 2013-15. Chris Puplick, who joined Bill Wentworth's staff in 1970, recalled that Ainsley would arrive in ministerial offices, demand to see ministers regardless of the circumstances and would bawl them out for their disloyalty or for what they had done or not done. She once had sharp words for Wentworth, who could not have been more loyal to Gorton, because his policies relating to Aboriginal 'land rights' had upset the Country Party.[12] Nevertheless, on the issue of access, the balance of public comment at the time generally favoured Ainsley. Editorials criticised Erwin's 'sour grapes', and journalists and ministers rejected Erwin's claims of being denied access to the Prime Minister. All ministers had a direct telephone connection to Gorton's office. Other stories observed that Ainsley as a public servant had no right of reply.

Universally disliked in Canberra political circles, the muck-raking journalist Frank Browne saw humour in the situation. He adapted the lyrics of Irving Berlin's very successful musical comedy – *Call Me Madam* – which opened with Ethel Merman descending a staircase singing 'The Hostess with the Mostess On the Ball'. Browne created his own eight-verse version – *Call me Dudley* – the second verse of which read:

> Then I bumped against young Ainsley,
> I was never in the race,
> Before I even knew it,
> I was sunk without a trace,
> And the mushrooms croon and ooze around King's Hall,
> AINSLEY GOTTO IS THE SHEILA ON THE BALL![13]

Erwin refused to go away. He made a further statement that 'for the good of the Prime Minister and the Liberal Party the Prime

Minister should get rid of Ainsley Gotto'.[14] On 14 November Eggleton urged Gorton to accept that for the time being it was preferable for him not to dignify those charges by having his name featured in the reports. 'The press is generally taking an anti-Erwin line. However, I must confess that I am less than happy about the treatment of some of the stories about Ainsley, and I am afraid there could be some "fall-out" once the sympathy associated with the initial impact has faded away.'[15] Peter Howson shared some of this view. He confided in his diary for 14 November that, while the public might despise Erwin for what he had said, 'the message is still getting home and is preventing a sympathy wave which might otherwise have gone to Gorton after last week.' Howson liked Erwin's criticisms of Gorton and 'particularly [of] the power and influence that Ainsley Gotto wields over him'.[16] The serial plotter met Alan Reid on 18 November and discussed the results of Erwin's disclosures about Gotto and comments from overseas about the need for a change of leadership. Howson wanted the Opposition to move a no-confidence motion 'which would have the effect of showing up Gorton in the House at this time'.

Joan Erwin had perhaps the last word at the end of 1969, and when she was still saying favourable things about her husband. In her Christmas and New Year message to her friends, which found its way into the press, she said that political life in Australia was a 'blackboard jungle' of 'questionable morality' and was 'no place for a considerate man'. Dudley had been 'unceremoniously dumped from the Ministry' but at least in His own way 'God has salvaged us from that den of iniquity. After a year of accusations and a great deal of smoke it seems incredible to me that the Australian public still doesn't suspect fire.'[17] Ainsley correctly surmised that Joan was having a crack at her.

Leaving aside Erwin's original explanation for his sacking, it is timely to look more closely at one of his claims. Eggleton had passed onto Gorton a question from the Melbourne *Herald* asking whether the Prime Minister had any comment on the charges by the former minister that Ainsley wielded 'undue' influence in the nation's affairs. Gorton wrote: 'No. The suggestions are too ludicrous to deserve comment.'[18] In 1984 Clyde Cameron, in his conversations with Gorton, referred to Howson's view that Gorton was unduly influenced by Ainsley Gotto. Gorton insisted that a private secretary could have only a very limited influence over him: '. . . you might ask them what they thought about something. But very rarely . . . I don't think you'd be swayed by what they thought, except as another example of thinking.'[19] Whether Gorton had deliberately or unconsciously given his former PPS the wrong title is unknown, but it is possible that he purposely downgraded her to a status where his comments were apt. It is more probable that Gorton was keen to stress that he made his own decisions and did not *need* contributions from anyone else. Yet, even supposing it was rare for Gorton to ask Ainsley for her thoughts on an issue, it would have been a rarer moment where she did not proffer an opinion.

There was one area where Ainsley certainly exercised a degree of 'influence' equating to 'power'. Standing over him, Ainsley could usually get him to do what for him were the tiresome aspects of his job: signing what had to be signed and taking notice of what had to be noticed. Ainsley had also become more confident about controlling access to the Prime Minister. Gorton might specify which ministers, MPs and senators he did not wish to see and might ask Ainsley to protect him from interruption while he was dealing with a specific issue. There remained plenty of room within that framework for Ainsley, on her own initiative, to control the traffic in and out of the Prime Minister's office, and she did so. Controlling his diary enhanced her authority, and she felt able to make the right decisions. Moreover, although a personal secretary might have some degree of 'influence' over the mechanics of a Prime Minister's job there would be no concomitant standing as a confidant in talks about policy and appointments. Given that by the end of 1969 Ainsley had replaced Betty Gorton as the Prime Minister's closest confidant, and that Gorton thought – unwisely – he had less need for Hewitt's constant availability and advice (a development noted by Eggleton[20]), Ainsley had become Gorton's principal sounding board and the one to whom he confided most of all.

Critics like Howson believed that 'a girl' should not influence appointments and policy formation. Howson would have been appalled had he known that, a few weeks after her appointment, Ainsley suggested Phillip Lynch should be promoted to the ministry ahead of Andrew Peacock. He probably regarded any exercise of influence as 'undue'. In 1994 Sir Robert Southey, another Old Geelong Grammarian and a staunch Gorton loyalist, said Ainsley 'carried out her duties very efficiently, with great skill in the face of a lot of unjustified and unfair personal and other criticism and I certainly didn't think that she exercised undue influence or an undue degree of persuasion over the prime minister. Not at all.'[21] Unfortunately, Southey was not asked what he understood by the word 'undue', and whether he thought Ainsley exercised influence short of its being 'undue'.

Others at the time thought that Ainsley's role was over-rated. Maxwell Newton determined she was 'no Cromwell in petticoats' and thought her influence was 'probably non-existent in matters of policy and marginal on issues of personalities'.[22] He placed her 'a very distant third' behind Gorton and Hewitt as a topic of conversation in Canberra's watering holes, and the 'least member' of Gorton's team behind Hewitt and Eggleton. Newton did see her as 'a fairly tough character in a predominately male world' but rated her no higher than 'the most ambitious, sophisticated and influential' of the secretaries in Parliament House. Clearly Newton was unaware of the exchanges between Hewitt and Gotto in the early days of Gorton's prime ministership and was ignorant of their outcome. He thought that Hewitt absorbed Peter Bailey's 'major functions' and 'Miss Gotto was left with the mechanical and routine remains'.

Newton was right on one score. He reckoned that Ainsley's enemies objected most of all to her youth though, like John McLeay quoted earlier, his language and intent was unambiguously sexist:

> If Ainsley Gotto were 43 rather than 23 years old she might be just another old battleaxe among that rather formidable brigade of maiden ladies mother-henning their bosses with teapot, typewriter and a telephone switch in the Ministerial suites at Parliament House, Canberra.

The critical point, however, is that Newton misunderstood the nature of Ainsley's influence and how it developed.

Two instances concerning McMahon are worth examining further. Within three months of taking office in January 1968, Gorton considered offering McMahon a diplomatic post or, at the very least, sending him to the backbench. He knew that the conspirator, leaker and liar would cause him trouble sooner or later. Visiting Warrnambool at the end of March Gorton met his good friend 'Bob' Southey, then the Victorian State President of the Liberal Party. They discussed the Prime Minister's plans for sacking McMahon including offering him a job outside politics.

Southey wrote to Gorton on 1 April to assure him that the NSW State President (Fred Osborne) and the Federal President (Sir John Atwill) could be expected to support the Prime Minister in his action against McMahon. At least that was the message, if not the words used. Southey admitted he was writing in 'Double-Dutch'; he dare not mention McMahon by name, just as he dare not use the telephone.

As she required of any letter addressed to the Prime Minister, Southey's missive was delivered to Ainsley's desk. She made two notations. At the top of the first page she asked the 'PM' if he wished to reply to it. Gorton wrote that he did not but wanted her to keep it handy. In the margin next to the first paragraph, where Southey referred to 'a course of action of great political sensitivity', Ainsley drew a line and inserted a question mark. It is possible that Gorton had not yet taken the PPS into his confidence on the plan to move McMahon out of the ministry. On the other hand, Ainsley's question suggests that she thought it appropriate and reasonable for her to be kept informed. As it happened, the plan came to nothing. 'John the Bold' proved on this matter to be 'John the Unready' and, as he acknowledged, Gorton eventually paid the price for his inaction.[23]

It was a different matter in November 1969 when Gorton was preparing to move McMahon from Treasury to External Affairs. Hewitt, formerly a Treasury official, was probably the prime mover though Gorton had long been exasperated by Treasury's failure to respond to requests or otherwise to take time in doing so. On this occasion Ainsley was taken into his confidence; the two of them talked about it over several weeks, and she pressed the case for moving McMahon. They were clearly of the same mind, but there was now a complication. The Prime Minister had baulked when he had a large majority and was enjoying the remaining days of a honeymoon in office, and when the three significant leaders of the Party Organisation were onside. Understandably, an electorally-weakened Prime Minister held principally responsible for the loss of 14 Liberal seats had very few available options. Sacking McMahon altogether was not one of them. Gorton, Hewitt and Ainsley all agreed that shifting McMahon to External Affairs was the right course.

Ainsley's 'influence' was evident in at least one substantive area of policy. Phillip Adams and Barry Jones had persuaded the Prime Minister to take an interest in the film industry and that interest developed into Gorton's support for a film and television school. Ainsley wanted him to go further still and, in 1970, Gorton committed the Government to an all-inclusive arts policy which saw him take a close interest in the new National Gallery in Canberra and in the appointment of its first Director. Ainsley was the intermediary through which the backers of the Gallery and of the Film and Television School were able to maintain the Prime Minister's interest.

Inevitably, there was gossip that went beyond the subject of 'power and influence'. Whitrod alluded to it in his recollection of the Bali 'incident' in 1968: in trying to establish Gorton's whereabouts he used the telephone rather than knock on the door of Ainsley's suite. So, did Gorton and Ainsley have an affair?

Not one of the former politicians, interviewed for my biographies of Gorton and Gotto and including those who disliked Gorton and disapproved of Ainsley's appointment, thought they did. The same is true of members of Canberra's Press Gallery. The gossips on the fringe of the fringe were unaware that Gorton as Prime

Minister had an extended extra-marital attachment to the widow of a very senior naval officer and that Ainsley's then preference for slightly older and very handsome men did not extend to one with battered looks and who was 35 years her senior. On the other hand, a few individuals assured me that they had good evidence of a physical relationship, the 'evidence' consisting of variations of what 'someone' who knew 'someone' who had been told by 'someone in the know'. I learnt for example, at fourth hand, that the pair of them had a 'love nest' behind a house 'somewhere' in one of the capital cities or, possibly, it was in a rural setting. I asked Gorton twice and Ainsley half a dozen times and both denied having had an affair and did so without the vehemence that immediately arouses suspicion.

When reaching the conclusion that there was no physical affair, I did not have access to Gorton's recorded conversations with Clyde Cameron of 1984. Cameron quoted Ainsley's comment to Ailsa Craig in *Woman's Day* of 30 March 1975 that she 'admired you excessively and had a tremendous affection for you'. Gorton agreed that she had 'an affection' for him and said he had 'an affection for her, a very strong one'. Cameron suggested that the comments they made about each other 'had all the ingredients for a romance'. Gorton agreed there were 'some ingredients' but then side-tracked himself by pointing out that the press never talked about whether Ainsley was in love with him or he with her. While Cameron accepted this point, he thought it not unreasonable for people to assume that Gorton was having an affair with Ainsley. Gorton agreed it would not be unusual, and some people might have talked that way to damage him. They would, however, be ignoring the fact that he was in love with his wife. 'And I do not want to say anything about Ainsley to damage her relationship with me in any way, because I had very very strong feelings for Ainsley, I really did like her terribly much. But I think they might consider that I also was very fond of my wife.'

The two men continued their exchange with Cameron saying that he used to watch Ainsley in the House and 'there wasn't any doubt that she adored you'. He felt that she loved him and that, if Gorton felt the same way, what was keeping them apart? Cameron answered his own question by reminding Gorton – and himself – that the former Prime Minister had said he was in love with his wife: 'presumably there was no room for two loves.' Gorton responded as someone experienced in extra-marital relationships: 'I was in love with my wife but I don't say exclusive love.' He and Betty had been married for more than 40 years, and 'the first flush of love . . . generally goes in about . . . five years at the outside.' Gorton agreed with Cameron that it was possible to have more than one love, and that he had special appreciation of Ainsley because of her loyalty to him in contrast to the disloyalty of some of his colleagues, and that contrast would have drawn him closer to her even if she had not been, in Cameron's words, 'young, clever, attractive, loyal'.[24] Whether or not there was a physical relationship, Ainsley Gotto and John Gorton clearly loved each other.

---

[1]   Interview: AG, 20 April 2017. The accepted wisdom in Coalition and Gallery circles was that Ruth Fairbairn was the driving force in the House of Fairbairn. See, for example, the *AFR* headline for 31 October 1969: 'Mr (and Mrs) Fairbairn's Gamble'.

[2]   Interview: Sinclair, 9 November 2000.

[3]   Gotto to Gorton, 3 Nov. 1969, Gorton Papers, NAA: M3787/1/48.

[4]   John Gorton believed, probably correctly, that Joan Erwin had prepared this sentence for her husband; he believed that Erwin was too slow thinking to come up with one like that. Reminiscential Conversations, Cameron-Gorton, vol. 1, p. 468 and vol. 2, pp 387-8. Gorton also said in

1984, 'I think it was a mistake to get rid of him, on my part, because he was a decent enough sort of fellow'.

5   *Canberra News*, 13 November 1969.

6   Interview: AG, 7 February 2017.

7   *Sun-Herald*, 16 November 1969.

8   Tony Street, whose father was one of three ministers killed in the aircraft crash at Canberra in 1940, won Corangamite in 1966. Fraser held the neighbouring seat of Wannon. Street was another 'mushroom' who later became a senior minister in the Fraser Government.

9   Interview (Linford): Erwin, 4: 8-9.

10   Gotto Papers, MS 9895/2/3.

11   *Herald* (Melbourne), 13 November 1969.

12   Chris Puplick to Hancock, 2 September 2018. Born in the London in 1948 and migrating to Australia with his family in 1962, Puplick would occupy prominent positions in the Liberal Party and was a Liberal Senator for NSW in 1978-81 and 1985-91.

13   Special Supplement, 'Things I Hear', 20 November 1969.

14   Press Clippings, 1969, Gotto Papers, MS 9895, Folio Box 2.

15   *Ibid.*, Folio Box 3.

16   Howson was mistaken if he regarded Erwin as an ally. Erwin despised the diarist who would sneak into Parliament 'like a little weasel' to do his jottings and who got his advice from the Melbourne Club. 'I can assure everyone [Howson] was no friend of mine'. Interview (Linford): Erwin, 4:9.

17   *Canberra Times*, 24 December 1969. Mrs Erwin did not mention that the 'den of iniquity' had given her two years on the Australian Council for the Arts and had recently appointed her – the only woman – to the seven-member committee to consider the appropriate location for the proposed film and television training school.

18   Press Clippings 1969-1971, Gotto Papers, MS 9895, Folio Box 2.

19   Reminiscential Conversations, Cameron-Gorton, vol. 3, pp 424-5.

20   Interview: Eggleton, 13 April 2018.

21   ABC, Transcript, The Liberals, 1994.

22   *Business Review*, December 1969.

23   The *Bulletin* of 20 January 1968 asked which Gorton he would be. For the Southey letter, see Liberal Party, Gorton Papers, NLA, MS 7984/15. For this episode, see Hancock, *Gorton*, pp. 161-2.

24   Reminiscential Conversations, Cameron-Gorton, vol. 2, pp. 389-93. See also *ibid.*, vol. 1, pp. 429-30.

138

8

'one of the most talked-about young women in Australia'

Ainsley Gotto kept a daily diary from the end of 1969 until her 24th birthday on 14 February 1970. Whereas her diaries usually just recorded future appointments and meetings she took time in this instance to report actions and conversations. It requires a knowledge of events and of people to follow everything but what is on the page tells much about Ainsley's participation in politics and about mood swings, the daily crises of office and the personality clashes.[1]

Ainsley observed how Gorton's spirits lifted after the election reverses and the leadership challenge at the end of 1969. On 21 January, Cabinet divided sharply over the McEwen-Gorton proposal for what became the Australian Industry Development Corporation (AIDC), an initiative whereby funds could be borrowed from overseas to enable Australian companies to develop Australian resources and to resist foreign takeovers.[2] Ainsley noted: 'PM elated at brawl on legislation, which he won.' Six days later she recorded: 'PM relaxed & happy – he's come to terms with being PM and instead of hating & fighting it, has started to enjoy it.'

Gorton was even happier on 28 January when Joh Bjelke-Petersen, the Country Party Premier of Queensland, accepted an independent inquiry into drilling to test for oil in Repulse Bay on the edge of the Great Barrier Reef. Ampol Exploration (Australia) Pty Ltd, which had arranged for a Japanese company to drill in Repulse Bay, announced in mid-January that it would cease operations pending a finding on whether drilling would damage the Reef. With the unions threatening to impose a 'black ban' on drilling, Gorton insisted that even 'slight damage' was 'too much damage' and wanted the Queensland Government to accept an inquiry. Bjelke-Petersen at first dismissed the necessity for any inquiry and then called for a broader one on the development of resources on and around the Reef. He backed down after Gorton hinted that the Commonwealth might initiate a case in the High Court over who controlled coastal waters. Ainsley recorded on 28 January 1970: 'V. successful day for PM & he enjoyed it.'

A striking feature of Ainsley's diary is her regular use of 'we' and 'us' when referring to the Government's positions and policies, reflecting her unself-conscious identification with John Gorton and her loyalty to him. Yet she could be critical. During the exchanges over oil drilling she commented unfavourably on Gorton's response to a telegram from Ampol:

> PM released a statement on Barrier Reef . . . last minute. I think ill-considered – statement. Didn't answer any points or suggestions Ampol made. Press are bemused and puzzled as to reason for statement. Want to know – is PM going to reply to Ampol? What's his attitude on its suggestions, etc. When will there ever be time to do things properly?

Gorton irritated her even more early in February when the RAAF flew him on an undisclosed trip to Lang Hancock's mining empire in Western Australia. The visit was so 'secret' that Ainsley had trouble persuading the Prime Minister to prepare a contingency statement should the press find out that he was meeting the controversial, very conservative and very rich Lang Hancock. She had firm views of her own. 'Still think he's been conned and shouldn't go.' Ainsley was further irritated upon discovering that Len Hewitt's secretary had been telling people that Hewitt was accompanying the Prime Minister to Western Australia. Gorton had previously told the Young Liberals in the West that he could not open their convention because he could not leave Canberra; they 'are going to be b. annoyed and I don't blame them'.

> Things moved very fast today and all the press had many details of the trip – who he was with, where he was and will file stories about stupid secrecy and this time, they're right.

To Gorton any fuss was immaterial. He was impressed by the extent of the mineral deposits and had listened sympathetically to Hancock's complaints about the Liberal Premier of Western Australia, David Brand, and the Minister for Industrial Development, Charles Court.

There are several references in the diary to Len Hewitt, nearly all reflecting Ainsley's exasperation with the man who would claim they had a smooth relationship. On 13 January Ainsley noted that Hewitt was being 'unhappy and peculiar' and wondered 'what I've done to tread on his toes about now'. On the same day, Hewitt told her she could not have a copy of the program for pre-budget talks over Industry, and Ainsley found out later that Gorton's personal secretary already had a copy: 'Another example of blocking.' On 2

February she thought 'Len quite peculiar again' and next day found him 'quite the reverse – it's probably deliberately disconcerting'. On Wednesday 4 February she wrote: 'Len livid because JGG[3] told me to use his office (which is actually mine anyway) he had the Department alter the entire office setup around his needs & what suits him, so Tony is out in the waiting room. B. ridiculous & typical.' Those who believed with the *Business Review* that Hewitt was the principal influence on the Prime Minister would have been surprised to learn that Gorton was happy for Hewitt to move away. Eggleton thought that Hewitt's change of location was to Gorton's detriment.[4] The Prime Minister needed the steadying influence the voice of experience could provide.

Ainsley occasionally referred to her workload. She spent most of Monday 19 January reading the Cabinet papers due for discussion the following day. This was the exercise she considered critical in highlighting for Gorton those issues or policy positions which might create 'problems' in the Cabinet Room. The papers for the Cabinet meeting of Tuesday 27 January did not reach her until the previous Saturday night. She started work on them while leaving a message for Gorton to ring her on Sunday morning. Bunting shared Ainsley's concern. He telephoned her to say that ministers would claim that the late arrival of the papers, and the complexity of issues involved in several submissions, excused them from being fully prepared for Cabinet. Ainsley told the Cabinet Secretary she would raise this matter with the Prime Minister on Sunday morning. After she did so, Gorton gave an order through her to Bunting to telephone all the ministers and tell them to read the papers.

Ainsley was always interested in appointments. On 21 January she recorded Freeth's appointment as Ambassador to Tokyo and the exchange whereby Plimsoll went to Washington and Waller returned to Australia to be Secretary of External Affairs. Freeth felt he was the victim of 'shabby treatment' by Gorton, and Ainsley was sad Plimsoll was leaving Canberra 'but McMahon wanted badly to get rid of him'. She had urged Gorton to find a job for Bill Arthur, a member of the Mushroom Club who had lost his seat in 1969 and was delighted when Arthur joined the private office to do research. She was very upset to learn of Barry Everingham's appointment as a minister's press secretary. It will be recalled how Ainsley believed Everingham had spread rumours about her having an abortion at the end of 1968. On 21 January she wrote: 'wrong appointment. Great consternation in the Gallery and dismay from us. Told Jean Lester [Betty Gorton's secretary] what a prick Barry E. is, she hadn't known. She told me "my abortion" was told to her last May by a Doctor's wife/ANU/ Doctor – jesus wept, when will they stop[?] . . . Must find out how Everingham got a clearance to work in a Govt Department – must be deliberate penetration.' [sic] (A similar situation would not have occurred on Credlin's watch.) Seven days later Ainsley returned to the subject of abortion: 'Mummy terribly upset as she was bailed up in town about my name appearing in transcript of Abortion Enquiry in Victoria – "The Ainsley Gotto of the Abortion Squad" – some people really are filthy.'

Ainsley's likes and dislikes were transparent. Her aversion for McMahon only increased after he 'complained bitterly' that Ainsley did not attend an Australia Day function he had organised; she had not been invited. More importantly, she had further evidence of McMahon continuing to reveal Cabinet secrets. On 8 February, Eggleton reported on a journalist's article and Ainsley wrote: 'We're sure the way he wrote it the leak came from Billy. I wonder more & more why the hell the Govt bothers to have a cabinet – why don't they just say to the press what they're <u>thinking</u> [emphasis in the original] of doing, it amounts to the same thing when you can't trust or rely on Ministers to respect confidential discussions.'

Ainsley was also aware that Malcolm Fraser was causing problems soon after his post-election elevation to the Defence portfolio. She observed him walking out of a January Cabinet meeting but she was not fully aware of its cause. Fraser was already gathering examples of what he saw as Gorton imposing his will on Cabinet. In January it was obvious that most ministers did not approve of the proposed AIDC though Fraser had to be careful because McEwen was the real proponent. Fraser was also angry with Ainsley because he thought she was involved in writing the sharp letter Gorton had sent him telling Fraser not to interfere in the administration of atomic policy, the province of Reg Swartz, the Minister for National Development. Swartz was an Ainsley favourite and 'very special' in Gorton's mind: he had been a prisoner of war and Swartz, an officer, had hit a Japanese guard who had struck one of his men.

Jim Killen was clearly a favourite. He often had meals at Getting Crescent or at a restaurant with Ainsley and her separated mother, Lesley, to whom he was becoming very attached. Ainsley was delighted to learn on 1 February that Margaret Guilfoyle was contesting pre-selection for Ivy Wedgwood's Senate seat in Victoria. A Guilfoyle supporter had informed Ainsley because of her 'strong interest and help in the Women's Division' of the Liberal Party. One MP whom Ainsley liked puzzled her. On 3

February she had a two-hour conversation on homosexuality with Don Dobie, the member for Cook in NSW. 'There is really something wrong [with] him – I don't know what.' Ainsley was almost certainly aware that Dobie shared accommodation with another man, and she was comfortable in the company of Bill Arthur whom she knew was gay.

At the time, Ainsley also liked Ray Coppin, the Commonwealth car driver who had served Menzies, Holt and Gorton and had taken on extra responsibilities at The Lodge. Someone in mid-January had 'poisoned' the water of the recently-installed swimming pool. A chemical analysis eased concerns; the added substance was non-poisonous, non-corrosive and non-soluble. On 28 January Derek Sharp of the Commonwealth Police implied it was 'an inside job' and gave Ainsley 'wild stories of things Ray has said & done – so mentioned it to PM. We don't think he did it.' In April Coppin was suspended from duty and in May jailed for six months for making fraudulent claims amounting to $2400. On appeal the sentence was reduced to a good behaviour bond and Les Irwin, an increasingly vociferous anti-Gortonite, offered to stand surety.[5]

On Saturday 14 February 1970 Ainsley wrote her final diary entry: 'Worked for 4 hours in the afternoon, but no tennis. We could win the Albert by-election. Vic rang at nine to say it's a cliffhanger but he personally thinks Heatley can pull it off.[6] Today I am 24 years old, and very tired.'

It is unfortunate that the diary did not extend to 25 February although what survives in the Gorton papers provides a good example of Ainsley trying to restrain her boss. The Government had no intention of granting a passport to the Australian journalist, Wilfred Burchett, who had lost his original document and now represented himself as a Cuban citizen. Nor would the Government order a judicial inquiry into its allegations that Burchett had earlier worked for North Korea and North Vietnam. Burchett had arrived in Australia – unimpeded – by private plane, and on 25 February Ainsley prepared a memorandum for Gorton in anticipation of parliamentary questions. Certain that Burchett was a traitor, Gorton wrote a marginal comment: he would not dignify 'the bastard' by saying there was insufficient evidence to prosecute him for treason. Fearful that Gorton might overdo his response Ainsley pointedly asked whether he intended to make 'a reasoned, middle-of-the-road, unemotional statement,' [emphasis in the original]. Gorton noted in the margin: 'unemotional but as vicious as possible.'

Several pleasant social occasions offered some respite from politics. Ainsley spent time on the tennis court with Gorton and his son Robin and Robin's wife Sue as well as with Don Chipp and Tom Hughes. On 3 January there was lunch at the Lodge with Edward Heath, the visiting Leader of the British Conservative Party who would defeat Harold Wilson in the General Election of June 1970. Ainsley also attended a dinner held in honour of the visiting American Vice President, Spiro Agnew. The major events revolved around the Royal Visit by the Queen, Prince Philip and Princess Anne at the end of April for the Cook Bicentenary. Ainsley joined both the welcome and farewell ceremonies at the RAAF Base at Fairbairn, attended a Garden Party at Government House, Yarralumla, and a reception at Parliament House. She accompanied the official party which travelled to Japan early in May to visit Expo '70. In addition to attending events associated with Australia's National Day at Expo, Ainsley was invited to a black-tie dinner at the Japanese Prime Minister's residence.

Ainsley was closely involved in the Trudeau visit in mid-May 1970. Prime Minister Trudeau of Canada was due to take an 18-day tour of the Pacific Region, starting with New Zealand and then visiting Australia in 15-20 May, followed by Malaysia, Singapore and Japan. The Australian visit was to begin with a weekend tour of the Great Barrier Reef followed by a night and morning in Sydney and two days in Canberra. Hewitt and Ainsley had clashed in the early days of planning. According to Ainsley's diary of 20 January, an official attached to the Canadian High Commission had met Hewitt to discuss the Trudeau arrangements. Their conversation included the proposed trip to the Barrier Reef. Hewitt spoke to her following the official's departure: 'Angry words afterwards, and he coldly told me you aren't going – is this his decision or an instruction (?).'

Closer to the event, the *Daily Express* in London of 3 April carried a warning: 'Oh Mr. Trudeau! Look what a row wiggling Miss Ainsley has got into over you.' She had created another 'furore' among Canberra's public servants because she had taken charge of the visit of 'swinging bachelor Pierre Trudeau' to Australia. According to the paper, there were many top officials who could expect to take that role, were better equipped to do so and resented the power the '32-year-old wields' (giving Ainsley's correct age of 24 would have enhanced the story). The *Express* proceeded to ask some rhetorical questions. Who vetted all Mr. Gorton's visitors before they could see him? Who got the blame when the Prime Minister sacked the Minister for Air? Who 'insists on Christian names for all', including those with knighthoods and titles? The answer was always 'Ainsley', and the *Express* warned the Canadian Prime Minister that, like it or not, she would address him as

'Pierre'.[7] Another British tabloid, the *Daily Mirror*, predicted on 14 April that Australians would see a meeting between the 'swinger' (Trudeau) and the 'wiggler' (Ainsley) as a 'tasty prospect'.

Ainsley had to forgo the Barrier Reef trip because of a political crisis in Canberra. The background was the Gorton Government's decision in January 1970 to assert Commonwealth jurisdiction over off-shore waters from the low water mark to the edge of the continental shelf.[8] It would introduce legislation to precipitate a State challenge in the High Court to determine whether the Commonwealth had constitutional power over the territorial waters. The Government also decided it was under no obligation to inform the States in advance of what was intended in the legislation. Ainsley correctly predicted in her diary on 21 January that the 'water legislation will cause a frightful stink, not helped by Fairbairn either'. David Fairbairn, when Minister for National Development, had – so he thought – committed the Government to consult the States before introducing the legislation. Labor supported the extension of Commonwealth power but moved a no-confidence motion citing Gorton's failure to honour Fairbairn's alleged promise. The House was to debate the matter on 15 May, the day Trudeau arrived in Australia.

On 14 May Ainsley learnt that the Labor Party had secretly called off the pairs for the vote on the Fairbairn issue. Phillip Lynch came to her office to say he had learnt that a Labor MP, possibly travelling to Perth, was told to return to Canberra but not to tell anyone. Ainsley immediately phoned Sir Donald Anderson, the Director-General of Civil Aviation, and asked him to confirm that the Labor MP had left on a flight to Canberra. She explained that this was a political matter and left it to Anderson to decide whether he could help. Anderson called back and confirmed the facts. Ainsley then arranged for Max Fox, the Chief Whip, to check with the Opposition Whip (her friend Gil Duthie) who said that the pairs were still 'ON'. By now there was another problem. Dudley Erwin had a broken foot and might have trouble reaching Canberra in time. Ainsley returned to Anderson who personally arranged for Erwin to be picked up by a training flight which was diverted to Ballarat and brought him to Canberra.

On the day of the debate and of the vote – 15 May – Gorton was due to meet Trudeau in Brisbane and, along with Andrew Peacock and Ainsley, was booked to join the Trudeau party for the trip to the Barrier Reef. Ivan Head telephoned Ainsley from New Zealand to say that the Canadians were concerned about the serious internal political problems and asked whether they should postpone or cancel the trip. Gorton told Ainsley to tell Head everything should go ahead as planned. Betty Gorton, accompanied by Andrew Peacock's wife, Susan, would meet Trudeau at Brisbane airport. Ainsley meanwhile spent a hectic day working with Max Fox 'to ensure we had our bases covered with whoever we could get back to Canberra – whether by commercial or VIP planes'.[9] In the event, Fairbairn absented himself from the House of Representatives on the crucial vote on a convoluted amendment motion prepared by Howson designed to preserve the Government while saving face for the anti-Gortonites like himself who had provoked the crisis in the first place. The Government agreed to consult the States and would not proceed with the legislation until the Budget session in August. John Gorton contacted Betty and Trudeau once the vote was assured.

Betty Gorton met Trudeau in Brisbane and, with Susan

Peacock, flew with him to Rockhampton where they boarded the *Coralita* and sailed to the Barrier Reef. It was a successful trip; Trudeau won the approval of local experts for his skin diving and Betty Gorton caught a substantial Spanish mackerel. Gorton met Trudeau when he arrived in Sydney on Sunday afternoon. A relieved Betty greeted Ainsley: 'Thank God you're here; Trudeau has not stopped asking about you.'[10]

That evening Sheila Scotter, editor of *Vogue Australia*, responding to Betty's request, had organised a small informal and private party for the Canadian Prime Minister. There was deliberately no reference to it in the official handbook for the Trudeau visit. The evening began with dinner on board the *Captain Phillip* and ended at the Taboo Night Club in Kings Cross. Scotter was embarrassed when the journalist, David McNicoll, broke his solemn promise to attend as a private individual. A photographer arrived at the Taboo and next day the *Daily Telegraph* carried the story on its front page, accompanied by a photograph of Trudeau dancing with Bobo Faulkner. Sheila Scotter sent her written apologies to the Gortons through Ainsley, whose presence at the party escaped notice but not the ardent attentions of Pierre Trudeau.[11]

There was a reception held in Kings Hall on the evening of 19 May. Three senators – Ivor Greenwood, Peter Rae and Harold Young, and their wives – issued an invitation to their friends to join them at the Hotel Canberra for 'a little hospitality and conviviality to put them in the correct physical and mental state to attend the Reception for Monsieur Trudeau.' Ainsley wrote at the bottom of her invitation, 'Senators Rae & Young insisted AG attend'. Rae and Young were rusted-on Gorton supporters. Greenwood was of a more conservative disposition. Ainsley had a readily-available escort: she went to the party with Ivan Head.

Her clearest memory of the reception centred on Susan Peacock's determination to corral Trudeau. She succeeded in getting him to the dance floor, but the Canadian Prime Minister returned quickly to Ainsley's side. Next morning Ainsley joined the party at Fairbairn Base to farewell Trudeau who by this stage seemed oblivious to anyone else. His flight to Singapore was due to land at Darwin, and he urged Ainsley to accompany him on that first stage. She could return on the next available flight to Sydney and then take one to Canberra. Ainsley wanted to go while sensing that accepting Trudeau's invitation would have long-term implications. Talking nearly 50 years after this moment she regretted backing off. Taking the flight to Darwin, she believed, might have changed her life. Ainsley was aware in making her comment that in May 1970 Trudeau was secretly engaged to Margaret Sinclair; they married in March 1971.[12]

From mid-1970 until the half-Senate election in November the Gorton Government was plagued by increasing internal opposition over its handling of Commonwealth-State arrangements and of anti-conscription and anti-Vietnam War demonstrations. Robin Askin, the Liberal Premier of NSW, and Sir Henry Bolte, the Liberal Premier of Victoria, remained constant critics of the Commonwealth's 'centralist' approach to financial matters and of any real or perceived intrusion into 'States' rights'. As a result, Gorton's decision in May to delay the territorial seas legislation became an indefinite postponement. The States were in no mood to compromise and the Government did not want to rely on Labor votes to carry a Bill through Parliament. It took the election of the Whitlam Government to establish Commonwealth sovereignty over Australian territorial waters. Gorton was also under attack for failing to deal with violent anti-war demonstrations and with draft resisters. Conservatives on the backbench could not understand why Tom Hughes, the Attorney-General, did not pursue prosecutions or introduce tougher measures to deal with violent demonstrations. They were not shifted by arguments for seeking a balance between political freedoms and lawlessness.

Ainsley kept warning Gorton about the murmurs she heard and the manoeuvrings she witnessed. She urged him to make peace with the dissidents. Gorton saw no point. Howson and his cohort did not like him, and he had no time for those Tom Hughes had dubbed 'troglodytes and termites'. Besides, Gorton did not believe they had significant support. More seriously, Gorton failed to recognise disturbing signs of which Ainsley was aware: Malcolm Fraser was becoming very disenchanted. On top of what she had witnessed in January-February, Ainsley also knew of Fraser's angry reactions to Gorton's attempts in July to call up the Pacific Islands Regiment to deal with unrest in Bougainville, initially without taking the matter to Cabinet. She also saw Fraser 'white-lipped with fury' after Cabinet knocked back his proposal for a defence force academy. Ainsley warned Gorton that the Defence Minister 'was going to be a problem',[13] though she was not to know how big a one.

Meanwhile, Ainsley continued to be a subject of media interest. *Pix* published an article on 20 June 1970 headed, 'Target of the Tongue Waggers', featuring her face as the bull's-eye on a sheet designed for target practice. The magazine promised to 'present the truth on the girl about whom all Canberra is talking'. It claimed that 'Ainsley-watching' was 'the new and absorbing Australian sport, played with great dedication by thousands of gossips and hundreds of inquisitive reporters'. *Pix* reported that Athol Guy considered Ainsley to be 'a very charming young lady' while some spoke of her loyalty and capacity for work. Others thought that 'Grotty', as she was nicknamed by 'many fellow workers', ruled with ruthless authority and used people. Apparently, Canberra journalists did not particularly like Ainsley. One said she was 'too aggressive' and another – strangely – thought her 'a colourless dresser'. *Pix* concluded that Ainsley 'doesn't give the slightest damn for Ainsley watchers'.

Eggleton persuaded Ainsley to talk to a journalist, Rosemary Munday, who planned to write articles on women whose lives were closely involved with politics. Eggleton explained that Munday was one of his 'chicks' who helped with the recent Royal Visit, and had proved to be 'responsible and sympathetic' in handling Royal Visit stories and had once worked for a Liberal minister in NSW.[14] Ainsley agreed to meet her and received top billing of the secretaries described and dissected in three articles headed, 'The Girls in the Power Game'.[15]

Munday described Ainsley as 'one of the most talked-about young women in Australia', acknowledging that some of the comments were not what a young woman might want to hear. Listening to talk in the lobbies, Munday had an image of a 'goddess' to whom backbenchers paid court, however insincere and begrudging, to gain access to the Prime Minister. With her 'headful of myths', Munday discovered 'a human being of many parts': 'Ainsley the unwilling centre of attention . . . Ainsley the cool, clear-headed, efficient private secretary . . . Ainsley the diplomat

. . . Ainsley the old-fashioned modern girl.' Ainsley knew she had been called 'disrespectful', 'rude' and even 'bitchy'. She explained how she deliberately hid her feelings, was obsessed with privacy, loved her job for its mental stimulation, derived satisfaction for doing it well and liked to drive her car fast because that required judgment. As for marriage, the question rarely asked in 1970 of alpha males approaching their mid-twenties, Ainsley responded, 'it will happen if it happens'.

Pointing out that Ainsley was hardly 'an average secretary' – she did very little typing – Munday placed her 'in the front seat of the nation's most strategic administrative post'. Ainsley, however, scoffed at the idea that she exercised power but accepted that she could manipulate situations. There was a part-public example of manipulation on 18 September 1970. Ainsley reckoned that a Moratorium rally on the lawns of Parliament House, to be addressed by Gough Whitlam on that day, might yield some compromising photographs. On her initiative, staff of the official Australian News and Information Bureau (ANIB) took photographs of the demonstration. One featured Whitlam appearing to address the crowd under or near a Viet Cong flag. The Opposition questioned both the authenticity of the photographs and the use of the ANIB for political purposes. Tony Eggleton took responsibility for ordering the photographs, absolved Gorton of any involvement, and stressed that the ANIB had been employed merely to preserve an official record.[16]

John Gorton needed a good result in the half-Senate election on 21 November 1970. Senior Liberals and Tony Eggleton continued to worry about Gorton's television image, but it was generally agreed within the Party Organisation that his campaign performance was a vast improvement on 1969. Gorton had a penchant for battle and he went in hard, assaulting Labor over law and order issues and defence and foreign policy. Ainsley travelled with Gorton for some of the campaign and was sitting at a table near the stage when fighting broke out at a meeting where Gorton was speaking in an outer suburb of Melbourne. Rival groups cannoned into her and Police had to intervene to save Ainsley from being pinned against the table. Still shaken after the event, she said it 'could have been nasty'. Although she was not hurt, 'I was glad help came so quickly'. The Melbourne *Sun*'s first headline for the meeting stated: 'Ainsley knocked down in fight.'[17]

Despite Gorton's best efforts, the Senate result was a disaster. The Coalition share of the primary vote of 38.2 per cent was the worst federal result for the non-Labor parties since the debacle of 1943. The saving grace was that Labor's primary vote stood at just 42.2 per cent, the real winner being the DLP which won seats in Victoria and in Queensland and, for the first time, picked up one in NSW. Unlike the 1969 result for the House of Representatives, no one could blame the Liberal Party Organisation for what happened in 1970. After all, as Ainsley explained, 'we' ran the campaign.[18]

1   Diary 1970, Gotto Papers, MS Acc15.126, Box 31.
2   Hancock, *Gorton*, pp 266-72. Cabinet finally approved the proposal early in February although it required some deft re-writing for the Cabinet Minutes to record an approval in the absence of majority Cabinet support.
3   Ainsley on paper and in conversation frequently referred to John Grey Gorton in this manner as she did for the rest of her life.
4   Interview: Eggleton, 13 April 2018.
5   *Canberra Times*, 21 April, 15 May and 18 June 1970.
6   Heatley, a former senator, did win the State seat of Albert in Queensland, taking it from the Country Party. 'Vic' was probably Vince Ockerby, the Party's General Secretary in Queensland. McMahon had told Gorton

the by-election would be held on 31 January. Ainsley recorded Heatley's amusement to receive Gorton's telegram of good wishes for the wrong day.

7   *Daily Express*, 3 April 1970. The *Express* identified the Air Minister as 'Leslie Erwin', confusing Dudley Erwin with Leslie Irwin.

8   Dec. 74, 21 January 1970. NAA: A5882, CO537.

9   AG to IH, 24 April 2001, J. G. Gorton: Book: Memos/Emails Etc., Gorton Papers, NLA, MS Acc03/185.

10   Interview: AG, 20 April 2017.

11   *Ibid.*

12   Interviews: AG, 20 April and 26 November 2017. Trudeau was 30 years older than Sinclair, and 27 years older than Ainsley. Referring to the Trudeau visit, Max Newton's *Weekend Business Review* of 27 October 1970 commented that Ainsley had developed 'a keen interest' in him but 'nothing has come of her hopes at this stage'.

13   Interview: AG, 20 April 2017.

14   Gotto Papers MS 9895, Folio Box 2.

15   Melbourne *Herald*, 26 September 1970.

16   Interview: AG, 17 December 2017; Eggleton Papers, NAA: M2903/88.

17   *Age, Australian, Daily Mirror* (Sydney), *Sun* (Melbourne) 17 November 1970.

18   Interview: AG, 17 December 2017.

9

'I'm so damn tired'

Given the Senate result, and the prospect of a House of Representatives election at the end of 1972, it was highly likely that John Gorton's leadership would be challenged in the Party Room at some time in 1971.

Despite the Senate setback, Gorton began 1971 by taking decisive and effective stands on issues that should have pleased his Liberal critics. At the Commonwealth Conference in Singapore Gorton stood by the decision of Edward Heath's Government in the UK to resume arms sales to South Africa, arguing that the decision was one for Britain to make. He defied attempts by Bob Hawke and the ACTU to prevent the export of merino lambs from Australia and rejected a proposed 15 per cent increase in fees put forward by the Australian Medical Association. When the Minsec mining group collapsed, Gorton mounted a rescue mission which saved Australian business from cascading bankruptcies. Yet, as he had discovered during 1970, effective action on some issues merely convinced the 'troglodytes and termites' that he was unworthy of high office. Rising inflation called for tough measures and Gorton was determined that the States understood and accepted the need to cut expenditure. The strong stand he took with the State Premiers, and notably with Askin and Bolte, rendered him more vulnerable. The Premiers of the two largest States, which between them sent a total of 39 Liberal senators and MPs to Canberra – constituting just over half of the Liberal Party Room – wanted Gorton removed.

Ainsley Gotto now realised that it hardly mattered what Gorton did or achieved; his internal Party opponents were a lost cause. Her attention, however, was temporarily diverted. Gorton had sent her to Singapore in mid-January 1971 to prepare the way for his arrival at the Conference. She returned briefly to Australia and flew back to Singapore with Gorton's official party. McMahon, the Minister for the (renamed) Department of Foreign Affairs, travelled separately on a commercial flight. On both trips Ainsley 'encountered chaos'. There was a marked contrast with the preparations and conduct of the 1969 London Conference. Ainsley sent a heartfelt letter after the event to Nicholas Parkinson, the Australian High Commissioner in Singapore, thanking him, his wife and many others. Without their help she would never have managed.

On 25 January Ainsley wrote to Ivan Head, who had been in Singapore with Trudeau, to issue a directive: 'if fate hates me enough and we are still in office in 1973, you will not allow the next Prime Ministers' Conference to be held in Ottawa' [emphasis in the original]. Judging by Singapore, it could only be 'as bad, if not worse'. She had spent so much time during the Conference apologising to Head 'for being caught up, tired, or just plain fed up. You must try and come quietly, here, very soon, and perhaps we can find that quiet spot without being interrupted or pressured or even mentally obstructed.' Things were warming up in Canberra, and the next Cabinet meeting 'will be long and arduous and pressures will continue to pile up one on top of another as they always seem to do until the House meets. I am so damn tired . . . I don't really know whether I can cope with it. Doubtless as always one will try to.' Ainsley sent Head an extract from a Gorton interview, saying that before he became too annoyed Gorton did say 'some rather pleasant things about your Prime Minister'.[1]

When Gorton met the Party Room on 2 February, the day the Country Party selected Doug Anthony to succeed the retiring John McEwen as Leader, he came under fire over the Senate election result. After three hours of torrid debate Senator Ian Wood of Queensland moved that the leadership be declared vacant. When Gorton called for a seconder there was silence. As Wood later remarked, 'on this warm sunny day the snowmen had melted'.[2] Yet just over a month later, half the Liberal Party Room bravely voted against Gorton – in a secret ballot. Although several major issues could have precipitated a crisis, it was the comparatively minor one of civic action policy in South Vietnam which led to Gorton's loss of office. Malcolm Fraser, one of his original backers for the Party leadership in 1968, became the instrument of Gorton's downfall in March 1971, an action which assured him of top place in Ainsley Gotto's list of villains.[3]

Fraser as Minister for Defence became concerned during February 1971 that the Army was not fully committed to the policy of 'civic action' in South Vietnam. He and the Army were giving different briefings to journalists on the subject. A journalist,

Robert Baudino, intended to publish an article on 2 March claiming that the Joint Intelligence Organisation was reporting on the Army's actions in Vietnam and that Fraser did not trust the Army's reports. The Prime Minister wanted to hear the Army's version and to offer his support. Gorton had tried but failed to contact Fraser before he met Lieutenant-General Sir Thomas Daly, the Army's Chief of the General Staff, for 15 minutes on the afternoon of Monday 1 March. Another journalist, Alan Ramsey, heard that Daly had accused Fraser of being disloyal to the Army and to its minister, Andrew Peacock. Questioned by Ramsey on the Wednesday, Gorton refused to comment on what Daly had or had not said. Ramsey took silence to mean confirmation and published the story in the *Australian* on 4 March. What had begun as a dispute between the Army and Fraser became one between Fraser and Gorton.

Tony Eggleton later recalled how some of Gorton's confidants, including Ainsley Gotto and Len Hewitt, thought 'Fraser needed to be taken down a peg'. The Press Secretary 'had picked up some snippets of conversation to that effect' and he believed that 'when the civic action blew up, they saw it as an issue on which they could cut Malcolm down to size'.[4] Yet, 'what they had in mind was some sort of a controlled burning-off exercise which unfortunately became a bushfire'.[5] Alan Reid added weight to Eggleton's assessment. He pointed out how Gorton, travelling to Shepparton for the by-election campaign following McEwen's resignation from the seat of Murray, seemed pleased that Fraser had been 'done over' when Gorton required him on 2 March to reply under his own name to the Baudino article, a reply dictated by Gorton.[6] Nevertheless, if Gorton did want to take Fraser down a peg or two his primary motive in speaking to Daly was his longstanding predisposition to go beyond 'normal channels' in seeking an explanation and to support those who had worn the uniform in war. It was that conversation with Daly, and the subsequent interpretations of it, which led to the leadership crisis of the following week.

After talking to Gorton on the afternoon of Friday 5 March, Fraser began clearing out his office. Gorton and Ainsley were totally unaware of what he was planning and doing. They had no idea that Fraser had written a resignation speech by Sunday afternoon, and discussed it with the Fairbairns, Sir Arthur Tange, the Secretary of Defence, and Admiral Victor Smith, Chairman of the Chiefs of Staff Committee. Gorton rang Fraser early on Sunday evening to warn him of the Channel Nine program *Meet the Press* put together by Sir Frank Packer's employees. Fraser reassured him: 'Don't worry about it boss – just have a good night's sleep.' He defended his deception by arguing he was under no obligation to give the Prime Minister prior notice of his resignation. Besides, two senior public servants had advised him he would be sacked if he revealed his hand. Together, Fraser's deceit and Gorton's failure to sniff the wind left the Prime Minister unprepared for what followed.

Ainsley was not involved in any plans for dealing with Fraser. She had been given something else to think about in the first week of March. On 4 March Eggleton sent Ainsley a note to say that her car 'is creating some interest again'. He had heard 'one or two rumblings recently about illegal parking'. He reported receiving a tip from a journalist relating to a planned police raid the previous day when someone in Parliament House had 'warned them off' taking action in relation to Ainsley's car. Apparently, some journalists sensed a story and wanted to know why the police ignored her car and who told them not to act.[7] Ainsley also had her mind on a matter of special interest to her. The artist June Mendoza was working on the portrait of John Gorton which was to be added to the official collection. Ainsley was delighted to discover that the man she admired would be on canvas as the man she knew. At the same time, with conspiracy theories providing regular fare around Parliament House, Ainsley was not immune from looking suspiciously at the outwardly innocent. She wondered at the time, and even more later, why Gorton's Press Secretary and the Minister for Defence talked to each other more often than their respective jobs required. Wisely, she kept her speculation to herself.[8]

Ainsley first appreciated the danger when, just after 3.00pm on Monday 8 March, a member of Fraser's staff hand-delivered a letter to her office. The letter announced Fraser's intention to resign because the Prime Minister's conduct indicated 'significant disloyalty to a senior Minister'. Fraser intended to deliver his resignation to the Governor-General on the following morning and would seek to make a statement after Question Time later that day. Ainsley took the initiative and typed a note for Gorton: 'You may wish to have a record of when you both saw and spoke with Malcolm Fraser last week.'

> You tried to telephone Mr. Fraser at about 7.30 p.m. on Monday evening to discuss the Baudino story with him.
>
> You saw Mr. Fraser in your office at 10.30 a.m. on Tuesday morning 2 March.
>
> Mr. Fraser returned to your office later that morning.
>
> You spoke to Mr. Fraser in Hobart at 5.15 p.m. on Thursday 4

March.

> You saw Mr. Fraser at approximately 3.30 p.m. in your office on Friday 5 March. He left your office at 5.00 p.m.

> You either spoke to him or saw him personally at the Lodge over the weekend. I don't know when.

> You spoke to the Minister just after 6.00 p.m. Sunday evening, 7 March to tell him about the "Meet the Press" Television Programme.[9]

Although Ainsley recorded Gorton's attempt to ring Fraser on Monday evening 1 March, she made no reference to Gorton's claimed attempt to contact him before or immediately after seeing Daly that afternoon.

On Tuesday morning, 9 March, Gorton tried in vain to persuade Fraser to withdraw his resignation, offering to admit his error of not denying the Ramsey story and to express confidence in his Minister for Defence. It appears that Fraser sought Tange's advice, and Tange warned him of 'buckets of scorn' should he stay in his post.[10] Gorton and Fraser spoke at a Party Room meeting where Howson, John Jess (Vic.) and Harry Turner (NSW) said they would cross the floor if forced into a vote of confidence in the Prime Minister.

By now, Ainsley was involved in some preparatory work. There is a typed document in her papers along with some notes in her handwriting dealing with the prospect of an Opposition motion of no-confidence in the Government rather than of one directed solely at the Prime Minister. It was calculated that, on Party lines, the Government would have 59 votes to Labor's 56. This assessment was based on the Government having its membership of 66 reduced by two because the Speaker was in the Chair and because McEwen's replacement would not be elected until 20

March. From 64 votes, a further four votes were taken off to allow for Government members being unable to reach Canberra in time. Even if Jess crossed the floor, the Government would still have 59 votes. Nothing was written about the Labor vote but, given that Labor won 59 seats in 1969, it may be assumed, with Jess added (Ainsley dismissed Howson and Turner as blowhards when it came taking action), that pair arrangements or absences accounted for the figure reckoned at 56. Clearly, 'we' had decided that the Government was not in danger. The Government did, indeed, survive but John Gorton did not. It appears that Ainsley had set herself the wrong question.

Two intriguing notes were attached to this assessment. A typed one referred to Jeff Bate, a known Gorton opponent, being delayed by floods. It read: 'forget about.' A second note read 'PM to see Dudley.' This note either recorded Gorton's intention to speak to Erwin or Ainsley's reminder to herself to tell or persuade Gorton to do so. Either way, Gorton and Ainsley both respected Erwin's ability to count. Nevertheless, they placed Erwin among the anti-Gortonites, as Howson certainly did. Curiously, however, Erwin made it clear in 1984 that he not only loathed Howson but considered it 'a damn shame' that the Party Room 'didn't give more support to Gorton' in the confidence motion on 10 March.[11] It is not known how Erwin voted on the day.

In his resignation speech of 9 March,[12] Fraser accused Gorton of violating the chain of command by directly consulting the Army without reference to the Minister for Defence. He also accused him of failing to 'kill' a journalist's story about Fraser's alleged disloyalty to the Army and to Peacock; by not doing so, Gorton had placed silence above loyalty to a senior colleague.

Fraser's third charge was that the Prime Minister had 'a dangerous reluctance to consult Cabinet, and an obstinate determination to get his own way'. He cited as evidence Gorton's attempt in July 1970 to prevent a Cabinet discussion of the proposed call-out of the Pacific Islands Regiment to deal with unrest in Bougainville.[13] Fraser concluded by saying that Gorton was unfit to be Prime Minister.

Gorton was measured in reply. He took the House through the sequence of events as he saw them. There were no recriminations or denunciations. Gorton said Fraser had been 'a good Minister for Defence' and it was 'a tragedy' he felt compelled to resign. Fraser's resignation had caught him completely by surprise, and he was not prepared for the allegation concerning the call-out, though he recalled being persuaded by Fraser's argument that a full Cabinet should make the decision. Confessing he was wrong not to have denied the story about Lieutenant-General Daly's alleged comment, Gorton nonetheless thought 'an enormous amount' had been built on this issue. He insisted it was only 'decent and proper' to defend the Army against undeserved criticism.

Gorton's speech was interrupted by a loud voice from the Press Gallery. Alan Ramsey shouted, 'You liar', when Gorton quoted him as saying, 'Fair enough', on being told that the Prime Minister thought it wrong to discuss what a third party (Daly) had said. While Ramsey was taking steps to apologise for his outburst, and Eggleton was working on the apology to make it suitably groveling, the House was debating a Whitlam motion to bring Ramsey before the Bar of the House. Sitting in her normal seat in the Chamber, Ainsley Gotto scribbled a note for Gorton: 'Why can't you announce that Ramsey has apologised to you –

you accept that – so the motion should not be carried.'[14] It was sensible advice. Whether it convinced Gorton or whether he had already made up his mind is not known. Gorton told the House he had heard from Eggleton that Ramsey had apologised, said the apology was good enough for him, and suggested the motion might be withdrawn, which it was.

According to Rosemary Munday, with Gorton under attack in the Chamber, Ainsley was in 'full flight', Munday adding the important information that she was 'dressed in midi culottes, purple shirt and boots'. Ainsley was swooping in and out of the House, scribbling urgent notes and snatching a few moments for a cigarette. Short of sleep, she was exhausted and on edge by the fateful Wednesday though 'had lost only a little of her starch'. Munday completed the picture by reporting that on Wednesday Ainsley 'went to work in a pretty daffodil frock and a string of pearls'.

On the morning of the vote, Ainsley spoke on the telephone to Sir James Plimsoll in the United States to say that Gorton could not speak to him as he had to attend a parliamentary party meeting on the leadership. Gorton had wanted to talk to Plimsoll about the National Gallery in Canberra. Plimsoll heard Gorton call out during his conversation with Ainsley: 'Tell Jim that it will be alright, I've got the numbers.'[15]

Whether Gorton was genuinely confident or not, he took three actions which undermined his position: he told an ill Duke Bonnett, a Queensland backbench supporter, there was no need for him to leave his sick bed and make a special trip to Canberra; he sanctioned the tactic of having two very junior Victorian MPs propose a vote of confidence instead of requiring the anti-

Gortonites to mount their own no-confidence motion; and he answered a question in the Party Room saying he would not ask the Governor-General to dissolve the House if the vote went against him. The first action cost him a majority; the second saved his opponents from declaring themselves; and the third removed the threat to backbenchers holding marginal seats.[16] Ainsley could not recall discussing Gorton's actions with him either before or on the day of the vote. In 2017 she acknowledged that Gorton had made the three serious mistakes.

Ainsley and Tony Eggleton waited in the corridor outside the Party Room. 'Miss Gotto paced up and down, hands clasped in front of her face'.[17] Inside the Party Room a succession of anti-Gortonites denounced their leader for acts of commission or omission. There were several intended killer punches. Malcolm Mackay (NSW) said the Prime Minister kept Liberal Party members waiting while at a nearby bar he drank and played darts with some locals. Peter Howson quoted Leopold Amery's charge to Neville Chamberlain – 'In God's name go' – either unaware or purposely hiding the fact that Amery was quoting Cromwell's demand of the Long Parliament. When the final vote was taken the result was 33-all. Gorton gave a casting vote against himself. McMahon comfortably defeated Snedden in the vote for the vacant leadership and, assisted by a wave of sympathy and guilt, Gorton had an easy victory over Fairbairn and Fraser in the election for the deputy leadership.

Max Fox, the Chief Whip, brought the results from the Party Room. McMahon's PPS, Kim Jones of Foreign Affairs, was standing not far from Ainsley. He saw her crying.[18] It will be recalled that the two of them first met during the hectic week arranging for visitors to be transported to Melbourne for the Holt Memorial Service. They saw a lot of each other after McMahon appointed a reluctant Jones his PPS and they got on very well together despite the distance between their bosses. Ainsley had no memory of shedding tears on the Wednesday. She did remember being angry with those who brought Gorton down and had trouble believing that he had stood for the position of Deputy Leader. More than most people in and around Parliament House on that day, Ainsley knew it would be a short-term appointment. When a distraught Reg Swartz walked into her office and asked, 'what have we done?', she could barely speak. In the meantime, Eggleton had announced the bare facts to the assembled media in Kings Hall. There was a gasp when he reported that Gorton was the new Deputy Leader. One journalist suggested he must be joking. Eggleton replied: 'I never joke at times like this.'[19]

After the event some of the press were very interested in what would happen to Hewitt and to Gotto. The *Daily Mirror* of 11 March was wide of the mark in suggesting that Hewitt would succeed Sir Richard Randall as Secretary of the Treasury. In the short term, Hewitt took the position of Secretary to the new Department of Vice-President of the Executive Council. He was subsequently appointed Secretary of the new Department of Environment, Aborigines and the Arts. It was headed by Peter Howson, whom McMahon, after a short delay, brought back into the outer ministry.

Rosemary Munday employed some fanciful tabloid hyperbole with her claim that 'the big question everyone in Canberra was asking' was 'What will happen to Ainsley?' According to one press report, she was still in bed at 8.30 am on Thursday morning, and greeted journalists wearing a dressing gown. She said it had been a long night and would make no comment except she would stay working for Gorton while he remained Minister for Defence.[20] Munday's article, headed 'Ainsley sticks to boss', clarified the situation for 'everyone in Canberra'. Packer's *Daily Telegraph*, which had pushed hard for McMahon, merely reported on 12 March that Ainsley's base pay would drop from $8000 a year to $7181. Some enjoyed her discomfort. An unsigned and undated handwritten note arrived from New Zealand: 'You have had your day of being Prime Minister you disgusting courtesen [*sic*]. You cheap skate.' The envelope was addressed to, 'The Ainsley Gotto, c/o Mr Gorton, Canberra, Australia'.[21]

Ainsley spent most of the Wednesday afternoon and evening clearing out Gorton's office and her own and sorting out what had to be retained as official files. She assured her own staff – referring to them fondly as her 'children'[22] – that they would be given reasonable time to move on. Initially, there was little to do as PPS to the Minister for Defence. On 17 March, Gorton left Australia accompanied by what Ainsley called 'Fraser stooges' to take over Fraser's pre-arranged trip to South Vietnam and southeast Asia. Ainsley spent some of her spare time over the next few days recording in a diary the comings and goings of ministers in the McMahon reshuffle.[23]

There was good and bad news. Chipp and Phillip Lynch dropped into her office on 17 March to tell Ainsley they were 'OK' and Ainsley learnt that Jim Forbes would have Education and Science ('an enormous surprise but good'), Snedden would be Treasurer and Nigel Bowen Attorney-General. She surmised that Killen, Hughes, Bury and Senator Annabelle Rankin would be sacked '& we don't know who else' (Bury lost Treasury but was appointed Minister for Foreign Affairs and Rankin went to New Zealand as High Commissioner). Ainsley heard that Fairbairn would be accepting appointment as High Commissioner to the UK once the Party found someone who could hold his NSW seat of Farrer. 'We're sure he [McMahon] won't leave us the present Lib. Service Ministers – Andrew [Peacock] will stay but be moved – & he'll probably put in Howson or Mackay or someone else to report back on John [Gorton] to him.'[24] Ainsley had also heard reports that Fraser and Howson were involved in machinations to make Gorton appear before a preselection committee for his seat of Higgins. If they succeeded and 'JGG' lost, Ainsley thought the Party could split 'wide open'. Letters of support continued to pour into Gorton's office a week after he resigned and when Ainsley spoke on the phone to him in Singapore Gorton 'sounded cheerful'. 'Fraser behaved like a B. today.'

Next day Ainsley recorded McMahon's sacking of Killen. She claimed 'people are disgusted that he waited until John was out of the country' before doing so. At this point, loyalty and anger warped her judgment: 'If we started a new party – more than half the Parliament would join it. A John Gorton party.' There was not the slightest chance of such an eventuality. At least Ainsley could offer sympathy; she took a distraught Killen out to dinner. There was better news. Peacock told her he had lost Army but was remaining in the ministry. Ainsley learnt directly or indirectly that many others were still 'in' but unassigned, and she also heard about Hewitt's new appointment. Chipp returned to Ainsley's office for a long conversation and to say he was 'finished' with Snedden.[25] Overall, for Ainsley the hard part was to sit on information. 'It's so awful when one knows what McM has in mind – and one can't say to the people involved – & has to pretend ignorance.'

Betty Gorton rang Ainsley early on 19 March to tell her of the statement she was giving to the Press Gallery. A journalist with the London *Daily Mirror* had rung Betty seeking confirmation that she was instituting divorce proceedings against her husband. Ainsley advised her not to put out a statement as it would be a sensational story: Betty responded, 'it is a sensation'. Ainsley promised to talk to someone and 'we' finally found the journalist responsible. Betty's son, Robin, having issued a formal denial told Ainsley that she was to be named as the co-respondent, a fact which Betty had not mentioned to her in the morning. Further on 19 March Ainsley recorded that Hughes has been sacked after a Cabinet meeting and McMahon had told him of being under a lot of pressure from the Party to remove him. 'It's so ridiculous. Jim [Killen] rang me and wants to leak it out – which I've advised against.'

Gorton returned to Australia on the morning of 22 March. He attended a Cabinet meeting that afternoon and kept Ainsley informed about the dissent directed at McMahon's support for the abolition of the Wool Commission. The Country Party ministers, supported by Gorton, wanted to retain it. On 2 April he told Ainsley that McMahon was thinking of returning the income tax power to the States. He would resign from the Party if McMahon did so. By this time Ainsley's judgment was back on track, as she realised that the grass roots of the Party would applaud McMahon's decision because they did not see the long-term implications which would be disastrous for Australia.[26]

Ainsley was hurt and in no mood for forgiveness. She might

divert Killen from taking rash actions of revenge, and try to restrain what Gorton called Killen's 'Irish', but separate tactical considerations did nothing to change how she felt about those responsible for undermining and destroying Gorton's leadership. Nor did she hold back. There were several private opportunities to let fly and at least one where Ainsley vented her feelings in a semi-public place. She visited the Hotel Canberra soon after midnight in mid-June 1971 where Sir Henry Bolte, in town for a Premiers' Conference, was holding court in the lobby. Observing that she was wearing 'a stunning yellow dress', a former Peacock press secretary claimed that Ainsley accused Bolte of hating, undermining and crucifying Gorton. The pair exchanged accusations for more than three hours while adding dollars to the drinks bill.[27]

No one reported the confrontation at the time but Ainsley remained the centre of media attention and especially in mid-April when she accompanied the Gortons on a trip to London where Gorton was to attend the Five Power Conference involving Britain, Australia, New Zealand, Malaysia and Singapore. Peter Cole-Adams in the *Age* of 15 April noted that the popular dailies – the *Daily Express, Sun, Daily Mirror, Daily Mail, Evening News* and *Evening Standard* – either featured pictures of Ainsley or 'resurrected' Erwin's comment, or did both. The *Daily Mirror* headline read, 'It wiggles, it's shapely, and it's in London'. The *Evening News* had its own front-page variation: 'A bit of a wiggle as Ainsley flies in'. Even the broadsheet London *Daily Telegraph*, which reported that the Five-Power Conference had agreed on new Commonwealth defence arrangements, and which devoted 10 paragraphs to the subject, placed that story alongside a photo taking an almost equal amount of space of 'Miss Ainsley Gotto,

24, secretary to Mr Gorton . . . arriving for the opening of the conference today'.

A *SMH* correspondent observed on 15 April that millions of newspaper readers could be forgiven for thinking that 'Miss Ainsley Gotto' had arrived for the talks with 'a Mr John Gorton rather vaguely in the background'. The *Australian* of 1 May dealt with the other end of the trip with a front-page photo of Ainsley striding across the tarmac at Sydney airport on her return from London and a stopover in Washington. In between, the *Daily Express* reported the essential information on 23 April that she was in the audience for the premiere of Dustin Hoffman's *Little Big Man* at a cinema in Shaftesbury Avenue.

Initially, the media in Australia had left Ainsley alone on one personal matter. That changed on 20 March 1971 when the Melbourne *Truth* reported a reference by the journalist John Boland on the HSV7 television program *This Week* to 'a matter of the heart involving two private secretaries'. Boland did not name them, but *Truth* did: Ainsley Gotto and Race Mathews, Gough Whitlam's PPS. Eight days later, the 'I Spy' column in the Canberra *Sunday Post* referred to Mathews 'squiring' Ainsley about town and reported talk of wedding bells.

Almost eleven years older than Ainsley, Race had joined the Labor Party in 1956, held positions as a primary school teacher and speech therapist with the Victorian Department of Education, served as a Councillor with the City of Croydon and, since 1960, had been Secretary of the Australian Fabian Society. He joined Gough Whitlam's staff in 1967 and, from the following year, he and Ainsley had a clear view of each other from their respective positions at the side of the Chamber. After a time, the younger

Capulet and the younger Montague, while arguing about politics, fell in love with each other. Both had a need for closeness when they got together late in 1970. Ainsley was worn out by work, distressed by the attacks on Gorton and was on her own; Race's first wife had died, leaving him with three small children. Race astutely observed that something was missing from Ainsley's life. For her part, Ainsley 'simply adored' this 'fascinating man'.

They could stay out of sight because Ainsley had taken a six-month lease on a house with a pool and a tennis court owned by friends of her mother. The house was in Kambah, an ungazetted new suburb on the outer edge of Canberra. Race said later 'we were very close. We were living together and we thought very seriously about getting married.' Ainsley had a different understanding. '*We* didn't talk about marriage: *he* did.' Ainsley described their time together as 'occasional' because both were 'frantically busy'. The difference between them, as she saw it, was that he wanted to marry and she did not want to stay at home and have babies. Ainsley was annoyed by the publicity and prepared a press release.

> I am not engaged to Mr. Race Mathews and I have no intention of becoming engaged to Mr. Mathews. Both Mr. Mathews and I have said this before and this constant harassment seems to me to border on persecution. When I make a decision to marry anybody I will make it myself – without the assistance of newspapers.[28]

Whitlam and Gorton tolerated the relationship, something their modern-day successors would never do. One Liberal, however, did have serious concerns. Peter Howson noted in his diary on 15 August 1971 that Race Mathews, endorsed to oppose him in his seat of Casey, was 'very friendly with Ainsley Gotto and might be spreading a lot of information from her around the electorate, which would be a problem'. Ainsley was not unhappy when Race ousted Howson in December 1972 though she was careful never to breach confidentiality. In the meantime, the Gotto-Mathews relationship had already eased its way into what became an enduring and very close friendship which in its halcyon days had helped Ainsley through the wretched months leading up to and immediately succeeding the change in Liberal leadership.[29]

1   For letters to Parkinson and Head, see Gotto Papers, MS 9895/2/5.

2   Interview: Wood (Ron Hurst, 18-20 October 1984), NLA,.TRC, 4900-84, 6:19-21.

3   For recent accounts of the lead-up to the leadership crisis, see Fitzgerald and Holt, *Reid*, pp. 221-40; Fraser and Simons, *Fraser*, pp. 207-25; Mullins, *Tiberius with a Telephone*, pp. 370-93

4   Fraser and Simons, *Fraser*, pp 213-14. The authors did not provide any documentation.

5   ABC: *The Liberals*, quoted in Mullins, *Tiberius with a Telephone*, p. 376.

6   Alan Reid, *The Gorton Experiment*, Shakespeare Head Press, Sydney, 1971, pp. 420-1.

7   Eggleton to AG, 4 March 1971, Gotto Papers, MS 9895, Folio 3, press clippings 1971.

8   Interview: AG, 17 December 2017.

9   Fraser – Papers Relating to his resignation from the Gorton Ministry, Gorton Papers, NLA, MS 7984, Box 14.

10 Peter Edwards, *Arthur Tange: Last of the Mandarins*, Allen & Unwin, Crows Nest, 2006, pp. 189-90.

11 Interview (Linford): Erwin, 4:1 and 9; 5: 16-18.

12 *CPD*, H/R, vol. 71, pp. 679-84.

13 For Tom Hughes' criticism of Fraser's representation of this incident, see Hancock, *Hughes*, pp. 186-7.

14 Fraser, Papers Relating to his resignation from Gorton Ministry, Gorton Papers, NLA, MS 7984, Box 14.

15 Quoted in Jeremy Hearder, *Jim Plim Ambassador Extraordinary: A Biography of Sir James Plimsoll*, Connor Court, Ballarat, 2015, p 230.

16 Gorton's demise did not, however, save ten anti-Gortonites – including Howson, Jess and Mackay – who lost their seats in 1972. Two of the ten stood as Independents having lost pre-selection. Just two Gorton supporters were defeated in 1972.

17 *Herald* (Melbourne), 10 March 1971.

18 Interview: Kim Jones, 20 December 2017.

[19]   Melbourne *Sun*, 11 March 1971.

[20]   *Canberra News*, 11 March 1971.

[21]   Gotto Papers, MS 9895/9/2.

[22]   Sydney *Sun*, 11 March 1971.

[23]   Diary 1971, Gotto Papers, MS Acc15.126, Box 31.

[24]   Fairbairn stayed in politics and was given Education and Science, Forbes went to Immigration and Peacock retained Army. Ainsley was right on one score: Mackay replaced Killen in Navy.

[25]   Despite Chipp's constant support for Snedden in leadership contests, the newly-appointed Treasurer did nothing in March to ensure Chipp's retention in the McMahon ministry.

[26]   For the above two paragraphs see Gotto Papers, MS Acc15.126, Box 31.

[27]   Peter Blazey, *Bolte: A Political Biography*, Jacaranda Press, Ryde,1972, pp. 214-15.

[28]   Gotto Papers, MS 9895, Folio Box 3. The above two paragraphs draw upon interviews: AG, 22 February and Mathews, 17 August 2017 and on Jenny Hocking, *Gough Whitlam: A Moment in History*, vol 1, The Miegunyah Press, Carlton, 2008, pp. 354-5.

[29]   In September 1972 Race married Iola Hack, a journalist and a feminist, one of ten women who formed the Women's Electoral Lobby and who managed to combine careers, marriage and children. See Iola Mathews, *Winning for Women: A Personal Story,* Monash University Publishing, Clayton, 2019.

AG on the far right, at kindergarten c1949: Gotto Papers.

The Gotto family c1951:
Gotto Papers.

Mother and daughters: c1959: Gotto Papers.

Kerrie's wedding, 1963; from left, Robert Webster (Lesley's brother), AG , Nan, Kerrie, Lesley, Deborah, Sid: Gotto Papers.

AG in the theatre, fifth from the left: Gotto Papers.

AG and Basil Dean: Gotto Papers.

Dudley Erwin: *Commonwealth Parliamentary Handbook*, 1968.

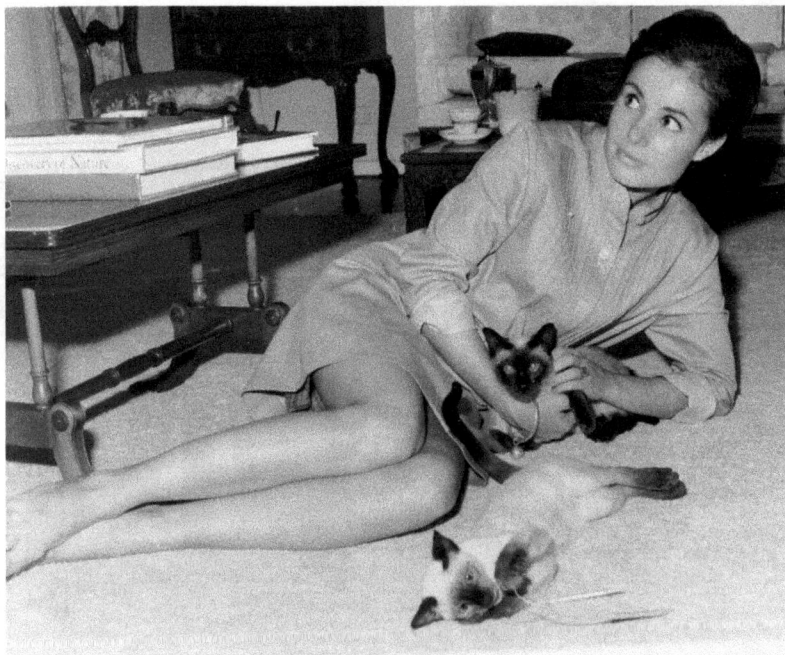

AG, February 1968: Gotto Papers.

PRIME MINISTER'S LODGE
CANBERRA

Have a good rest and get well soon

Betty.

Betty Gorton's message to AG, December 1968: Gotto Papers.

Some of AG's friends, the Mushroom Club; standing from left: Don Jessop, Bill Arthur, Tony Street, John McLeay, Don Chipp, Bruce Graham, Bill Bridges-Maxwell, Fred Chaney, Jim Killen, Tom Pearsall, 'Duke' Bonnett; in front, Tom Hughes and Andrew Peacock: Tom Hughes Papers.

Election night 1969: standing from left, Tony Eggleton, Michael Gorton, John Gorton; seated from left, Paula Gorton, AG, Betty Gorton, staff member, Gotto Papers.

Woman's Day cover, 18 October 1971: Bauer Media Limited.

Ainsley and Bill Pollock, Monaco, 1973: Gotto Papers.

Ric Mauran, mid-1970s:
Gotto Papers.

Ainsley in the Outback, c1985-6: Gotto Papers.

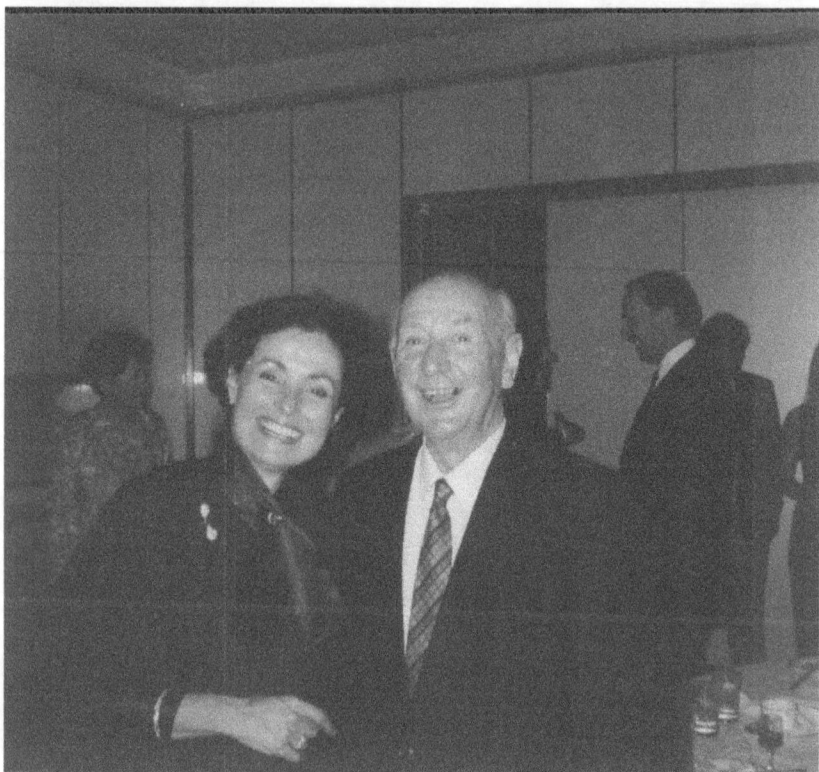

AG and Reg Swartz (Paul Keating in the background),
Gorton's 80th birthday party
Gotto Papers.

AG and Nick Carson, Gorton's 90th birthday party: Gotto Papers.

AG and Nick Carson at lunch at Whale Beach with Lady Renouf 4th from the left, date unknown: Gotto Papers.

AG, Gorton and Lady Gorton, Gorton's 90th birthday: Gotto Papers.

Three friends: Ainsley, Pru Goward and Glen-Marie Frost, Gorton's 90th birthday:
Gotto Papers.

A reunion: AG, Sir Lenox Hewitt and Gorton, Gorton's 90th birthday:
Gotto Papers.

AG and Helen Coonan, Gorton's 90th birthday: Gotto Papers.

10

Woman's Day

On 1 August 1971, the day McMahon sacked Les Bury as Minister for Foreign Affairs, Alan Reid published his book, *The Gorton Experiment*. Reid wrote most of the story while Gorton was still Prime Minister, with a 54-page postscript covering his final weeks in office. As Paul Hasluck pointed out, the main part of the book was designed to assist the destruction of Gorton as Prime Minister, and the postscript was meant to ensure he would not remain as McMahon's rival.[1] Reid claimed that Gorton as Prime Minister had achieved nothing constructive, had dominated or ignored his Cabinet, undermined Harold Holt, dispatched his rivals, Hasluck and Fairhall, squandered his inheritance and destabilised his party.

Gorton had previously been in contact with Harry M. Miller, the management consultant and theatrical producer, about writing his autobiography. Miller now urged Gorton to respond directly to Reid. With Ainsley pushing Gorton to accept, Miller negotiated a contract whereby Gorton would be paid the considerable sum of $60,000 for six articles to be published in Rupert Murdoch's

Sunday Australian. Murdoch gladly seized the opportunity for a quick and newsworthy response which he believed would assist a Gorton comeback.[2] Miller suggested an apt title: 'I Did It My Way'.

In the first article, published on 8 August, Gorton focused on the VIP affair and 'the curious and totally unsubstantiated tale' of how Ainsley Gotto, Dudley Erwin and himself allegedly collaborated to replace Holt as Liberal Party Leader. Everything Gorton wrote on these two subjects had been aired before. Media and political attention concentrated, therefore, on two paragraphs where Gorton breached Cabinet solidarity to demonstrate that McMahon and Fairbairn had breached Cabinet solidarity. Taking four days to pluck up the courage, McMahon requested Gorton's resignation as Minister for Defence. Gorton replied with a laconic, 'OK'. A journalist invented the story that Ainsley Gotto cried when Gorton broke the news,[3] thereby giving her further reason to detest the fourth estate. His comment to Ainsley that tears were better for her image did nothing to appease her. If the journalist had been anywhere near Gorton's office, he would have heard the laughter as the occupants enjoyed the moment when the little man did something he thought was big.

Magnus Cormack, the new President of the Senate, was worried. He sent a note to Ainsley on 21 August from the Australian Club in Melbourne.[4] He saw her as someone who had 'served most loyally to a man for whom I have a high regard and affection'. Cormack had known Gorton since the late 1940s, persuaded him to leave the Country Party for the Liberals and engineered his preselection for the Senate. He had never sought to penetrate his friend's reserve but wanted Ainsley's help 'in trying to restrain him'.

Cormack feared that the articles would have Gorton dismissed as 'sulking like Ajax in his tent before Troy' and clearly saw Ainsley as one of the few who could dissuade him from self-destruction. Yet John Gorton was having far too much fun for anyone to shift his course.

By this time, with further Gorton articles in the pipeline, there were rumours about Ainsley being ready to write her memoirs. On the day of the Gorton sacking, the editor of the Melbourne *Herald* telephoned her and followed up with a letter repeating his suggestion that, if she ever thought of writing about her time in the 'political arena', she should first consider discussing it with the *Herald*. On 15 August, when Gorton's second article appeared in the *Sunday Australian*, the front page of the *Sun-Herald* carried a photograph of Ainsley with Harry M. Miller at Sydney airport. Under the headline – 'AINSLEY GOTTO TO TELL HER STORY' – the paper reported that 'the controversial secretary of Mr John Gorton ... is planning to write her memoirs', adding that 'Canberra observers' believed her story 'could be political dynamite'. The book publisher, Rigby Limited, sent Ainsley a telegram on 17 August seeking the first option on her manuscript, and Sun Books on 24 August contacted Miller for a similar purpose. Miller told Ainsley that the Rigby proposal was 'ridiculous' and advised her to 'forget about it'. By that stage, Miller had received two offers for a paperback and one for a hard cover.[5]

Wisely, in view of the time it would take to write a book, Ainsley followed Gorton's lead and Miller's advice and agreed to contribute to articles about her experiences. She signed an agreement whereby Sungravure Pty Ltd would publish four articles in the popular weekly magazine, *Woman's Day*. Taken over by John Fairfax &

Sons Pty Ltd in 1953 Sungravure, in addition to *Woman's Day*, also published *Pix*, *People* and, later, *Cosmopolitan*, as well as printing and distributing comics for many other Australian publishers. Roger Wood,[6] an urbane Englishman and the Managing Director of Sungravure, decided to enter the bidding after Joan Reeder, editor of *Woman's Day* since 1957, had lunched with Ainsley. Wood knew that *Woman's Day* could not match the major publishing houses but showed Miller how the story would have a different treatment if published in a woman's magazine. Next day, Wood and Ainsley had a casual talk in Sydney over drinks, and Wood and Miller then engaged in seven hours of negotiations and reached agreement at 4.00 am on Thursday 19 August.

In the contract with Sungravure, Ainsley agreed to assist in the preparation of four articles, each not more than five pages in length. She assigned the copyright and publishing rights of the information and photographs she provided to Sungravure, agreed to accept any reasonable request to promote the articles, including the taking of photographs for publicity purposes, and to give Sungravure the first option to publish any book she might write relating to her experiences in the Commonwealth Public Service. A key clause proved to be 6 (c): 'the Publisher shall submit copy to the Author and the Author shall approve or reject in whole or in part such copy. Only such material contained in approved copy shall be published in "Woman's Day" or sold for publication overseas.' The significance of this clause will become apparent later. Within seven hours of execution, Sungravure would pay Ainsley $15,000 and then $7,500 each on the second and third anniversaries of the Agreement.[7] The return was much lower than the rumoured $40,000-$100,000.[8]

Reeder appointed Ailsa Craig, a very experienced senior journalist to work with Ainsley.[9] Craig later called it 'the hardest assignment of my career'. Covering a Royal Tour or interviewing Jackie Onassis or Princess Margaret would be so much easier. The problem, as Craig saw it, was 'the Gotto feeling for dignity'. She had sold her story but, when she started telling it, wished she had not. 'Quite unrealistically, she regarded it as an invasion of her privacy.' It was not simply a matter of protecting her own skin. Over some six weeks, Craig saw a lot of Gorton and Gotto together and was struck by Ainsley's admiration and affection for her boss, mingled with pride for someone she regarded as a great Australian. She soon recognised that Ainsley was also terrified for Gorton's reputation. 'Rather than embarrass or hurt him in any way, she would have given up the whole thing. There were many times when I wished she would.'[10]

Yet Ainsley did want to tell her story. She set out her motivation in two private notes. One was a formal and restrained response to a letter criticising her decision to speak out.[11] Ainsley explained she was not writing a book; it would be 'improper' at this time to write an account of a government for which she had worked. Rather, there will be a series of articles, not written by her but by a journalist based on the journalist's observations and talks with her. She knew there would be those who approved and those who disapproved, and that 'has characterised any action I am supposed to have taken for the last four years'. Except for one interview with a journalist – only given after pressure – she had not sought publicity.[12] She was not and never had been in public life. Nevertheless, she felt that someone who has been constantly discussed and gossiped about had a right to speak and in speaking she would make sure no harm would be done to Mr Gorton.

The second note reflected years of pent-up bitterness and frustration.

> Too much of the filth and dirt of political Canberra has rubbed off on my name. The Ainsley Gotto legend sickens me. I have been accused of just about everything from being the Christine Keeler of [Canberra], seducer of Ministers, to having a love affair with John Gorton himself. Gossips have said that Betty Gorton hated me, that I wielded such extraordinary influence over her husband and I could pick and choose his friends.

Ainsley referred to the 'countless times' she had been upset and angry at the attacks on her, most notably when her supposed friend, Dudley Erwin, 'caused me to be called Miss Wiggle all over the world'. She was now determined 'to put the record straight', not just about herself but about the 'most amazing' man she had ever met. It was 'horrible' to see him torn to pieces by high-powered people who sought to destroy him, perhaps through her. She saw it happening and could not stop it. 'Now at last I can do something about it. I intend to do so.'[13]

Ainsley soon learnt that the voices of disapproval had not gone away. Freida Fox of North Sydney sent a handwritten and undated note to 'A. Gotto (Typist)' at Parliament House. She had read 'with horror & absolute repulsion' about Ainsley's 'latest exploit. Haven't you committed enough trouble & unhappiness to Mr. and Mrs. Gorton, without writing your "so-called memoirs ["?].' Fox called Ainsley 'a tin-pot typist with a swollen head' who was only after money. 'If you were my daughter, I'd paddle your posterior so hard you'd eat off the mantelshelf for a month.'[14] The journalist Ron Saw asked in the *Daily Telegraph* of 17 August, 'What in God's name could Ainsley Gotto have to say that would be worth $40,000?' He could not imagine her saying anything that

Gorton had not said already. Besides, Miss Gotto was 'smug . . . probably impertinent ... certainly a flibbertigibbet' but, most of all, he found her 'irritating' because her name kept cropping up in places where it had no business to be. Now he was supposed to get excited about what 'The Typist Said to the Minister'.

On 25 August, Sungravure sent Miller some suggestions for a publicity release. Describing *Woman's Day* as a 'mass circulation weekly', Roger Wood said he was delighted to secure the rights ahead of 'some formidable rivals' and he was now busy in Europe negotiating world syndication rights. He described her as:

> a remarkable young woman who strode the Canberra corridors of power with considerable charm, considerable achievement, and considerable skill. There is hardly a political incident she did not witness, or become involved in. There is hardly a political personality in Australia today she does not know.

Wood identified two important questions: 'Was she influential? Was her influence decisive as has been alleged more than once?' He concluded: 'Miss Gotto's story will tell us.' Joan Reeder had introduced politics, arts and relationship issues to a cooking, knitting and gossip magazine, and focused on women of achievement. [15] Taking account of upbringing and 'exceptional good looks', she said Ainsley 'would be an extraordinary girl even if she had never been the Prime Minister's secretary'. Reeder thought it 'oddly right' that two ambitious and determined people were drawn together in a relationship 'that shaped the political life of Australia in such a vital period of its history'.[16]

Robert Mayne, writing in the *Sun-Herald* on 5 September, contributed to the expectations. Under the headline – 'AINSLEY GOTTO TO TELL ALL' – he claimed that her memoirs would be 'a time bomb that may explode under some of the best-known names in Australian politics'. Canberra was 'still agog' to learn what she had to say. Mayne reminded his readers that an 'incredible number of stories' had been circulated about Ainsley, including the claim she had a voice in policy formation, and assured them she wanted 'to set the record straight and tell the truth about those years'.

Anticipating Ainsley's reaction, Ailsa Craig sent her a telegram saying she 'cringed too' on reading the *Sun-Herald*'s 'tell-all' story.[17] Ainsley did not like the article but what had upset her was the suggestion, made while Wood was overseas, that she might approve a comment in her name for the *Sun-Herald* story announcing the *Woman's Day*'s successful bid. She was 'shocked and distressed' to think that anyone could seriously propose that she 'should put my name to what I regard as gutter journalism'. Further, in Wood's absence, strong suggestions were put to her that the story should have 'by Ainsley Gotto' on it. She needed to discuss this and other aspects with Wood. Ainsley asked for, and presumably secured, a meeting with Sungravure's managing director in Sydney on the following Monday to iron out these matters.

According to Craig, the 'real trouble' started after Ailsa had spent seven days on her own composing the four episodes. Ainsley sub-edited them, fighting 'over almost every sentence'.[18] She had two abiding concerns: to protect Gorton and to preserve her privacy. The articles were written in the third person but contained many quotations from Ainsley taken from taped interviews. Ainsley insisted on removing some of what she said, and Clause 6 (c) of the contract gave her control over the final publication. In one instance she spoke on tape of Peter Howson referring to a photograph when lunching with MPs at Parliament House: 'I see

Ainsley Gotto's come back from London with John, but where was Betty?' Ainsley pointed out on tape that Howson knew perfectly well Betty Gorton had travelled to and from London [in June 1971] 'with us'. Ainsley wanted the story to be told but thought that Gorton might suffer indirectly. She insisted on removing Howson's name. In the published text Howson is identified only as 'a man who is now a minister', probably on the assumption that readers of *Woman's Day*, unlike close Canberra watchers, would not be able to identify him. Ainsley removed the sentence from Craig's text where it referred to Howson's pending contest with Race Mathews for the seat of Casey. The sentence read: 'Ainsley Gotto has strong Liberal Party affiliations and leanings, but she would obviously not be displeased by a Labor win in Casey next year.' That sentence might hurt Gorton and would certainly hurt Ainsley should she seek Liberal preselection.

Another person who contributed to the sub-editing did not have the power of removal. Typically, John Gorton was not interested in arguing over interpretations; Ainsley and Ailsa must tell the story as they saw fit. Shown a version of the printed text, he proffered a few amendments which showed Ainsley in a better light, all of them accepted. He intervened at one point, for example, to bolster Ainsley's argument that she did not act in a manner unbefitting the Principal Private Secretary of the Prime Minister. In Part Three, Ainsley categorically denied the charges of 'Johnning' him in public or of stalking into a Cabinet Room meeting saying 'John, I've got a message for you'. Gorton wrote a paragraph amplifying the situation: she never went into the Cabinet Room or the ante-room unless she was sent for, and she never entered the Prime Minister's office while a meeting was taking place. Ainsley would have been thrown out if she had done so. She might occasionally send notes to the Prime Minister, but an attendant took them in.[19]

While Ailsa and Ainsley worked their way through more than 20,000 words of text *Woman's Day* started whipping up interest in the forthcoming 'Ainsley Gotto Story'. The process began on 6 September 1971 with a front cover and five pages broaching the question, 'What Makes Ainsley Gotto tick?' The readers of *Woman's Day* were offered the prospect of nerve-tingling answers to critical questions: 'Why does Ainsley Gotto slam taxi doors? Why does she command the attention she does? Is she really the ruthless, power hungry young woman her critics say she is?' If she tells the full truth of her time in the Gorton years, 'oh brother that'll be the story'. The next five issues provided brief reminders that an 'astonishing story' would soon be told about a 'fascinating' and 'attractive enigma'.

As the Gotto-Craig exchanges dragged on, *Woman's Day* tried another approach to retain attention. On 4 October it reproduced head shots of four women – Jackie Onassis, Empress Farah of Iran, Audrey Hepburn and Ainsley Gotto – and asked what they had in common. The answers: they were internationally known, had captured the public imagination, bore a close resemblance to each other, had the same enigmatic smile and always appeared 'graceful, well-groomed and enviably poised'. The stories of three of them had been told the world over. 'Soon, the fourth, Ainsley Gotto, tells HER story in *Woman's Day*.'

Publication of the four articles began on 18 October 1971. June Mendoza was appalled by the front cover featuring a picture of Ainsley in consultation with Gorton. 'Ainsley, do you think "Woman's Day" strained every muscle or did it come naturally to them not only to take <u>the</u> most unflattering photo of <u>both</u> of you from <u>every</u> possible angle [emphases in the original]; but to actually print the damn thing on the cover as well!'[20]

The first article engaged in some scene-setting with the image of 'a scrap of a girl, sunburnt, skinny, self-possessed' eating a steak sandwich while 'perched' on a window seat in Air Force One, the Presidential jet which Lyndon Johnson had made available to bring the Gorton retinue from Honolulu. 'Her name was Ainsley Gotto. She was barely 22.' Much of the article focused on Gorton. She respected him 'utterly' but could never find the right word to describe what was 'very special' about him. It had nothing to do with sex appeal, while his charm alone could not explain the willingness of men and women to go without meals or sleep to get things done for him. 'Perhaps it's because you feel the greatness of the man.' Knowing that he was trying to do something 'big' you were drawn into helping him achieve it. Given these feelings – Craig wrote of 'a note of veneration in her voice' – Ainsley felt both sorrow and anger that people like Fairbairn and Howson tried to stop him from doing what was right for Australia.

McMahon was another villain; he wanted to destroy Gorton politically. He would never have asked her to work for him when he became Prime Minister, and she would never have done so. 'Put simply, I don't like him.' As Craig correctly saw it, Fraser figured as 'the blackest exhibit in the Gotto gallery of villains'. Ainsley thought him one of the least liked men in the parliamentary party: 'aloof, arrogant – a loner. I dislike him intensely.' Fraser's enduring sin for her was to betray a trust, telling Gorton on the Sunday night that everything was all right and to have a good night's sleep, and then resigning and provoking a leadership crisis on the following day. Ainsley did not, however, tell all. Had she done so, the Canberra Gallery might have taken notice of another aspect of the Fraser story. Her sub-editing included removing the sentence that immediately preceded 'I dislike him intensely': 'When I think that once when Malcolm was very drunk he tried to make a pass at me – ugh!'[21]

Ainsley's second article, published on 24 October, focused on work and personal relationships, ending with the implication that some Canberra wives closed ranks against her. It began with the story of how Ainsley worked with Erwin to secure Gorton's election to the Party leadership and covered her appointment as PPS. The article recounted her upbringing alongside strong-minded sisters, protecting herself from an inferiority complex by cultivating what many would see as an aggressive manner of speaking. Several sentences described how she came to find her element in the Whips' office where she formed friendships with many MPs and with Dudley Erwin and his wife, Joan. Ainsley described her first days with Gorton and praised Tony Eggleton and Len Hewitt for helping her settle in. She talked at length about Erwin's attack on her, wondering whether 'he'd had a few drinks and was over-emotional' and was probably 'feeling sore'. Ainsley thought that in blaming her for his downfall, Erwin had overlooked the point that Gorton made up his own mind about appointments and dismissals. She speculated further that Erwin wanted a scapegoat; 'perhaps he couldn't face the reason why', namely, that he 'wasn't good at the job'. Nonetheless, 'it was an extraordinary accusation to make against me, particularly when he and his wife had been so close to me and my family'. It was all 'pretty vicious'. After his outburst, Ainsley and Dudley said no more than 'good morning' if they met in the corridors of

Parliament House, and Ainsley had never spoken to Joan Erwin since Dudley was dismissed. The article concluded on a surprising note: Ainsley spoke of her 'mixed feelings' about Susan Peacock. Once very close, Susan neither spoke to her nor rang her for some time after Ainsley ceased to work in the Prime Minister's office.

Although Part Two of the Gotto story included a long passage on the Erwins, it would have been longer still if Ainsley had agreed to retain the several paragraphs covering the fractious Dudley-Joan relationship. Much of this section was devoted to what Ainsley recalled as Joan's increasingly neurotic behaviour in the latter part of her husband's term as Chief Whip. 'Perhaps part of her problem is not having children. I don't know.' Having lived in New York, the second Mrs Erwin was miserable living in Ballarat, and hated Australia 'with all these little ladies with their tin pot hats and mentalities to match'. In tears, she kept threatening to return to the United States. After one late-night slanging match on the telephone, which Ainsley witnessed at the Canberra end, Dudley said he would pay her fare. Throughout it all, Ainsley went out of her way to bring the frank-talking Joan into broader social company and believed that Mrs Erwin liked her and her mother. Joan's very public Christmas card was something of a shock and Ainsley accepted for publication that the reference to 'no smoke without fire must surely have been a crack at me'. In the original and removed version, she said the comment 'does seem to mean that she was accusing me of having an affair with the PM'.

Alongside another photograph of her, the front cover of Part 3 bore the message of Ainsley continuing to tell the story 'ALL AUSTRALIA IS TALKING ABOUT'. In this article, Ainsley covered the Gorton-Liza Minnelli meeting in Sydney, the accusations that she called the Prime Minister 'John' in public and prevented ministers from seeing him, her relationship with Betty Gorton, the things said about her which were really aimed at John Gorton as politics became more 'vicious', the 'horrible' letters she received, and how she became a target for the sick and dirty minds who made obscene telephone calls to both Ainsley and her mother. Ainsley referred to the Fairbairns who clearly did not like her and who often made unpleasant cracks about her. She quoted Gorton's description of the David Fairbairn he called a friend as 'pedestrian, conservative and slow thinking'.

Part 4 began with a description of perhaps the last drinks party in the suite Gorton occupied as Deputy Leader of the Liberal Party. Friends were wandering in and out and conversation flowed. Bob Hawke, then President of the ACTU, was a new arrival. He had come to wish John Gorton the best of good fortune. Ainsley fetched Hawke a drink and the two were soon sparring verbally. She kept interrupting one of his long anecdotes and Hawke told her to 'shut up'. Ainsley said she would not 'shut up' but a smiling Gorton asked her to be quiet, and she accepted silence. She told Ailsa Craig that Hawke was obviously clever, but he frightened her. 'Too much power unchecked is unhealthy for anyone.' Their first meeting was not propitious, particularly as Hawke called her a 'nit-wit', albeit in fun. The occasion was important for another reason. Craig pointed out how that week marked the end of the 'glamour days' for Ainsley: 'she was now just an ordinary secretary.'

Ainsley received a bundle of letters praising her loyalty, honesty and courage.[22] A few sent their own poems. Many expressed their support for Gorton, and wanted him back in office, contrasting the 'manly' and 'sagacious' Gorton with the 'snake-in-the grass'

Fraser and the 'creepy crawly worm' McMahon. One described Ainsley as the 'mostest, just as J.G.G. is the greatest'. Older men and women predominated. Lt Colonel A. V. Palmer of Bendigo, who subsequently published two volumes on mining in his city, told Ainsley that she should not be alarmed that he was sending her a second letter. He was aged 64 and a grandfather and 'no gay cavalier'. One woman regretted that Ainsley had found it necessary 'to explain and humiliate' herself for the privilege of being the former Prime Minister's Private Secretary. In her reply, Ainsley said she did not find it a humiliating experience. Indeed, given the kind letters she had received, she felt that most who read the articles 'have been very pleased that I have set the record straight in relation to the many unfair and untrue stories that have been written about me'.

The trolls were also active. One bravely identifying himself as 'Mr Brown' wrote:

> You have told us how you have enjoyed your Boy Friend John Gorton . . . but I for one particularly notice you havent told us about the sex experience you have had with the Right Honourable John Gorton and just how good he shapes in the Cot . . . Now then Ainsley old Girl you make be a clever little Office Girl and an A.I. in the Cot too . . . [but] for God sake dont start fooling yourself and think that by writing those few stories in Womans Day that you have fooled the rest of the World, but its no doubt its that Box of yours which is the sole cause of bringing down Larrickin John. [*sic*]

Did *Woman's Day* get value for its money? At one level the answer must be 'No'. Ainsley's fierce defence of her privacy, her concern to protect Gorton's reputation and conviction that it was improper and illegal for a former employee to reveal government secrets meant that the four published pieces did not 'tell all'. In fact, they told very little that the Canberra Press Gallery did not already know or remember. The articles did not even address the two questions Wood had posed, namely whether Ainsley was influential and whether her influence was decisive. Not surprisingly, therefore, the *Woman's Day* articles were barely mentioned on radio or television or in the newspapers. On the other hand, the magazine's readership – around 540,000 copies were sold each week – did learn something more of what went on in Canberra, and learnt something more about the personalities, and especially about those Ainsley disliked. From the *Woman's Day* perspective, the articles were a success in creating a slight bump in circulation and assisting Joan Reeder's ambition to increase the proportion and quality of articles devoted to people and personalities.[23] Reeder saw Ainsley as a celebrity, someone who was very different and who, as a young woman, had already lived an interesting life at the top end of Australian politics, and who would continue to move among the rich and famous around the world. *Woman's Day* adopted her as a person and a personality whose life ahead was something its readership should want, and did want, to know about. Hence, as will be seen, Reeder and Ailsa Craig followed Ainsley to Monaco.

[1]   Hasluck, *Light*, p 158.

[2]   Gorton Papers, NLA, MS 7984/32; personal communication, Rupert Murdoch, 30 Aug. 2000.

[3]   *Daily Mirror*, 13 August 1971.

[4]   Gotto Papers, MS 9895/2/7; 'The Very Private Ainsley Gotto', *Muse*, June 1986.

[5]   Gotto Papers, MS 9895/2/10.

[6]   An Oxford graduate, Wood served in the RAF during the Second World War, edited the *Daily Express* (UK) when aged just 32 and, after his time in Sydney and a further stint in Fleet Street, he succeeded as executive editor in more than doubling the circulation of Rupert Murdoch's *New York Post* in 1977-

87.

[7] Gotto Papers, MS 9895/2/9. For the Wood-Miller negotiations over the contract, see Glenys Bell, *National Times*, 11-16 October 1971 and *My Story: Harry M. Miller as told to Denis O'Brien*, Macmillan, South Melbourne, 1983, p 192.

[8] *Sun-Herald*, 5 September 1971.

[9] Graduating from the University of Sydney with first class honours, majoring in Latin, English and Zoology, Craig published a satirical novel on the Communist Party, joined Fairfax in 1951, was London correspondent of the *SMH* (1954-7) and returned to Sydney to hold various positions with *Woman's Day*. For her subsequent career, see *SMH*, 19 January 2013.

[10] *Woman's Day*, 15 November 1971.

[11] For the two notes, see the undated handwritten version on House of Representatives notepaper and her draft letter to Peter Donovan of Mount Druitt, 28 September 1971 in Gotto Papers, MS 9895/2/9.

[12] She had in fact given two interviews – one to Richard Walsh (1969) and one to Rosemary Munday (1970).

[13] Gotto Papers, MS 9895/2/9.

[14] *Ibid.*, 2/5.

[15] See the Reeder obituary in the *SMH*, 28 June 1999.

[16] Gotto Papers, MS 9895/2/10.

[17] *Ibid.*, 2/9.

[18] For changes made to the text, see *ibid.*, Folio Box 1.

[19] Gorton did take the opportunity to protect his reputation. He changed, 'By the time John Gorton lost the Liberal Party leadership . . .', to read 'By the time John Gorton voted himself out of the Liberal Party leadership'.

[20] Gotto Papers, MS 9895, 2/9.

[21] *Ibid.*, Folio Box 1.

[22] For responses to the articles see especially Gotto Papers, MS 9895/2/9.

[23] The *New Journalist* for November-December 1972 placed 'people and personalities' fourth of the five reasons women read *Woman's Day*, as opposed to third of five in the case of the larger publication, *Women's Weekly*.

11

'What you need is an Ainsley Gotto'

On 3 February 1972, an advertisement appeared in the 'Positions Vacant' columns of the *Sydney Morning Herald* seeking a:

Sec.- Executive

Job of the Year

Location: Europe

With or without French, if you are a top flight Secretary (no shorthand) but good typing skills, poised, well groomed and interact effectively with people, you'll thrive on the challenge of this outstanding position. Let your initiative and self-motivation find satisfaction, you'll travel Europe/North America, arrange meetings, Press releases and handle research. Salary Open.

Ailsa Craig wrote in *Woman's Day* for 6 March 1972 that the advertisement 'might just as well have said: "If you're an Ainsley Gotto, this is the job for you".'

The advertisement was inserted on behalf of Drake International, a global human resources company first built on the concept of 'Don't Pay A Full-Time Salary For A Part-Time Job'. Robert William ('Bill') Pollock, the President of the company, was born in Winnipeg, Canada, in 1929. He graduated in 1951 from the University of Manitoba with a Commerce degree and co-founded Drake International in Winnipeg with Jim Shore, another young entrepreneur whom he met at Burroughs Corporation (later, Unisys). Drake expanded rapidly into all the major cities of Canada and, in 1959, moved into the United States, the United Kingdom in 1960, and Australia in 1965. In 1967, Shore and two managers were killed in a plane crash. Separated from his wife and with no children, Pollock, now the sole owner of Drake and a multi-millionaire, lived and worked in Monaco when not visiting Drake offices around the globe. He worked long hours seven days a week and, for two years, had been looking for someone to save him 200 days a year by taking some of his workload and sharing some of his responsibilities.

Arriving in Sydney, Pollock was presented with the names and details of a few respondents to the advertisement of 3 February. He interviewed a couple of them and decided they were not what he wanted. Someone said to him, 'you need an Ainsley Gotto'. He asked: 'What's that?' He was given an explanation but thought no more about it until he reached Melbourne where a friend in the Young Presidents Organisation asked how his search was faring. Told that he not found anyone suitable, the Young President said, 'what you need is an Ainsley Gotto'. Pollock decided it was time to explore this matter.[1] Contact was established through a friend of Ainsley's whose cousin worked with Drake International. The moment was opportune. Ainsley had been talking to Sir John Atwill, the Federal President of the Liberal Party, and Charles Lloyd Jones about joining the Board of David Jones but Lloyd Jones felt that the other Board members might think she was too young. At the time, there were no other options in sight in Australia, and it made sense to consider going overseas.

After talking to John Gorton, Ainsley agreed to meet Pollock. She had lunch with him at the Southern Cross Hotel in Melbourne on 10 February 1972. Ainsley learnt at first hand that Pollock was very good at selling a line and that line, as she recalled, meant she would be his right hand and involved in making and implementing policy. There was an 'added incentive'. Pollock owned the company; he could do what he said he would do.[2]

At first, she declined the offer while pushing the proposed salary well beyond her current Public Service remuneration. Pollock at first offered her $12,000 and then raised it to $15,000 with an annual review. Ainsley had further discussions with Gorton who acknowledged there was not much of a future in working for him. Assuming McMahon lost the 1972 election, the best Gorton could hope for was a shadow portfolio in the Opposition. Nevertheless, if Gorton had said he really needed her to stay with him, she would have done so. At a small party, held in Gorton's parliamentary office on 16 February, Ainsley announced she would be resigning from the Public Service to take a job with Drake International at Monte Carlo in the Principality of Monaco. She submitted her resignation from the Commonwealth Public Service to take effect from Friday 10 March.

The story splashed across the press in Australia and in London, with Gorton quoted as saying that Ainsley's departure was 'like losing my right arm'. Tony Eggleton wrote to Ainsley on 17 February describing himself as her 'London press clipping agent'.[3] Pollock in Melbourne soon had a direct experience of the media interest. On 17 February, the day of the great flash flood in Melbourne, Pollock arrived late for a meeting to learn that the ABC wanted to interview him. He was perplexed. Why was Ainsley Gotto considered so important? He wanted to decline but Ron Urwin, the Australian manager of Drake, told him a refusal would be bad for business. Next morning, the receptionist at his hotel warned Pollock that the press was waiting to interview him. He was met in the foyer by a pack of photographers and journalists. Pollock was 'surprised' and 'overwhelmed' by the attention; he had no idea that Ainsley 'would be featured so much'. The headline in the *Australian* for 17 February – 'Ainsley leaves Gorton' – remained fixed in his mind. As he soon discovered, the media attention lasted for months after the initial appointment.[4]

In Ballarat, Dudley Erwin (or his wife) added two newspaper stories of 17 February to Erwin's collection of press cuttings, each referring to Ainsley's new appointment. Alongside them there is a hand-printed heading: 'And so ends the life story of "Miss Wiggle" in Australian Politics'[emphasis in the original]. In Melbourne, John Sorrell interviewed Lady Clarke, the wife of the 3rd baronet, Sir Rupert Clarke, the Consul for Monaco. The Clarkes were good friends of the Rainiers and loved the palace and the Hotel de Paris where they stayed on their holidays each year. Lady Clarke said, 'Ainsley will have a simply scrumptious time living in that jewel in the sun'.[5] Ron Urwin added a note of caution:

> She's a girl who's used to having her finger on the pulse of things and now she is facing the frightening situation of having to learn all our terminology and a business which is completely strange to her.[6]

Kirwan Ward, writing for the *Daily News* in Perth on 23 February, was at first dismissive. When the first stories about 'Miss Gotto' came through, he 'instinctively resented the idea of an over-possessive, over-presumptuous private secretary pulling the strings that make Australia jump'. Yet, after seeing her on television the previous evening he was not sure she could not do a better job than those she worked for. 'I would have to think very hard to remember any other woman who has been half so impressive on telly, half so poised, half so intelligent and – the rarest quality of all – so thoroughly able to take care of herself in a situation that so often brings out the worst in the interviewed.' Australians had been told that we have a shortage of top management, yet we are letting 'top management material' in Ainsley Gotto leave Australia and all that interests anyone is how much of her salary will be tax-free.

With the attention focused on Ainsley's new job it is unlikely that many took much notice of Claudia Wright's story in the Melbourne *Herald* on 17 February. One night, Ainsley and John Gorton had gone to the Sydney home of Gordon Barton. The founder of an interstate trucking company, Barton had established the Liberal Reform Group in 1966, the forerunner of the Australia Party and the Australian Democrats, and he was the proprietor of *Nation Review* and Angus & Robertson. Germaine Greer, in Australia to publicise her book, *The Female Eunuch*, was also present. She later told Wright:

> I had a snappy argument with Ainsley Gotto who turned up with John Gorton at a dinner in Sydney one night. She said to me . . . . 'I really don't see what women's liberation is all about . . . I'm perfectly liberated in the circumstances.' I [Greer] mean that was hilarious . . . and I thought to myself . . . how can you think you're liberated . . . everything that ever happens to you is the result of your position. I was in somebody else's house so I didn't say that to her . . . I might have upset her lacquered casque of hair.

Greer 'was interested to see the two of them' and was to an extent impressed by Gorton who seemed to accept that women in

Australia were oppressed and who accepted the necessity for child care centres for working mothers.

As Ainsley recalled, she had asked Greer to tell her what 'Women's Liberation' was all about. Germaine said if she had to do that Ainsley would not understand. Ainsley decided Greer was 'quite rude' and consumed by self-importance and she was glad when the evening ended.[7] A Gotto-Greer encounter in 1972 could never have involved a meeting of minds. Ainsley had never read anything about feminism and was not interested in what she saw as abstract cerebral activity. She did, however, have very definite views on one subject: neither laws nor political campaigning could establish the 'equality' that mattered, namely, 'equality of performance'.

Ainsley attended many farewell parties, one being a special dinner with Gorton and his closest allies: Bonnett, Chipp, Guilfoyle, Hughes, Killen, Peacock and Wentworth. She arrived at the airport on 14 March carrying a mink coat and, courtesy of *Woman's Day*, a bunch of flowers. Asked what advice she would give aspiring secretaries, Ainsley offered five words which explained much of her own success: 'Work hard and get lucky.' She declined to say whether her ex-boss had said goodbye to her in Sydney but did say she had sold her new Volvo for a good price. Ainsley refused to be drawn on who would win the next election or whether she would write a book. She left Australia with mixed feelings. 'I am a little sad to be going.'[8]

Boarding her flight to Los Angeles, Ainsley was surprised that she and Urwin were assigned seats in Economy. Bill Pollock alone of Drake employees travelled First Class. A steward presented Ainsley with a bottle of champagne sent by Gorton who later posted some press clippings covering her departure. Next to one from the *SMH* depicting Ainsley carrying the coat he wrote: 'I gather this has given rise to a strong story that I gave you the mink.' Next to Packer's *Daily Telegraph* photo of Ainsley at the airport with her 'Parting Smile' – it looked more like a half grimace – Gorton wrote: 'still doing their worst.'[9]

Arriving in Los Angeles, Ainsley was asked to take the notes at a meeting of Drake executives. She felt out of her depth taking down words and sentences which meant very little. There was no plan to ease her into an understanding of the language and substance of the Drake business. She would have to pick it all up in the course of a 16-18 hour day and a hectic travel schedule. Ainsley had signed a contract with Pollock and Ewart Hodgins, the Drake Treasurer, where, as the 'Executive', she agreed to serve in the capacity as determined by the 'Employer' (in effect, Pollock) and use all her best efforts to promote the interests of the 'Employer'. The provisions for termination consisted of six weeks' notice in writing for both sides and Ainsley was to receive a salary of $A8,000 plus allowances of $7,000, as well as further allowances for which vouchers were to be submitted.

Within two-and-a-half months of leaving Los Angeles Ainsley had visited Toronto, New York, London, Cote d'Azur, Nice, Monaco, Munich, then back to Monaco and from there travelled to Beirut and the Persian Gulf, across to Osaka and then to Sydney. When the *Woman's Day* team of Ailsa Craig and Cec Lynch, the photographer, met Ainsley in Monaco in April. she had not yet found the time to look at the famed Grimaldi palace where the Rainiers lived. She was renting a room at the Europa Residence where Pollock occupied a lavish penthouse.

Ainsley soon discovered that, while Monaco was tax-free, it was inordinately expensive. A tenant renting an apartment would have to furnish it from scratch, even supply light fittings, and had to pay an annual charge for the concierge. Ainsley could not afford a car, and the first-class air travel and the Commonwealth cars of her previous life were now pleasant memories. Eventually Ainsley took occupancy of an apartment on the seventh floor paying FF 26,000 for a one-year lease.[10] She had two bedrooms, two bathrooms, a sitting room and a kitchen and a grand view of the coast from her bedroom. In no time she furnished it with characteristic good taste.

Bill Pollock and Ainsley flew to Australia in May 1972 for a three-week visit to look at the company's branches in Sydney, Melbourne, Adelaide and Perth. Drake had organised an informal gathering of press and radio representatives to meet Ainsley at the Wentworth Hotel, Sydney, on the afternoon of 25 May. Bob Nelson of Sungravure was concerned because *Woman's Day* planned to publish its article on Ainsley in Monaco in the first week of June. He pointed out it would be a breach of Ainsley's contract with Sungravure for her to cover similar ground at this press conference. It was agreed that she would confine any remarks to her activities with Drake and her homecoming impressions, while explaining that her contract prevented speaking about her life and experience overseas and especially in Monaco. Ainsley could not pose for pictures but there were no objections to cameramen photographing her during the conference. Nelson believed that difficult questions could be easily parried, and with a sweet smile she could say that her story would be out in *Woman's Day* next week.[11]

The press conference was an outstanding success from all points of view. The *Australian* on 26 May headed its report, 'Ainsley gets a film star welcome', noting that Elizabeth Taylor could not have done it better than Ainsley arriving in a Lamborghini for a grand press reception amidst TV cameras and flowers. The *SMH* article of the same date was headed, 'Miss Gotto – executive sans wiggle', and reported that she conducted herself in a manner Princess Grace might have envied: 'She was MGM regal.' The female reporters of the two papers differed slightly in referring to her apparel, one favouring a red wool suit and the other a suit of flame orange. Lenore Nicklin of the *SMH* commented on Ainsley's new vocabulary which included phrases like 'profit analysis' and 'quality control' and concluded that Ainsley's new world was very different from her old one. In one sense, however, she had returned to a pre-Gorton life. Ainsley said she had done more typing in the last two months than in all the previous four years. Apparently, no one at the press conference detected any significance in this fact. She hid it all by describing her new job as 'a mental holiday where there is no penalty if you happen to be a female who is active, contributing and uses her mind'. No one commented on the ambiguity within that sentence.

Woman's Day published its piece on 5 June with Ainsley photographed on the front cover in Monte Carlo alongside a leader, 'Ainsley Gotto's New World'. Underneath, there was a line advertising another celebrity, 'The Sonia McMahon We Got To Know'. Ailsa Craig's article described the life of 'The New Girl In Monaco', focusing on her constant travel since leaving Australia. Ainsley was at pains to explain that while the job presented her with an exciting challenge, she was a little homesick and was missing her family, friends and her dog (a Labrador had been 'hired' for some of the Monaco photos). She also missed Canberra and working for Gorton. Ainsley felt 'a bit uptight' getting used to the language – like the word 'dialogue' being used as a verb – and relying on others to help with French; 'all the same the job's a terrific challenge. It's terribly exciting.'

Joan Reeder wanted to publish a follow-up story about Ainsley in Monaco and, over lunch with Bill Pollock, sought to persuade him to write a piece. Pollock would later tell Ailsa Craig that Reeder was 'rather a "Drake" person'. Apparently in all seriousness, Pollock explained to Reeder by letter on 24 June that he had responsibilities to an 800-member company, and time spent on the article could result in a loss of profits. Besides, Ainsley herself 'is an expensive commodity to employ and as I have, she also has, a profit centre in terms of the Company. In other words, so much of the Company's money is expended on her, both in terms of salary and air fares and hotel bills, that she, like myself, must justify and recoup that outlay, not only in balance sheet terms, but also to the rest of the Company.' Pollock was also worried that anything he might say of 'value' to the company may be struck out. If, however, the article had enough Company content, without being overdone, then the time he spent on the subject could be treated as profitable to Drake. Ainsley saw this correspondence, confirming her suspicions about the world she had encountered. Pollock never did write the proposed article.

Reeder and Craig retained their hope that Ainsley might contribute more to *Woman's Day*. They had suggested she keep a diary, but Ainsley excused herself early in August from any immediate action. There were personal problems at home: her parents' divorce and her mother's car accident from which Lesley took time to recover, 'plus trying to cope with work and a few other things as well just about fixed me'. Besides, she had just returned to Monaco from London, Montreal and Toronto and was about to return to Toronto: 'that particular place does not move me in terms of writing a potential column.' Ainsley had become more concerned about an article and some accompanying photographs published in the London *Sunday Times* at the end of 1971. She had agreed to be photographed provided the films were processed in Australia and would not be published until she had cleared them. Ainsley also understood that the woman who arrived with the photographer would not be interviewing her. Her recollection of this arrangement was 'very clear and strong', and Sungravure 'could well imagine her shock to see the photographs and the quite incredible story which accompanied them'.[12]

Not many would have known what Ainsley meant by 'a few other things' in her letter to Reeder and Craig. The young woman, who had spoken so warmly about Drake to the press conference in Melbourne and had told *Woman's Day* that she had a 'terribly exciting' job, felt frustrated and ignored in Monaco. On 14 July 1972 Ainsley began to tell the other side of her Drake story in a three-page typed memo sent to Pollock and marked ('<u>FOR YOUR EYES ONLY</u>'). [13]

Ainsley told Pollock that there was 'a very strong and real verbal communication problem' between them; hence the formal memo. Her starting point was that unless they could iron out some areas there was little point in her continuing to work with him. What Pollock needed, she wrote, was 'a bright, not too intelligent, shorthand writer/nursemaid type. This I am obviously not, nor do you pay me to be that.' What he originally offered her

– '(t)he challenge, the achievement potential' – was not there and, after 'serious and careful searching', Ainsley decided that there was no deficiency in willingness or ability on her part. Rather, the deficiency lay with her employer. Ainsley had absolute freedom to commit her productive hours. She had no dependents of any kind. Yet Pollock had not used, or had 'somewhat abused', this resource. She spent her time taking notes at meetings and changing bookings; she did very little else. Aware of her own shortcomings – she did not specify them – Ainsley was also aware of what she could do 'if allowed'. What she was 'allowed' to do hardly earned her the title of 'Executive Assistant'.

There were many specific complaints. Pollock kept brushing her off and treating her as his 'decorative appendage', not to be taken seriously. She had never before been in a situation where 'there has been so little respect . . . for the individual, or for that individual's intelligence and ability'. She accepted he was the 'rule-maker' but that position 'doesn't carry with it rudeness, lack of flexibility, lack of understanding, or lack of respect for anyone else in dealing with them'. Ainsley wanted to be given substantive things to do and the chance to exercise initiative, and to use her 'active' and 'fairly good' mind. She and Pollock needed to sit down together and work out what could be done; 'there was no point in continuing unless it can be ironed out with some degree of dignity and sense'.

Six weeks after delivering this memo Ainsley noted that it had not been addressed. Judging by a copy in Ainsley's papers of a second and undated two-page memo, probably written late in 1972, she and Pollock did eventually have a discussion.[14] Ainsley believed that it boiled down to one proposition: 'I am unsuitable for the job you originally hired me for' and 'I haven't performed it.' They apparently discussed alternatives, including a role in public relations or the creative field. That idea raised other problems. 'How are the people in the company going to react . . . when I obviously am not really working for you as your Executive Assistant any more?' Pollock raised the possibility of her working under Ron Urwin in Australia. Ainsley asked whether Urwin would want the sort of 'people problem' her presence would probably create for him. Ainsley returned to the underlying question of her July memorandum: 'do you want to continue (or start) to work with me, or would you rather not?' She thought she was coming to a job with an '80% Executive Assistant Function, and 20% secretarial', with more emphasis on the latter when they were travelling. She was sorry if she had misunderstood the arrangement and especially for herself because she had invested a lot of emotion and indeed my own money to reach the stage where they were both asking – 'what can she do?'. If Pollock wanted her to go, 'let's have it out on the table so that neither of us "waste" the next month or so, only to come back to where we now are'. Ainsley pointed out what she could offer:

> Initiative
> Intelligence and judgement
> Capacity
> Enthusiasm (rather blunted at the moment!)
> Ability to handle without direction
> Commitment
> Need to achieve
> Able to learn
> Time
> and a rather peculiar personality.

She concluded by asking whether something could be made of those qualities to give her both responsibility and accountability.

Ainsley's memos are revealing on three counts. First, Gorton's management methods and style provided the reference point by which she judged Bill Pollock. Indirectly, Ainsley spelt out what she saw as Gorton's virtues as an employer: he listened, took notice of her opinions and took her seriously, treated her with respect for her mind and for what she could contribute and let her have a go on her own. Secondly, Ainsley did not think it relevant that she had entered a business world for which she had no background, training or expertise, other than six months spent as a secretary-typist with a Canberra furniture removals and storage company. It was one thing to claim she had been brought into Drake under false pretences; it was quite another to expect an elevated role in a successful international company after spending a few months as an apprentice. Thirdly, given that she was very unhappy and feeling overworked doing menial tasks, why did she not return to Australia? The simple answer is that Ainsley could not accept failure. In difficult circumstances she had a habit of fighting back while concluding that any fault really lay elsewhere.

It had become an unhappy year. Ainsley was now a stone heavier. Hence the *Daily Mirror* headline for 18 October 1972: 'Ainsley Gotto's wiggle is becoming a wobble.' The good news was that her younger sister had, to a degree, sorted herself out. There was a hitch when Debbie rang her father to tell him of her plans to marry Mitchell Burns, a talented saxophonist, and asked him to 'give her away'. Sid said he 'wanted nothing more to do with [your] disasters'. As Sid's former wife remarked: 'Succinct as ever.'[15] Ainsley was not overly impressed by the nude photographs of Debbie published in *Pix/People* ('Entertainment for Men') on 2 August 1972, or by her nude modelling for an art class @2.17 an hour. Yet under the headline, 'For One Gotto, A Quiet Life', the

Canberra News of 29 June carried a story about Debbie's new life in a broken-down shearer's cottage about 22 miles from Canberra where she and Mitchell were building a life together. Debbie had just made a singing appearance on a bill featuring *Billy Thorpe and the Aztecs*, and the poster she had designed for the concert had become a talking-point, not least because a few Canberra shop owners thought it too sexually explicit for display in their windows.[16]

Needing rest and recuperation, Ainsley returned to Australia at the end of 1972 to be with her family and friends over Christmas and New Year. She moved into a South Yarra house owned by Terence ('Terry') Whelan, a Melbourne company director and a wealthy descendant of 'Whelan the Wrecker', the company which demolished many late 19th century Melbourne buildings. Ainsley had met Whelan through their mutual friend, Athol Guy. For her, the house was perfect: discreet and tastefully furnished, its walls displaying original works by Sidney Nolan, Arthur Boyd, Albert Tucker and Brett Whiteley. Billy Snedden and his wife, Joy, arrived one evening for what became a party to celebrate Snedden's one-vote majority on 20 December in the contest for the Liberal Party leadership after Labor won the 1972 election. Ainsley did not think it boded well that Snedden stayed drinking until 4.00 am.[17]

Lesley Gotto rang the Whelan home on 23 December with the news that Debbie had been killed in a car accident. She and Mitchell had been coming to Melbourne for the family Christmas. According to police reports, Debbie was driving their 1972 Volkswagen Kombi Van at an estimated 55 mph along the Hume Highway at about 2.00 am on 23 December when, just north of Jugiong, it struck a large tree limb that had been blown onto the road during a storm. The van skidded for about 70 yards, tipped onto its offside and collided with a tree, trapping Debbie in the driver's seat and killing her almost instantly. Mitchell Burns was taken to Yass Hospital suffering minor injuries. Both were wearing seat belts, Debbie had been driving for seven years and no alcohol or drugs were involved.

Whelan came into the room where Ainsley was sitting, silently handed her a large brandy and left her alone. The newspaper headlines of 24 December identified Debbie's family connection: 'AINSLEY GOTTO'S SISTER DIES IN CAR CRASH' (*Sun-Herald*); AINSLEY'S SISTER KILLED IN SMASH (*Sunday Mirror*). A death notice in the press said Debbie's 'goodness and understanding and wonderful humanity provided such an inspiration for so many'. A memorial service was held in St John's Church of England, Reid, Canberra, on Boxing Day. Ainsley found solace from the letters she received, including a very warm one from Senator Margaret Guilfoyle,[18] and from meeting many political and social friends in Canberra, Melbourne and Sydney. Returning to Monaco, and sitting alone in her apartment, she realised she had become very angry with God as well as with Bill Pollock.

[1]   Interview: Pollock, 17 March 2017.

[2]   Interview: AG, 21 March 2017.

[3]   Gotto Papers, MS 9895/9/13. Eggleton had taken a position as Director of Information at the Commonwealth Secretariat.

[4]   Interview: Pollock, 17 March 2017.

[5]   G. Dudley Erwin Papers, NLA, MS 7862, Box 2; *Sun Herald*, 16 February and *Herald* (Melbourne), 17 February 1972.

[6]   *Herald* (Melbourne), 15 April 1972.

[7]   Interview: AG, 29 June 2017.

[8]   *SMH* and *DT*, 15 March 1972.

[9]   1972 file, Gotto Papers, MS 9895, Box 3.

[10] Gotto Papers, MS 9895/6/2.

[11] For the negotiations between Harry M. Miller and Bob Nelson on this delicate division of subject-matter, see Gotto Papers, MS 9895/11/1.

[12] *Ibid.* 6/2.

[13] *Ibid.*

[14] *Ibid.*

[15] Lesley Gotto to AG, 9 August 1972, Lesley Gotto folder, Gotto Papers, MS Acc07/127, Box 4.

[16] For Debbie see Gotto Papers, MS Acc07/127, Boxes 2 and 4, and *Pix/People*, 20 July 1972.

[17] Interview: AG, 29 June 2017.

[18] Gotto Papers, MS Acc07/127, Box 2.

12

Getting a life

Ailsa Craig wrote to Ainsley on 19 October 1973, having heard from Lesley Gotto that she was now happier in her job, 'I should hope so! If ever I saw a girl who hated the way she was [earning] a big salary it was my little Flossie. As things were the last time I saw you, no wonder! That nice, kind, generous, sterile boss of yours would be enough to drive any creative mind crazy.' Craig heard that Ainsley was visiting Australia in December and raised the possibility of a story for *Woman's Day*. She also asked about Ainsley's 'love life'. She observed Monte Carlo was not fertile ground. It was a place 'where most males appear to be superannuated'. She should get over to France: 'At your age it's important.'[1]

Ainsley did find love – briefly, but in Australia, with a slightly older, former Geelong Grammarian who had graduated from two universities and presently worked with a tobacco company. She later described him as 'one of the best looking . . . charming men I have ever met in my life . . . tall, blonde and worth a bomb . . . any woman would look at [him] and faint'. She was instantly attracted to a man she found witty, amusing and intelligent, as well as being a 'bushie'. Ainsley sought advice from Don Chipp on how 'to play it'. Chipp advised his 'dear little sister' to hasten slowly and earn respect 'by what you do, not what you say'. It was a tall order, but Ainsley was 'mad about him'. She likened his effect on her to that of Basil Dean. From Ainsley's viewpoint, both men were right for her; it was just the wrong time for each of them: the Gorton and Pollock jobs required her full attention.[2]

A relationship which did seem to change everything began with a dinner on 19 September 1974 at a Monte Carlo restaurant. Aristotle Onassis was dining there on the same evening. According to Ainsley's diary there were, in addition to herself, three Canadians at the table: Pollock, George Gardiner and Richard Mauran. Gardiner was a Toronto businessman and philanthropist and a notable racehorse breeder in Canada. In 1954 Mauran – Ainsley originally spelt his name as 'Moran' – had co-founded the Swiss Chalet BBQ, which expanded into a chain of chicken restaurants. Five years later, he and a partner opened a hamburger restaurant, and launched what became Harvey's hamburger restaurant chain. Mauran was married but separated from a woman who bore a striking resemblance to a young Elizabeth Taylor. Although Mauran was very good at making money, Pollock disapproved of his taking two months off a year to go sailing.

Ainsley's diary in the following days recorded several references to Mauran. They sailed together in his yacht and dined and lunched in fashionable places including La Colombe d'Or in Saint Paul de Vence, featuring original works by Matisse, Picasso and Chagall on its walls and paintings by unknown artists. Although 'Ric', as she called him, left for Geneva on 30 September the relationship continued to gain momentum, and Ainsley's 1975 diary[3] recorded assignations in Monaco, Geneva, Paris, the Italian Riviera, Toronto and Gstaad and they included meeting Ric's two children.

Ailsa Craig was right in saying that Ainsley seemed happier at Drake, but there remained an underlying discontent still present when she left the company in 1978. Ainsley expressed her feelings at the beginning 1974 in response to a Pollock memo sent to 'promotable, and preferably transferable personnel' asking them to show how 'we can ensure that you are in the most effective role possible within the organisation'. Ainsley explained that, apart from helping the Treasurer focus more effectively in his role and reviewing and restructuring the Monaco office, she had made no significant contributions to the Company. For her to do more would depend on Pollock providing direction. As it was, she sometimes wondered why she was on the payroll and queried where she was going. She did, however, have ideas about giving her 'more corporate responsibility, more direct involvement and responsibility for trouble shooting situations [and] problem areas'.[4]

Ainsley expanded on her responses in private notes she composed while in Melbourne on Drake business in May 1974. She did not want to work for 'line people' or feel she worked twice as hard as everyone else because she did not have weekends or public holidays off. She did not want to be typing and dealing with telexes. What Ainsley did want was more 'international spread', more stable hours, 'more <u>normal</u> time off and the opportunity to do more problem analysis and have more decision-making responsibilities'. Observing that the males in Drake were offered positions in the Young Presidents Organisation and were presidents of companies, she asked, 'what is there for AG 2-3 years down the line [?].' It was important '<u>not</u> to waste a year of my life like I did in 1972' [emphases in the original] and equally important to return to Australia twice a year to spend time with her family. She also needed a higher salary because her cost of living expenses were greater than in Australia, and her personal travelling was very expensive. In Monaco she had no personal life; her life was 'all work'.[5]

On separate notepaper Ainsley listed five unsolicited job offers. One from a retail house offered a very attractive salary with fringe benefits which included discount buying. She had two proposals from media outlets. One, a 'v. firm offer', was for her own national current affairs program with very lucrative remuneration possibly rising to $100-200,000 over two-five years plus travel, a car and a built-in contract designed to her satisfaction. The other media offer was a job with the *Herald and Weekly Times* involving both television and newspaper work. The fourth proposal was for Ainsley to be the CEO of a small marketing promotion company with responsibility for day-to-day management and reporting to a hands-off owner. The fifth consisted of a parliamentary seat which did not offer much financially or an assured future but would give her the chance 'to participate in the mainstream of life'.[6]

Other possibilities came and went. Richard Walsh, now of Angus and Robertson, had approached her at the end of 1972 to write a book on how to become a successful female executive. At the same time in 1972-3 a London-based employee of Angus and Robertson suggested a book about secretaries. Ainsley was attracted to both projects, but her interest faded when she thought about the time required. In May 1973 the head of Mahoney Hayes Enterprises Pty Ltd approached his friend, Maurice Silverstein of MGM, suggesting he might consider Ainsley for a film role. He described Ainsley as someone who photographs 'beautifully' and 'is a very capable actress and ballet dancer'. He sent a nine-minute film edited from a TV interview to give 'Morrie' an idea of her style, and wrote a letter to Silverstein's wife, the Australian actress

Betty Bryant who played the leading lady in *40,000 Horsemen*, describing Ainsley as 'a great lady', 'one of us' and 'a very bright darling girl'.[7] Nothing came of the approach.

She formed a warm friendship with an Australian dentist. Rex Lipman, happily married to Eve and a father of five, was a decorated commando from the Second World War who made his name in dentistry, banking, tourism, hotel management, thoroughbred racing and philanthropy. Lipman suggested that he and Ainsley might go into the travel business together. Lipman and his friend, Bill Pollock, were due to meet for the 1977 Melbourne Cup and Lipman wondered if Pollock had brought 'my favourite little Drake' with him or left her home to mind the shop. Lipman warned Ainsley that 'I will cut your pretty little throat if you are not in London in January [1978] and at that time dentists, developers, drakes and others can all take several paces to the rear and let the dog see the rabbit'.[8]

Ainsley's name continued to be mentioned in connection with a parliamentary seat. Through Drake, she provided secretarial assistance for the Liberal Party in the double dissolution election of 1974. She was sufficiently interested to raise the candidate issue with Tony Eggleton after he became the Party's Federal Director in 1976. The two happened to meet in Toronto where they discussed the possibility of Ainsley contesting pre-selection for the Federal seat of Cook in south-east Sydney. Don Dobie won Cook for the Liberals in 1969, lost it to Labor in 1972, just lost to Labor in 1974 but regained the seat in 1975 with an absolute majority. There were two reasons why Ainsley considered Cook: she thought her profile might turn a marginal seat into a safe one and it would be a minor consolation to remove a former friend who had supported

McMahon in opposition to Gorton.

Eggleton was mildly encouraging. He thought Peter Solomon, who managed elections for the NSW Division of the Party, would be interested in her availability for a seat in NSW, especially in a pre-selection contest 'against the member we were discussing'. He warned she would be 'chancing her arm a fair bit'. Malcolm Fraser, now Prime Minister, would have reservations but would not intervene in NSW pre-selections. Eggleton advised Ainsley to seek personal reassurance from Solomon, perhaps in writing. 'I would be very cautious unless the NSW Division is prepared to give you some sort of informal guarantee.'

Ainsley did contact Solomon and presented him with a list of 17 questions.[9] Solomon told her there was a good chance of forcing Dobie to a pre-selection and the Organisation would not try to stop it and would not feel obliged to support Dobie. Ainsley learnt, wrongly, that Dobie had just 20 per cent support from Liberals in the electorate and none in the machine or in Federal Parliament.[10] On the other hand, only some in the Party machine would support her. To Ainsley's surprise, she learnt there were 'lots' of negatives about 'AG'. Solomon told her that one of the Party's prime requirements of a pre-selection candidate was knowledge of the Party itself. Ainsley's questions about its procedures suggested there was much she did not know. She also raised the possibility of standing for the Senate but the outlook there appeared bleak. Overall, Ainsley would have gathered from the exchange that, while her name was very familiar, it would require a lot of learning and lobbying for her to have any chance of defeating Dobie. Living in Monaco was not a good starting point.[11]

While Ainsley was looking at Australian politics, she was

shifting about in her relationship with Mauran and with Drake. There was a major step forward when she and Ric took a trip together from 9 January to 22 February 1976. They started with a two-week hunting safari in Kenya, flew to (Southern) Rhodesia (now Zimbabwe) and to Victoria Falls, took a flight to Johannesburg and boarded the famed Blue Train to Cape Town before stopovers in Sydney, Fiji, Honolulu and Chicago with the adventure ending in Toronto. Ainsley believed that this trip finally persuaded Bill Pollock that the relationship was becoming serious.[12]

The time spent on her African safari convinced Ainsley that she needed to change her life and her lifestyle. Drake was demanding more of her than she was now prepared to give.

Ainsley raised with Pollock the possibilities of her either resigning or taking a prolonged leave of absence. Pollock was anxious to keep an executive assistant whom he had appointed a director of several Drake companies, who was playing a key role in recruiting senior managers and had proved adept in dealing with trouble spots. By July 1976, the pair had ruled out resignation or taking leave of absence and settled on an arrangement whereby Ainsley would work for months in blocs, was relieved of the 'mechanics' of her job such as typing and telexing, and would spend 80 per cent of her work time on 'value items' such as international recruiting at the senior level and problem-solving situations. Pollock still had a problem: how to reconcile Ainsley's months of time-off with corporate needs. As he explained in a memo of mid-1976, the company needed her to be available when it had a project for her, to be available throughout the project and for it to be completed before Ainsley stopped working. Ainsley's proposals for time-off took no account of what Pollock regarded as axiomatic.

Nothing was resolved over the following twelve months. Pollock and Ainsley exchanged further memos in July and September 1977, and Ainsley did make a concession. The company had been having problems and, in organising her time off, she would rather 'make what contribution I can until we get back on track and you are therefore "easier" to work with – and then revert to having my objectives as a primary priority'. Pollock dictated a 16-page response. At one level he was unstinting in his praise. Ainsley's support had been 'exemplary' and, more recently, she had 'lent a strong hand' in dealing with various top-level management changes. Yet while Pollock had attempted to meet her requests, Ainsley had ignored his verbal and written efforts to commit herself to establishing a plan redefining her role in the Company. None of her recent projects appeared 'to have come to any fruition'. Ainsley may have been busy but not so her 'cost centre justifies itself within the Organisation'. She had not made 'a positive contribution which is measurable in terms of results against pre-determined objectives'. Pollock wrote that he had 'dialogued' this point to Ainsley 12 months ago. He now recognised he 'was relying on someone who did not want to be relied upon'.

Pollock could have exercised his option under her contract and sacked her, but Ainsley was an asset, albeit a wilful one, and he wanted to retain her. They needed, therefore, to develop a cost-effective plan to avoid 'a pattern of miscommunication, missed objectives, missed deadlines'. Following this exchange of memos, Ainsley agreed in September 1977 to perform her role as Executive Assistant for a period of nine months, establish a plan to replace herself on 30 June 1978 and, short of 30 June 1978, to discuss whether she might in the time available assume another role or no role at all. She intended to reply to his long memo when she returned from leave early in October. There is no record in her papers that she did so.[13]

By September 1977 Ainsley's relationship with Ric had foundered and then recovered. They went on a less successful African safari at the beginning of the year, had a week together in Barbados after which Ainsley flew to Australia via Rome where she stopped off and wrote a letter to Ric.[14] This letter, whether sent or not, offers valuable insights into a confused state of mind. She thanked 'my very special man for sharing and allowing me to share such lovely and special times with you'. Ainsley wanted to spend more time with him but only when things were 'normal' and she was not tired or exhausted and just wanting the world to go away so she could sleep. There were three main problems. First, she valued her independence and hitherto, with one exception (not identified), had 'never cared very much for any length of time if someone passed out of my exist [*sic*] as I always had my life to go on with which was always of paramount importance'. Now she felt vulnerable. Secondly, there was a barrier: Ric retained another life with his friends and his wife. Whereas she had shared her friends he had not done the same, 'and at times I hurt'. Thirdly, there was 'my strange streak of Victorian prudism'. She hated checking into hotels and feeling she had to sneak behind doors. She had told him when they first met she didn't like being 'a mistress' and, while she could go along with it for a while, 'it causes conflicts within me' and shows in 'moodiness, unhappiness, crankiness – call it what you will, but I don't think it is something I can suppress entirely, or forever'. That was why, partly, she wanted to give him up especially as she, unlike him, could not live emotionally from day to day.

Ainsley wrote another letter around mid-December 1977. She referred to their being together for three-and-a-half years, and that they had said good-bye to each other so many times. Ainsley acknowledged they were different people wanting different things and with different principles of living and caring for others. He played games, especially in relation to his wife, and she did not. She recalled Ric telling her in Versailles a year earlier that women did not change – they always wanted material things – but material things were all that he had given her. 'Thank you for so many things – and be happy – and enjoy your choice of principles and style of life, which can never be mine.'

Within six weeks, however, Ainsley was prepared to accept that Ric could change. The couple went to Acapulco at the end of January 1978 for what proved to be another turning-point in Ainsley's life. They returned to Toronto on 21 February prepared to undertake a 'trial marriage'. Two days later Ainsley met Pollock.[15] She reminded him that in Los Angeles in March 1977 he said he would do anything to make her happy, provided it was reasonable. Ainsley explained her personal situation for which she needed time-off for travel and for making the marriage work. Her preference was to take leave of absence for about six months rather than resign. Although she told friends at the time that she was finishing with Drake altogether, Ainsley was clearly looking for a safety net in case the trial marriage fell apart. According to Ainsley's record of the conversation, 'RWP (Pollock) stressed that AG should feel she could come back to the Company at any time, and that those words were really meant'. Ainsley would take an unspecified leave of absence on 30 June and, in the meantime, concentrate on finding a new secretary for Pollock and a 'top Investment man' for the Company. She would also tie up all the loose ends relating to directorships, credit card cancellations and related matters before she left.

Ainsley waited until 17 April before breaking 'the big news' in a very long letter addressed to 'Lesley, Kerrie, Nan and Daddy'.[16] She would be taking an unspecified leave of absence from Drake because she and Richard had decided upon a 'trial marriage'.

> He's finally realised he's in love with me and wants us to live together and see if we continue to make each other happy – and I've agreed but on the basis that I want to get married, so that's why it's a trial marriage.

It may not work, 'but both of us think it will and that we can make each other happy, which is really all that matters in this world'. The worldly-wise would have heard alarm bells if they had read the next sentence: 'Ric is still not divorced, but when he feels the time is right for him to do so, will.' Ainsley, however, was 'unconcerned on that score' though she did add, 'for the moment'. 'We' (that is, Ric) had bought a house of five storeys and a basement in London at a very fashionable address: 49 Chester Square, Belgravia. Tony Curtis, the Hollywood star, was the previous owner. Chester Square was to be their permanent home, Ainsley omitting to tell her family that owning a residence in the UK entitled Ric to a UK visa and assisted tax avoidance in Canada. Mauran had agreed to keep Ainsley's apartment and her maid in Monte Carlo should it not work out and he had bought 'a super silver Porsche 924' which she planned to bring back to Australia later in the year and, as a returning resident, would sell 'for a hopefully huge profit'.

After 'a marvellous week' in London she was 'finally beginning to believe it's all really going to happen'. The strange thing for her was 'worrying about the sort of dishwasher I want, and what staff I want to hire, rather than Melbourne Drake's profit picture! . . . And everyone is saying how pretty and happy I look, so I guess I must be radiating it out.'

What is striking about the remaining paragraphs of the letter is that so much was about a projected new lifestyle which the trial husband was, or would be, financing. They looked at a small villa with a pool surrounded by sea at Cap d'Ail, adjacent to Monaco, where Greta Garbo had once lived. It appears that Ric did not share Ainsley's enthusiasm for the place and the purchase did not proceed. Ainsley attended the Grand Prix at Monaco, where Ric had moored his boat, and Ainsley's quests included Liz Gibson, a former Pollock girl-friend, Roddy Kinkead-Weekes, a former English county cricketer, and the Australian-born Lady Tryon ('Kanga'), a former special mistress of Prince Charles. Ainsley was then due for major serious dental work in Monaco for which Ric was paying. Among the coming attractions, Ainsley and Ric would be sailing around the Greek Islands for seven weeks, visiting Venice in September for the famed Historical Regatta, spending time in Australia and then choosing between sailing around the Virgin Islands, reliving the Acapulco experience or skiing in Europe.

Ainsley told her family that she was taking unpaid leave of absence from Drake while remaining on the payroll, so her residency did not change. Ric would pay what was required for that to happen. Officially, so far as Drake was concerned, she was taking time-off for personal travelling. 'We really havent [*sic*] told anyone what we're doing, and don't intend to, as it is really no one else['s] business, and I dont [*sic*] want any questions from the

Press about my "style of life" until I try it and know whether it's going to work, and then what we do from there.'

Ending the letter, Ainsley acknowledged that her news was a 'bombshell', albeit more one for Ric. He said he never wanted to get married again, never wanted to live with anyone, never wanted to commit to anyone again, and so on. 'In fact it's shattering for him to discover that he's in love with me, wants to live with me [,] anyone else bores him, etc. Lovely for me though.' The thought of lazing about in the Greek sunshine in July and August made her believe, 'I'm enormously lucky, it must really be my year . . . to be happy'.

The year 1978 was also a good one for her mother. Lesley had started some new lives as a Christian Scientist and as an arts administrator. She had been the foundation director of the Queensland Festival of the Arts[17] and a pioneer of the Crafts Guild of Australia. In Brisbane she met James Brett Nutting, who had adult children of his own, was just two years older than Lesley and a wealthy figure in the Queensland building industry. Lesley and James were married in Brisbane on 5 August 1978 according to the rites of the Presbyterian Church. Kerrie and Ainsley were present, the latter arriving just hours before the event after flight delays in Athens and Bahrain. Lesley now referred to herself as Lesley Gotto Nutting. Sid, meanwhile, had bought a house in the Canberra suburb of Farrer, extended his repertoire of gourmet cooking, continued working in the theatre and formed a relationship with a woman he had met through the theatre. Yet his surviving papers tell a sad story. Sid remained deeply in love with Lesley and kept chastising himself for never communicating his feelings to his wife. As for Ainsley's beloved Nan, she was getting old, her stronger affections were now directed towards Lesley, her son Robert, the new arrival James Nutting and Ainsley's sister, Kerrie. Nonetheless, Ainsley did manage to see Nan again and for the last time when she and Ric arrived in Brisbane for Christmas 1978.

Ric had been in New York, leaving Ainsley behind in London to settle in with a new butler and a new housekeeper; she was not sure how they would get on. After staying with the Nuttings over Christmas, Ainsley and Ric flew to Melbourne on 29 December. They had rented a house in Portsea owned by Liz Gibson's brother and, to enhance comfort, Liz had found a young woman to cook and look after them. Set in a quiet street and back from the road, the house was ideal for their purposes. They could relax undisturbed and yet entertain friends either staying in or visiting Portsea.

Richard's son arrived – 'we could cope with that' – but one Saturday, two strangers, a part-time female journalist and a male photographer, turned up at the front door. The woman said she knew Race Mathews and asked if he had mentioned her name to Ainsley, which he had not. Mathews was furious on later hearing the story. It appears that the two visitors had previously contacted Harold Holt's widow, Zara Bate, and other people in Portsea to find out where Ainsley was staying. Now that they had made contact, would Ainsley mind if the photographer took a photo of her? Reluctantly, she agreed. It was better to get something done and get them out of the place. After taking photographs, the unwanted visitors departed, after which a driver arrived to take young Richard to the airport for flights to Canada and to England. Ainsley and her lover sat by the pool and played backgammon in the warm, secluded garden. She had removed all her clothes while Ric wore just a shirt and a hat.

Soon, a familiar clicking sound alerted Ainsley to a further intrusion. The photographer had gone into the next-door neighbour's house, placed a stool against the high fence dividing the properties, leant over it and was taking pictures. On seeing the camera, Ainsley grabbed a towel and raced inside, while Ric pulled on his shorts and confronted the photographer. Ainsley was so upset she could not go to a drinks party that evening. The saving grace was that they were not caught making love but, as she later discovered, the photographs were very candid and not flattering. In a distressed state, she contacted a barrister friend in Melbourne who told her that current Victorian law provided no protection and she should visit a doctor he knew to get some pills to deal with anxiety.

Ainsley took this advice but by now was aware that the photos were likely to appear in the midweek edition of the Melbourne *Truth*, a paper which regularly featured topless females and had published full-frontal female nudes. Speed was essential, and she telephoned David Haines, a Melbourne businessman whom she had met during the 'Get Gorton Back' campaign of 1971-2. Haines in turn contacted his own barrister, Cliff Pannam, QC, who persuaded Justice Beach of the Victorian Supreme Court to grant an injunction preventing Southdown Press, which published the newspaper, from reproducing the photographs. A negotiated settlement ended the matter, and a legal bill of $885, which Ric paid, seemed a worthwhile expense to save Ainsley from acute embarrassment and to recover the photographs, already cropped for publication, as well as the negatives. Ainsley's loathing of the media now encompassed the paparazzi. It was hardly reassuring to know that she remained enough of a celebrity to attract the attention of what she called 'the worst of the low life'.[18]

Despite this incident, she looked back on the Portsea interlude as a pleasant one without ever matching the excitement of the year before at Acapulco. At the beginning of February, Ainsley and Ric left Australia for a few days in Hong Kong before flying on to London. Ainsley had an obligation to fulfil before resuming the luxurious travel Ric could provide. She spent several days from mid-February to mid-March posing for the June Mendoza portrait she had commissioned, probably at Ric's expense. After the final sitting, she joined Ric in Nassau on 16 March followed ten days later by time in Fort Lauderdale, Florida, where he owned a house. From 5 to 17 April, the couple sailed around the Virgin Islands in Mauran's boat after which Ainsley returned alone to Chester Square on 22 April.

She remained, nonetheless, in public view. The Brisbane *Telegraph* of 25 April 1979 had a second level Page One headline, 'New Wiggle brush with fame'. The accompanying article referred to the Mendoza portrait which was presently hanging in the Royal Society of Portrait Painters exhibition on London's Mall Galleries near Buckingham Palace. More people, according to the report, were looking at 'the lovely lady in the low-cut dress, with the faraway look in her eyes' than at the nearby portrait of Prince Charles. One man was overheard remarking to his wife that he did not like Gotto's 'hard' eyes that did not match 'the soft sensitive lips'. Nonetheless, like 'countless others', he kept looking. The *Telegraph* concluded that, in far-off London, 'the Gorton connection still surfaces'. A friend, Viscountess Downe, told Ainsley that, of all the modern portraits, 'it is a winner . . . head and shoulders above anything else in the exhibition'.[19]

Ainsley's diary for 1979 indicates that she was making up for the Drake years of working 16-18 hours a day.[20] There was rarely a day when she was not dining or lunching or having drinks with the titled, the well-known and the well-off, some of whom became close friends. There are frequent references to Roddy Kinkead-Weekes and his new wife Annabelle, to John Lewis, her lawyer, who owned The Sloane Club, to Viscount and Viscountess Downe of Wykeham Abbey in Yorkshire, to Baron Tryon and 'Kanga' who lived in Wiltshire and Rebel Russell, the Australian woman who became an executive film producer and whose credits would include *Priscilla, Queen of the Desert*. Ainsley had previously encountered the 2nd Baron Crathorne when she and Ric were house hunting in London in 1978. An hereditary peer who sat with the Conservatives in the House of Lords, Crathorne had created an independent fine arts consultancy. At the end of 1978 he invited Ainsley to join a weekend shooting party in North Yorkshire. Crathorne was a useful contact as Ainsley was keen to furnish Chester Square with *objets d'art*. Ainsley also became a client and good friend of Robin and Odile Kern of Hotspur, Robin being a third generation antique and art dealer. There were visitors, too, from Australia: the Nuttings and Snedden, now Speaker of the House of Representatives. Bill Pollock also dined at Chester Square.

By mid-1979, Ainsley's relationship with Ric was failing. Ric did not intend to re-marry while Ainsley, who wanted marriage and (probably) children, resented every time she felt obliged when ordering wine or groceries to give her name as 'Mrs Mauran'. She wrote a letter to Ric when home on her own in 49 Chester Square

she never wiggled, was unaware of 'wielding power' and called the rest 'nonsense – the folklore of reporting'. The paper quoted Caird: 'With her background we felt that Ainsley would bring a fresh approach to current affairs – she produces a special brand of chemistry on television.' Ainsley explained that, although approached by Australian television, she had chosen to work with Granada 'because they have the reputation of not only being a big and successful company, but of having the courage to take on some fairly unusual animals'.

Margaret Jones complained in the *SMH* of 19 June that while the *Daily Mail* could speak to Ainsley the Australian press could not. She had vanished from her Manchester hotel. The Granada press office was apologetic. It did not know her whereabouts except that she was 'somewhere in England'. The office said that 'Miss Gotto' would not give any more interviews. The interview with the *Mail* was 'a one-off thing' and hedged with all sorts of safeguards. 'Miss Gotto is wary of the press. She thinks she had rather a bad time with them in Australia.'

Today Tonight went to air on 23 June. Ainsley's responsibilities included finding interviewees and preparing scripts, both tasks hindered by her lack of local knowledge. There were certainly some explosive issues, including the trial and sentencing of Peter Sutcliffe, the so-called 'Yorkshire Ripper', convicted of killing 13 women and of seven attempted murders. Ainsley collected a mass of papers on the related questionable practice of 'cheque book journalism', seeking a legal opinion from her own lawyer on the subject.[9] Ainsley also covered labour relations and unemployment, the perennial issues in the North-West, as well as the attempted assassination of Pope John Paul II and the nine-day rioting early in July in the Toxteth ghetto of Liverpool, and the further rioting at the end of that month. This latter subject was of pressing interest, and not only within Granada's bailiwick of North-West England, because the riots occurred in part because of the poor relationship between the police and the black community and because they raised questions about the policies of the Thatcher Government.

Ainsley had star billing for *Today Tonight* but, after poor ratings, it was dropped in August. She was then assigned to a team of presenters, researchers and technicians responsible for the weekday program, *Granada Reports*. Although Ainsley attended all the monthly meetings of the team, there is no evidence in the often-detailed minutes of her ever saying anything. She tentatively suggested in a memo to Caird that he might circulate an agenda in advance, yet nothing appeared to change while she worked for Granada. Caird wrote a commentary on the highs and lows of each week's 'performance' of *Granada Reports*, and regularly praised the work of several individuals. He mentioned Ainsley just once, referring to the film she had assembled on a play, set in 1911, about the 'Pit Brow' women of Leigh and Wigan who worked on the surface of collieries up to the mid-1950s. Caird described her work as 'very enjoyable and informative'.[10]

If anything, the complaint that Ainsley did not 'fit in' strengthened as the year went by. She resented it but could hardly deny that London was where she spent time with friends and where she visited galleries, restaurants and the theatre and where, during 1981, she was being pursued by an enraptured millionaire businessman from Miami. To quash the complaints and to reduce costs, Ainsley decided to move out of the grand Midland Hotel in Manchester at £31-70 a night and take a three-month lease of a furnished flat in central Manchester at £140 per month. She took occupancy on 19 November. Five days later she handed a well worked-out proposal to Caird that Granada should 'adopt' the troubled area of Toxteth, which now had a Thatcher Cabinet minister who had become the *de facto* 'Minister for Merseyside'. Granada could deliver weekly or fortnightly reports on the progress, if any, of attempts to resolve the 'Battle of Toxteth'. On 27 November, three days after making her submission, Mike Scott and Rod Caird informed Ainsley that Granada would not be exercising its option to renew her contract. They said she was 'too posh' for the North-West of England. In effect, she was dismissed.

Ainsley went back to her flat. Angry and unable to sleep, she drafted a memorandum for Scott.[11] Their meeting was 'a shock' and should not have been one. The total feedback she had received at Granada consisted of two nice comments (including Caird's) on pieces she had done, 'an unjustified blast at some incorrect information' she had given out on air without anyone bothering to check the circumstances with her, and two justified criticisms of her style. Hence her 'amazement' when told that she did not fit into the North-West. She asked if viewers had switched off (she did not believe they did), and if there had been letters of complaint (she saw just one). Moreover, in a region of 'so many different nationalities and colours, I'd have thought I fitted in better than most'. There were two other issues: performance and comparative fairness. Since October Ainsley had been on screen five times in presenting the Liverpool end of the program. If there had been no improvement in her screen appearances she could accept the view 'that I can't do it'. She believed her work had improved over the five screenings, particularly in the last two. In any case, were two other named presenters judged on five screen appearances or allowed to get over their nervousness and develop their own style?

'Next, I'm frankly sick to death of comments about my image.' If Scott and Caird had spent time talking to her over the last three months they might have discovered that their idea of her image was 'bullshit'. She might own a big house – it would have been more accurate to say she lived in one – but her interest was not that house or the social life of London but the job with Granada. Despite her lack of training, feedback and encouragement, she had tried 'to fit in' and had tried to do, and had done, a good job. Contrary to the image, she did not hate Manchester; indeed, she had just acquired a flat in the city. 'I'm sorry I can't change my name, or the way I look and dress and if that's different than other people, tough . . . I am what I am and that's why I have been able to do some of the unusual things I have done. And will continue to do.' She knew better than most the negative side of employing her but 'it was management's job to recognise an unusual resource, and harness it so it is well utilised, rather than brush it aside because it is a little different or difficult'. As it was, there had been '(a) lot of effort and adjustment from my side, and precious little from yours'.

Ainsley was not sure in 2017 whether she delivered her letter to Scott. She was not 'normally rude' and probably held it back after re-reading the letter the following morning.[12] Either way, management remained unmoved. For Granada, the only question was whether Ainsley would leave before the expiry of her existing contract. Scott thought she might find it easier to go immediately and to use any remaining entitlements as 'time off'.

The Head of Programme Services, acting for Scott, confirmed in writing that Granada was not exercising the option of a further contract, and noted that 'you have elected to work on as you want the available time to persuade us that we should reconsider our position'. Ainsley confirmed that intention. Once again, if in different circumstances from those applying in her exchanges with Pollock in 1972-3, Ainsley was not of a mind to admit failure. Her underlying argument mirrored the one used against Pollock. Management did not know how to exploit an uncommon resource.

When it became obvious that Granada had no intention of reviewing its decision, Ainsley sought to stage-manage the wording of any public announcement. Critically, she wanted to turn a dismissal into an agreement to part company. Ainsley's version took the following form: Ainsley's short-term contract was not being renewed because Granada could not find the right format within its regional programs 'to suit her particular background and talents':

> Although I am naturally disappointed that we have not been able to come up with a clear format with which we are both happy, I have enjoyed my time both in the North West and at Granada. I found it instructive and stimulating. I'm looking forward to applying the many things I've learned about television in the future.

The *Daily Mail* could not resist one more reference to an old favourite: 'The wiggle girl is moving on'. The *Mail* reported that her final assignment involved the actor Omar Sharif who was attending an international bridge tournament in Manchester. Ainsley concluded her last broadcast by saying that *Granada Reports* will return tomorrow 'but I won't be as I'm off to warmer climes. I've thoroughly enjoyed my time in the North-West, and thank you for letting me be with you. Merry Christmas and goodnight and goodbye.'[13]

The satirical magazine, *Private Eye*, had its own way of saying goodbye. It began its account on 1 January 1982 by noting that Ainsley Gotto, 'who has warmed the hearts of some of the world's most distinguished men with her knowledge of Ugandan Affairs', had been sacked by Granada TV. Scott had told her that she was 'too posh for the vulgar cloth-capped viewers of the North-West'. *Private Eye* claimed that Gotto replied that Ron Caird, described by the *Eye* as 'a sickly incompetent lapsed Marxist', had wrecked her potentially brilliant career in television by employing her on trivia. *Private Eye* quoted Ainsley as saying that Caird was 'wholly lacking in judgement', a statement invented by the *Eye* to allow it to remind readers that Caird once said there was 'a certain magic chemistry between Miss Gotto and the camera'.

Ainsley sent a handwritten note to 'Paul' (Sir Paul Bryan) apologising for failing to write earlier to thank the Bryans for recently including her in a party and to inform him of the decision not to renew the contract on the grounds of her being 'too posh'. She acknowledged that her time at Granada had not been 'easy' from many points of view, but it was an experience 'I wouldn't have been without'. She thanked him for being instrumental in getting her the job. Bryan replied with his own handwritten note. He had already heard the news from Scott and was 'very sorry and frankly surprised' because he thought it was all working out well. At least Ainsley did not think it all 'a waste of time'.

In 1986, when Ainsley had returned to live in Australia, she was interviewed by *Woman's Day* for an article published on 4 April of that year. Apparently, Ainsley did not object to the publication of the following sentence referring to her departure from Granada: 'Deciding she was not suited to regional television work and bored with life in Lancashire, Ainsley moved out of television into what she laughingly refers to as her "retirement".' Ainsley was, indeed, unsuited to regional television and she may well have been bored by life in Lancashire, but she resolutely denied that in 1981. It was inaccurate, however, to give the impression it was her decision to leave Granada. Nor was it true to say she 'moved out of television' on leaving Lancashire. She tried for three years to find another spot in the industry.

Two months after the above statement was published, an interviewer for *Muse* magazine recalled the *Private Eye* comment that Granada's Programme Controllers had decided 'Gotto's manner was "too posh" for the viewers of north-east London [*sic*]'. It is unlikely that Ainsley was responsible for the geographical inaccuracy, but she was almost certainly the source for the interviewer's further statement that Ainsley 'accepted the dismissal with grace and a nonchalant shrug'. Apparently, Ainsley had eventually acknowledged the reason for her departure from Manchester.[14]

Yet when interviewed for business magazines in 1993, Ainsley provided different versions of her departure. She told *Independent Business Queensland* how she had been at a friend's dinner party in London and was 'sounding off about the media to one of the other guests who suggested: "If you can't beat them, join them."' Then out of the blue she was given a screen test with Granada Television. 'I thought it a bit of a joke at first but when the station subsequently offered me a contract I found myself working in television.' She not only had her own program; she was learning about all the aspects of the business.

> After about ten months, I became the anchorman for a North of England regional news and current affairs program with a viewing audience of about 4.5 million people. It wasn't really my scene though and I decided to leave. I was more interested in national and international affairs.

Ainsley gave *Business Queensland* a slightly different version of the same theme:

> With serious reservations she accepted [the Granada appointment], renewed the contract once, but declined it the second time round. Manchester current affairs, she felt, did not give her the global scope she was used to.[15]

The plain fact was that Ainsley did not decide to leave Granada. The decision was made for her. Failure, however, was unacceptable so failure could not be admitted, especially by someone seeking to impress. Yet the unvarnished truth was not seriously demeaning. Very simply, connections and a screen test had landed Ainsley in a job for which she was not qualified and for which she was ill-prepared. She was, as she said in her letter to Scott, an 'unusual resource' but both the employee and the employer had to commit in every way to reap the benefits.

[1] Interview: AG, 13 September 2017.

[2] AG to Bryan Cowgill, 25 March 1980, Gotto Papers, MS 9805/7/4.

[3] China Trip 1980, Gotto Papers, MS 9895/8/2-3.

[4] Gotto Papers, MS 9895/7/4.

[5] For these letters, see LGN Correspondence 1980s, Gotto Papers, MS Acc15.126, Box 9.

[6] Gotto Papers, MS 9895/7/1.

[7] For the drawn-out negotiations, see *ibid.*

[8] Miller to AG, 1 July 1981, Gotto Papers, MS 9895/7/4.

[9] *Ibid.*, 7/3.

[10] *Ibid.*, 7/1.

11 *Ibid.*

12 Interview: AG, 24 May 2017.

13 Gotto Papers, MS 9805/7/1.

14 See Nikki Barraclough in *Muse*, June 1986.

15 *Independent Business Queensland*, vol 1, no 2, 1993; *Business Queensland*, 5 July 1993.

14

'an Australian of some renown'

After leaving Manchester, Ainsley spent the next three years expanding her circle of contacts and exploring career options. For all the activity and the seemingly endless encounters with the well-connected, Ainsley established nothing of substance before making what became another major change in direction after flying to Australia at the end of 1984.

Before then, there had been other changes in her circumstances. Ainsley found a tenant to take over her lease on the Manchester flat, and she moved out of 49 Chester Square which Mauran had sold to Chase Manhattan. As Ainsley explained to a daughter of the Australian diplomat, Sir Nicholas Parkinson, a five-storey mansion was too big for one person. After living for some months in an apartment of the Sloane Club in Chelsea, owned by her legal friend John Lewis, she moved to a house which Mauran had acquired in Felden Street, Fulham. The new house had two advantages over Chester Square: it had just one flight of stairs and there was a garden. Ainsley also told her friend that she was planning a two-week holiday and business trip in Australia negotiate a deal with an Australian television company.[1]

Ainsley had spent the New Year with the Downes at Wykeham Abbey, after which Viscount Downe had made another television approach on her behalf.[2] He had spoken to Lord Buxton, a director of East Anglia TV, after a dinner at Castle Howard. Downe explained to Buxton that 'a special friend had found... Granada did not work' and he had heard that 'East Anglia was a gentlemanly organisation'. Buxton was delighted by the description. Downe asked Buxton if he might encourage 'the relevant manager to consider a new recruit'. The conversation was not difficult. Buxton knew Downe's Norfolk relations well and the two men shared an interest in National Parks. Naturally, Buxton said he could not influence any decision but 'would make sure that the right man took [Ainsley's] interest seriously'. Ainsley should write something to which Buxton could respond. Downe also provided her some useful information about Buxton, namely, that he was also Chairman of Independent Television News (ITN) and a direct descendant of the leading anti-slavery campaigner Sir Thomas Fowell Buxton.

Ainsley saw Buxton on 8 February 1982 and met David Nicholas, the Editor of ITN, and his deputy on 19 March. Nicholas explained that ITN had a 'tradition' whereby regular anchor presenters 'have a solid background in newsgathering and are capable of going out on location and reporting events as part of a hard news team'. It is unclear why Ainsley took so long to respond but she wrote to him on 13 October 1982. Acknowledging that, while she did not have a hard journalistic background, 'I do have a unique experience at senior levels in government, politics and international business as well as a real journalistic period at Granada which I hope you will agree justifies your giving me a screen test and an interview'. Eight days later, an assistant to the Editor referred to the abundance of correspondence they had received and said it may well be a while before they got back to her. There is nothing in Ainsley's files to indicate there was any follow-up on either side. Ainsley had, however, taken the first step: in 1981 she joined the National Union of Journalists as a probationary member and became a full member from July 1983. Ainsley did have a screen test with another company, possibly in the United States and possibly in March or early in April 1982. She reported that, while the head of the station thought it was 'terrific', the executive producer did not like it; so that, short of firing the producer whom Rupert Murdoch had personally hired, she will not be part of the program.[3]

Ainsley's trip to Australia in April 1982, shared in part with John Lewis, did not seem to involve much business. There was a visit to Lizard Island at the northern end of the Great Barrier Reef followed by time spent in Brisbane, Melbourne and Canberra, sometimes in the company of Gorton loyalists. Back in London, Ainsley flew to Nice in mid-May for the Cannes Film Festival on 19 May 1982 where she met Rea Francis who worked for the Australian Film Commission and who would become one of her closest friends. Francis introduced her to the Hollywood producer Al Schwartz. For the next two days Schwartz squired Ainsley to drinks and dinners, and phone calls and flowers followed her back to London. On one day early in June Ainsley received calls from both Schwartz and Mauran.[4] Ainsley flew to New York later in the month and met up with one of what were now two millionaire Miami businessmen in pursuit. Within a few days she went to dinner parties and films and visited a museum, all the time either meeting or taking calls from the persistent Al Schwartz.

On 5 July in London Ainsley had lunch with George Walker, having at Cannes attended the black-tie premiere of his film, *Return of the Soldier*. Walker was a product of London's East End who became a boxer, a gangster's minder and convicted criminal. He later acquired another life consisting of a diverse property empire financed by banks attracted to a charismatic, publicity-seeking and risk-taking entrepreneur.[5] At the same time, Walker had also developed an interest in film and television. Over lunch, he and Ainsley developed the idea of a program of interviews with prominent figures in international news. They talked first of approaching Menachem Begin of Israel and Yasser Arafat of Palestine, while others listed by Ainsley included Giscard d'Estaing, Fidel Castro, John Vorster and Colonel Gaddafi. They decided, on Walker's recommendation, to engage a boxing promoter and an international entrepreneur, one to approach Begin and the other Arafat. Nothing seems to have happened for two months and Ainsley discovered that Walker was not easy to pin down or, sometimes, even to find. She later tried another tack by approaching Reese Schonfeld, one of the founders of CNN in the United States. The original program of interviews never eventuated.[6]

From mid-1982 until late 1984 Ainsley frequently travelled between the UK and North America, visited Rome, Monaco and Paris, and had a three-week holiday with an unidentified companion in Puerto Vallarta, the Mexican resort on the edge of the Pacific Ocean. She made return trips to Australia, periodically dined with Ric at private clubs in Belgravia and Mayfair and fashionable restaurants such as La Popote in Knightsbridge, absorbed the varied attractions of living in London and entertained local friends and overseas visitors in the tasteful surroundings they came to expect. Vicki McKenzie in *Women's Weekly* of July 1983 described Ainsley's lifestyle as 'chic and sleek'. At home in Felden Street – McKenzie noted that Ainsley also lived in Monaco and Fort Lauderdale – there was champagne on ice, sculptures by Salvador Dali and Jan Brown in the drawing room and antique Chinese paintings and works by Australian artists on her walls. Ainsley had her hair done by Hugh Green who was the preferred choice of some Royals. She bought exquisite and expensive jewellery from the celebrated designer, Charles de Temple, in Piccadilly Arcade. Ainsley had 'discovered' Jasper Conran when he was just 19 and became one of his early private customers before he moved well beyond her price range. She wore a collection of Conran clothes for the *Weekly* photo shoot.

Kerry Packer's Australian Consolidated Press had sought to interview Ainsley because there was 'considerable interest in Australia' in Ainsley's professional successes since coming to Europe, her TV work and her future.[7] In her *Weekly* article, McKenzie described Ainsley as 1.55m tall and, weighing 44 kg, said nobody could ever describe her as 'shapely' and she did not have much to 'wiggle'. Yet 'Ainsley is still extremely attractive with her striking dark good looks and freckled elfin face . . . her mind as sharp and her energy as high as ever'. McKenzie relayed the almost obligatory first impression of 'an imperious, rather brusque, woman'. She followed with the equally obligatory discovery that, 'on further acquaintance', Ainsley was 'a warm-hearted, sincere person who cares passionately about everything, especially telling the truth. Behind the clipped words, and no-nonsense manner, you discover a lady who is intensely shy and fanatically private.'

McKenzie observed that Ainsley's diaries were 'full of witty, well-known and frequently titled names'. Ainsley met one of these 'names' at a dinner in December 1982. The new Australian High Commissioner, Sir Victor Garland, invited Ainsley to join a party at Stoke Lodge which included Sir Robin Day. Born in 1923, Day served in the Royal Artillery in the Second World War and read law at Oxford where he became a memorable president of the Oxford Union. Day tried the Bar and other forms of employment before joining ITN in 1955. An obituarist described Day on his death in 2000 as 'a national institution' and 'the most outstanding television journalist of his generation'.[8] Day had transformed the television interview because he asked direct and searching questions of the leaders and the also-rans in politics. He became, in his own words, 'the Grand Inquisitor', whose hallmarks were a polka-dot bow tie and heavy horn-rimmed spectacles (the comedian Frankie Howerd called them his 'cruel glasses'). Robin Day would become one of Ainsley's most ardent admirers. As ever quick off the mark, he sent her a card on the day after the Stoke Lodge dinner: 'What a gifted & gorgeous lady you are.'

During 1983-4 Robin Day was a regular dinner guest. His Australian-born wife, then a Law don at Oxford, accompanied him twice in the early part of 1983 but they had separated by the end of the year. Day wrote many thank-you notes, beginning with one after a dinner where Snedden and Donald Trelford, the editor of the *Observer*, were among the guests. Day was at his least effusive: 'You are a brilliant & beautiful hostess full of style & sparkle'. More typical was the letter he sent Ainsley in January 1985 telling her what he missed while she was in Australia:

> Your sparkle, your charm, your electric vitality, your flair, your verve and all the several inexplicable things about you which make you so infuriatingly fascinating . . . I also miss you for your kindnesses to me, your tolerance of my intolerable ways. You have been a truly beautiful friend & my fondness for you is great.

Ainsley became immensely fond of Robin Day but there was never any intention of having a relationship with him. Day frequently expressed his disappointment.

He did his best, however, to help Ainsley get into television. Day recommended her to his friend Peter Jay. Son-in-law of former Labour Prime Minister, James Callaghan, and himself a former British Ambassador to the United States (1977-9), Jay was the founding chairman of *TV-am*, a breakfast television station. Day described her as someone new and who had warmth and style and a broad knowledge of news, current affairs and business. Ainsley wrote to Day on 1 February 1983 referring to 'the power of your personality' because Jay had met her for a drink and she subsequently appeared on his program to talk about exploited secretaries. Day's recommendation that Jay might try Ainsley as a presenter did not eventuate, probably because Jay was sacked later in 1983. On her side, Ainsley tried hard to arrange for Day to cover the 1983 Federal election in Australia, but his BBC schedule ruled that out. At least one connection worked. Ainsley received £150 after being interviewed for the program 'David Frost – Live from London' – for transmission to Channel Nine Network in Australia on 11 June 1983. She crossed paths with Frost quite a few times.

Ainsley's major assault on the television industry occupied some two years. Among the Australian plans was a proposal with Stefan Haag, a director, designer and arts administrator, who had previously worked with Lesley Gotto. Haag and Ainsley aimed 'to produce an in-depth look at Government and Politics throughout history and man's ongoing search for the ideal structure governing society'. There were to be two programs based on interviews with academics, historians and politicians, the second involving 13 episodes designed to appeal to a ready market. Ainsley's exact role was not clear but would be central. Haag described her as 'an Australian of some renown . . . with an uncommon international network of contacts in the upper strata of persons in diverse fields such as banking, the arts, politics, industry and the media'. Ainsley was uniquely qualified because of her deep interest in politics and because of her Granada experience as an interviewer on various programs. As the approach would be 'international', the ABC would have a stake in the worldwide sales of the two programs.

On 10 June 1982 Stefan Haag informed Ainsley that he had taken Professor Leonie Kramer, Chair of the ABC, to lunch to press the case. He got no further than a contact with the Director of ABC TV who proved elusive, but he did meet the Director of Features who wanted to see a proposal on paper. Although no openings were available until well into 1983 Haag wanted Ainsley to provide tapes of her work from Granada as well as a written proposal. He asked a fair question: did Ainsley really want to proceed, because there had to be patience? Nothing of substance eventuated at Ainsley's end.

In September 1984, in London, Ainsley met Peter Charlton, the Chairman and CEO of the McCann-Erickson advertising company. For a few months thereafter, the pair discussed on the telephone or by mail the idea of marketing video material in Australia collected from the television companies in the UK. They talked about upfront fees for exclusivity, royalties on video cassette sales, fidelity contracts based on exclusivity and extra fees for exclusivity in New Zealand. During their exchanges, Charlton suggested that Ainsley might return to Australia and do a television series and he had approached Channels Seven and Ten with that idea in mind. Specifically, he put a plan to Channel Seven of an hour-long women's program going to air for 13 weeks. Charlton wanted Ainsley to be the presenter and sought her ideas on the issues to be addressed. Charlton reported that Channel Ten had shown interest in a program such as 'Ainsley Gotto's London' or 'Ainsley Gotto's Monaco' and, as Ainsley would be in Australia in January 1985, they might then explore that possibility.

If Harry M. Miller could not persuade Ainsley to take up similar ideas, then Charlton had little chance of success. It was not that the Granada experience had made Ainsley wary. In keeping with her temperament, she was just more interested in working behind the scenes to place quality British programs and archival material before American and Australian viewers. Ainsley had already been working with a business partner to this end. Ainsley could tell Charlton on 12 November that London Weekend Television (LWT), which held the ITV franchise for Greater London and the Home Counties, could give her company exclusive rights, depending on the price, to its material for transference to the video market in Australia. Within a month Charlton had to tell Ainsley that 20 video shops had shown little interest in LWT programs. In February 1985 he told her that Channel Nine was not interested.[9]

Ainsley had irregular but above-adequate sources of funds. She made use of her inherited artistic interest by designing interiors for friends in London, Los Angeles and Monaco, and for Ric Mauran's house in Fort Lauderdale. Ainsley did some well-paid work for Bill Pollock who was worried about the London branch of Drake. Between January and March 1982 Ainsley worked 13 full days and 11 half days for the company.[10] She also worked as a consultant for companies involved in mining, satellite and cable television and the print media. She was in contact with Sir Richard Storey, Bt, Chairman of the Portsmouth & Sunderland Newspapers, about raising capital to assist with setting up a Croydon Cable service – she was too late getting back to him and another company had made the deal. Her international political contacts appealed to the corporate sector who employed her as a lobbyist. In 1984 Sir Ian McFarlane, Chairman and Managing Director of Southern Pacific Petroleum, paid her to attend the International Herald Tribune Conference on Oil and Money on his company's behalf. She sent him a bill and well-prepared notes at the end of the year and received a fee of $US12,000 plus expenses of GBP£1013-00.[11]

Ainsley had many contacts with the British Conservative Party. Early in August 1984 Cecil (later Baron Parkinson) and Ann Parkinson were dinner guests at Felden Street. Parkinson, a Thatcher favourite and a former Party Chairman, had fathered a child by his secretary, Sara Keays, with whom he had conducted a 12-year affair. He resigned as Trade Secretary in October 1983 and the child, Flora, was born on 31 December. Day wrote to Ainsley after the dinner: 'Cecil does pound on. Sooner or later we got to S Keays – and by name . . . Ann seemed very cheerful.'[12] The rising star, Chris Patten, a future Cabinet minister under Thatcher and John Major, and the last British Governor of Hong Kong, was another contact. They had both attended the Tory Conference

AN AUSTRALIAN OF SOME RENOWN'

in Brighton in October 1984 and had returned to London before the IRA bomb blast which was intended to assassinate Margaret Thatcher and did kill five people and injure another 31. One of Ainsley's Tory friends, Jonathan Aitken, had alienated Thatcher after dumping her daughter, but joined the Cabinet under John Major, served a prison sentence for perjury and took Holy Orders. Aitken and his then wife, Lolicia, were occasional dinner guests at Felden Street. Through Snedden, Ainsley met and became friends with Viscount Tonypandy who, as George Thomas, was first elected to Parliament in 1945 as a Labour member for a Welsh seat and later served as Speaker of the House of Commons (1976-83).

Ainsley retained her links with Gorton loyalists and continued to pay membership subscriptions to the Liberal Party. On 17 October 1984, Ainsley wrote to Andrew Peacock, the Leader of the Opposition since Bob Hawke's victory over Malcolm Fraser in 1983. Hawke had called an early election and Ainsley wanted to wish Peacock well for the campaign. She knew it would be difficult but 'I am hopeful that with your usual brilliance, you will more than pull it off'. Ainsley also said she expected to be staying with her mother for about six weeks at the beginning of 1985.[13]

She did not tell Peacock, or anyone else, about her intentions. Too many ideas and plans had come to nothing. Ainsley was very serious-minded but was not given to serious stock-taking or planning, let alone delivery. She knew what she would *like* to do, namely, to find a role in the television industry where she could make use of her 'unique experience at senior levels in government, politics and international business'. Disposed to believe that this 'experience', coupled with being 'of some renown' and well-connected, Ainsley was confident that something would eventuate.

She was not, however, prepared to sacrifice a packed social life to train or otherwise prepare herself in advance of an offer.

1   AG to Sheena Parkinson, 8 April 1982, Gotto Papers, MS 9895/7/4.

2   Downe to AG, 4 February 1982, *ibid.*

3   AG to John Kitching, 5 April 1982, *ibid.*

4   1982 Diary, Gotto Papers, MS Acc15.126, Box 31.

5   For Walker, see the obituary in the *Telegraph* (UK), 25 March 2011.

6   Gotto Papers, MS 9895/7/4.

7   General Correspondence 1983-1984, Gotto Papers, MS 9895/1/2.

8   Dick Taverne, *Guardian*, 8 August 2000.

9   For the Charlton contacts, see Gotto Papers, MS 9895/1/4.

10   1982 Diary, Gotto Papers, MS Acc15.126, Box 31.

11   General Correspondence 1984-1985, Gotto Papers, MS 9895/1/3.

12   Robin Day to AG, 7 August 1984 in *ibid.*

13   *Ibid.*

15

'I'm not unhappy, no, with the way my life has turned out'

Ainsley left London on 22 December 1984 to visit family and friends in Australia. She joined her mother at the Nutting household on Bribie Island. Lesley introduced her daughter to Lee Carroll, a visitor from the United States. Four years younger than Ainsley, Carroll had obtained an Associated Arts Degree in California, trained as a lead and bass guitarist and had worked with American acts and, in Australia, with Arthur Blanch (Best Country Male vocalist in 1985) and Smokey Dawson. Lee and Ainsley quickly established a rapport. Carroll wanted to see something more of Australia, and particularly of the Outback, and Ainsley was of the same mind.[1]

John Gorton, a widower since May 1982, arrived at Bribie Island on 21 January 1985 and he and Ainsley later met up with the Australian actor Ray Barrett on Stradbroke Island. Gorton and Ainsley then joined Lee Carroll in Tamworth for the Country and Western Music Festival where Arthur Blanch was performing. They also had a meal with Ian Sinclair, the Leader of the National Party, and his wife Rosemary. The Tamworth visit had some uncomfortable moments. In a letter written much later Ainsley observed how Gorton 'did not enjoy the company I was with' but said Carroll 'very much enjoyed meeting you!'.[2] Leaving Tamworth, Gorton and Ainsley visited Hamilton Island before the former returned to Canberra and Ainsley and Carroll set out on 1 March 1985 for their Outback experience. They started driving to Roma and then to the Arcadia Valley and on to Charleville.

Ainsley left the expedition several times over the next twelve months to meet social engagements, starting in Melbourne, Canberra and Sydney before flying to London at the end of March. There she found that the renovations for Mauran's new acquisition in Eaton Square, Belgravia – bought to replace the house in Felden Street – were well behind schedule. Ainsley stayed with long-standing friends such as the Downes and the Tryons and met others in London, including Robin Day, had dinner with Ric Mauran at an exclusive private members' club in Mayfair, and next day the couple lunched at the Ritz with Ainsley's sister Kerrie to celebrate the latter's 41st birthday.

After Lee Carroll arrived in England, Ainsley and he set off on a grand tour of Europe starting in Paris and visiting Monaco for the Grand Prix. Ainsley would later tell the Moores in Canberra that it took much soul-searching before Lee decided to come with her to Europe. For her, it meant seeing more of Scotland, Wales, France, Italy, Greece, Switzerland and Holland than she had seen before. It was also 'very special to be with someone who was seeing Europe for the first time'.[3] They returned to England in mid-

June. Carroll flew back to Australia via Los Angeles while Ainsley remained in the UK until the end of September to keep watch on the renovations. She spent more than three months having lunches, dinners and overnight visits with friends in London and around the country. She saw Ric a few times and dined at the Canadian High Commission with Joe Clark, the former Conservative Prime Minister, who had briefly ousted Trudeau's Government in 1979.

Ainsley returned to Australia late in September and re-joined Carroll on their Outback adventure which this time took them from Townsville to Winton in Queensland's central west and then to Alice Springs, Kalgoorlie, Esperance and Perth. Ainsley was back in London at the end of October where there were more dates with Ric and with Robin Day, and dinners at La Popotte and nights at Annabels. While in London, Ainsley learnt early in November that Kerrie would be marrying a second husband, Philippe Elseasser, within a few days. Kerrie was out when Ainsley delivered a wedding present on 6 November. Philippe did not ask her in, and Ainsley learnt later in the day that she was not invited to the wedding. Lady Downe intervened and told Kerrie that if she did not invite her sister then the Downes would not be attending. All was resolved, and Ainsley was appointed a witness. Just before returning to Australia in mid-December, Ainsley had a memorable dinner with Robin Day and Aidan Crawley. Aged 77 years, Crawley had been to Harrow and Oxford, enjoyed a first-class cricket career during the Depression, been a prisoner of war and a Labour and then a Conservative MP in the House of Commons. Crawley had also been a journalist, an author and a television executive and editor. He and Ainsley immediately established a warm friendship which lasted until Crawley's death in 1993.

The Carroll-Gotto expedition resumed by taking in Geraldton, Carnarvon, Tom Price, Marble Bar and Port Headland. While travelling on the Gunbarrel Highway in the Northern Territory, Ainsley had noticed an investment advertisement inserted in a newspaper by Max Archer Interiors. Ainsley rang her mother to suggest that the family company, Gotto Enterprises, should look at the idea, not realising that the investment involved interior design. When Lesley enlightened her, Ainsley contacted Archer by telephone and set up two pre-Christmas meetings in Brisbane which set her on another career. Talking with the much older Archer, Ainsley saw an opportunity to work with colours, fabrics and design, something she loved to do when working for friends in the northern hemisphere. The bonus was that Gotto Enterprises would be an equal partner with Max Archer Interiors in a business which brought her into the field of commercial design where she would not be a salaried employee working for someone else. The terms of the arrangement were first worked out at the December meetings where Edward ('Ted') Benson, an accountant who had worked for Ainsley's mother, was also present. Everything was settled by the time Ainsley started work in the following April.[4] At no stage did she feel that a total absence of technical qualifications in design constituted a barrier for entering the interior design business.

On 15 March 1986 Ainsley resumed her 'discovery' of Australia by flying to Broome and, with Carroll, visited the far north-west before returning to Brisbane in mid-April. The expedition was now complete. Reflecting on her experience, she said the Outback fed 'my soul'; encountering it gave her 'a sense of perspective, spiritually as well as visually. The real Australia is still out there... not in these concrete monoliths that people call cities.' Although still uncertain during 1986 about whether she could live full-time in Australia, travelling through the Outback had fortified her sense of identity as an Australian, though she would see little of it thereafter.[5] Thirty years later Ainsley's discovery of the Outback was her sole favourable memory of her contact with Lee Carroll.[6]

Ainsley was genuinely surprised by the media attention she received after starting work with Max Archer. The *Courier-Mail*, long interested in this Queensland-born 'celebrity', published an article on her just before she left for Broome. Three magazines – *Woman's Day* (14 April), *Muse* (June), *Prime Time* (October) – followed suit in 1986. All started out with two explicit or implied questions: what has happened to the once-famous 'wiggle' who had worked with John Gorton; and how does she now feel about the past?

Ainsley told the *Mail* that she was 'baffled' by the media interest in what was 'a lifetime ago'. She made two things very clear: the criticisms and innuendo never hurt her, and she had never considered herself a role model for other women. Ainsley thought of herself as a professional in whatever she did; being professional came first; being a woman was secondary. She spoke of her belief in 'equality of performance' not in an equality whereby a law required everyone to be treated equally. While she did not elaborate on the meaning of 'equality of performance' her views had remained unchanged since 1972 when she clashed with Germaine Greer. Beyond getting lucky and working hard – the advice she gave secretaries in 1972 – she saw no need to reflect upon a situation where an ambitious male could advance far without experiencing her kind of luck in being appointed to

John Gorton's office. For Ainsley in 1986 it was all relatively straightforward. She lived for the present and for her new job with Max Archer.[7]

Writing in *Muse*, Nikki Barrowclough reported that Ainsley was disturbed by the questions asked of her when back in Australia. It was as if her past was her whole story. She imagined a gravestone reading: 'Here lies the end of Ainsley Gotto, who died in 1972 when she left the country.' Ainsley told Barrowclough that the Gorton years were 'exciting, stimulating, stretching and very satisfying'. She did not miss the past but did miss the excitement. At the same time, Ainsley wanted interviewers to see that she had been active in many post-Gorton pursuits. Two magazines received the message: she was 'an internationally successful businesswoman' (*Woman's Day*) and 'a very mature and sophisticated businesswoman of considerable talents and experience' (*Prime Time*). *Muse* quoted her saying that the 'great mixture' of people she knew included 'some very successful [ones] in the world's eyes'. Perhaps Barrowclough expressed suspicion that Ainsley was feeling uncomfortable about what happened to her after the Gorton years, about her seemingly disjointed life since 1972 and about settling for a business partnership on the Gold Coast. Hence Ainsley's comment: 'I'm not unhappy, no, with the way my life has turned out.' According to her interviewer, 'an outsider can still speculate on what really lies next for her.'

What Ainsley did become was a woman of property. She took a loan of nearly $370,000 from her stepfather's company, J. B. Nutting Investments, and bought an apartment just outside Surfers Paradise overlooking the Broadwater. While Lee Carroll worked on the structure of the building, Ainsley focused on simple and plain design lines and neutral colours for the interior. She liked elegance, but comfort was more important, and she wanted 16 Midshipman Court to be 'a home not a house'.[8]

Ainsley's more important acquisition was the joint purchase in February 1987 of 102.7 hectares (265 acres) of land at Smith Road, Bonogin, near the town of Mudgeeraba in the hinterland of the Gold Coast. Ainsley and Lee paid a purchase price of $165,000 plus stamp duty, legal costs and other expenses of $5,629-50. Although they were equal owners, Ainsley contributed 56.4 per cent of these initial costs, again assisted by a loan from J. B. Nutting Investments. (By 1988 Ainsley owed the Company $519,000.) She later claimed to have been almost solely responsible – to the extent of $60-80,000 – for the rates, maintenance and improvements which included buying a generator, gyprocking the tin shed and painting it, installing carpets, clearing part of the land, establishing gardens and gravelling roads. She did not put a value on Carroll's labour. All this money and weekend work turned a metal clad shed into a two-bedroom cottage with a kitchen, a dining room and a lounge room with a bathroom/laundry and a veranda. Visitors to the property, who included John Gorton, were struck by the way Ainsley had furnished it with the taste and accoutrements like those installed in the houses she occupied in London.

In March 1991 a valuation summary of the property described it as comprising some moderate sloping ridges and knolls with one area in the north-east cleared for pasture. It was heavily timbered and access to it from the road was poor. The one available service was the telephone. 'The property is presently used as a secluded rural home site.'[9] It might also have been described as a 'retreat'.

Allan Pidgeon, a good friend she met on the Gold Coast in the mid-1980s, saw the farm as representing Ainsley's 'Bohemian phase' which also involved managing Carroll's band and carrying some of the equipment to performances.[10]

Ainsley tried her hand at other operations. She joined a consortium with Diane Cilento, previously married to Sean Connery, to make what became an unsuccessful bid for an FM radio licence on the Gold Coast. Ainsley also belonged to a syndicate which bought a likeable but dud racehorse. Politics remained important. In 1988 Ainsley arranged a major function for the Liberal Party on the Gold Coast, and two more functions in the following year. The 1989 events were designed to 'help repair the damage' caused on the Gold Coast by the leadership coup in May when Andrew Peacock replaced John Howard as Leader of the Liberal Party. The Liberal brand had been damaged because John Moore, the Queensland conspirator who was actively disliked in the Gold Coast business community, had gloated on the ABC's *Four Corners* program about the success of the coup.[11]

The partnership with Max Archer did not survive for long. Ainsley bought him out and set up her own business – Ainsley Gotto International (AGI) – with its headquarters in Southport on the Gold Coast. At the same time, Ainsley increased her bank mortgage to $180,000 to support an overdraft of $60,000 in order to run the business. AGI advertisements described Ainsley as 'a well-known Australian identity' whose movement into design was 'an easy and natural transition from a career carved out of major challenges and personal achievement'. According to AGI, Ainsley had 'a lifelong passion and involvement in interior design and decorating' and brought 'an appreciation and a wide breadth of knowledge and understanding to the Australian design practise [*sic*].' She also had a record of completed design projects undertaken in Monte Carlo, Nassau, Los Angeles, Florida, London, Toronto and the south of France. The unsuspecting were left to assume that the jobs were undertaken by a qualified and experienced professional.

Business Queensland for 27 September 1992 published a list of the 'Largest Commercial Interior Design Companies in Queensland', ranked by value of interior design work and the number of full-time staff. AGI was ranked 15th out of 17. It had two offices in Queensland and none elsewhere in Australia. AGI spent 85 per cent of its time and effort on interior design, employed two designers full-time and five part-time, did 70 per cent of its work for business while its specialities were architectural and project management. AGI had completed three major projects, one of which, the Hinchinbrook Island Resort, won an Australian Tourism Award in 1991.

The Sydney gossip columnists knew where Ainsley was living and working. Mark Patrick reported in the *Sun-Herald* of 17 January 1988 that 'Surfers' hot interior decorator' and her 'constant companion, the dashingly handsome Lee Carroll' attended 14 hours of partying in between performances by Frank Sinatra, Peter Allen and Kerri-Anne Kennerley. Two women who became very important in Ainsley's life – Helen Coonan, a lawyer and future Liberal Senator and Howard Government minister, and Glen-Marie Frost, who already had a long career in business as a consultant and often featured in the social pages – were also there, along with their husbands. Dorian Wilde reported in the same paper on 17 July 1988 that 'the freckle-faced femme' had been telling friends that she and 'her boyfriend, businessman Lee Carroll will be seeking the rustic life in the hills behind Surfers'. The *New Idea* of 24 September 1988 said Ainsley looked remarkably happy. The magazine described her business as 'a runaway success', she was building 'a dream house' in the mountains and owned a home in 'fashionable Belgravia' and a 'luxury Surfers Paradise home'. In addition, Ainsley had 'a new love': 'Lee Carroll, a brilliant American guitarist who had a group on the Gold Coast.' Inevitably, Ainsley was asked about marriage. She professed a belief in the institution while saying everything looked different when aged 42 and not 22. Just the same, 'Lee and I have talked about it, but we'll see what happens in the future'.

There was a very different story hidden from public view. Far from being a 'runaway success', AGI was barely surviving. It never earned enough to pay Ainsley a taxable personal income. Moreover, by 1988 Ainsley was deeply worried about her future with Carroll. She originally felt the need for his sake, and probably for hers, to boost his confidence. She reassured him in a letter that he was 'gentle, strong, sensitive' and said her male friends saw him as 'a multi-talented, warm, gentle funny man' whose company they enjoyed. Glen-Marie, however, saw him as just 'an ordinary bloke'.[12] Ainsley pressed on. She had the habit of 'talking up' the qualities of those with whom she kept company. Believing that he was jealous of what she had achieved, Ainsley declared herself envious of Carroll's musical ability and of so many other things. Another Ainsley letter – undated, but probably written in 1988 or early in 1989 – reveals something more disturbing:

> Does it ever occur to you to try & work out why I drink so much? It's really very simple. I do it so I can sleep - & therefore cope with your rejection of me as a person, as a woman & your tolerance of

me as an unquestioning provider of meals, laundry & money. And frankly, I am both worth, and deserve more. If I'd been less afraid I would have pulled the plug a long time ago.

The rejection 'as a person, as a woman' was not only very hurtful, it was also puzzling. She had never experienced rejection before. Anyone who could confess in another letter that 'the somewhat passionless cuddles are sorely missed' must have been hanging on in desperation. Ainsley's fear was real enough, but she was not prepared to say later in her life whether the fear was predominantly one of failure or of being left alone.[13]

Her friends overseas knew she was unhappy. In December 1988 'Ginny', Viscountess Petersham, wrote after hearing from a mutual friend who had been in Australia that Ainsley had been having 'a rotten time'. Like so many who knew her in England, Monaco and North America, Ginny believed that Ainsley was 'the last person that deserves that'. She told Ainsley that there were a lot of very concerned friends on the other side of the world and suggested she join them and to try and have a happy Christmas.

Ainsley drifted through the following months until, in Sydney doing AGI business in 17-19 September 1990, she received a phone call from Carroll to say there was something he needed to discuss with her. Ainsley noted in her diary for 19 September, 'LC (Lee Carroll) told AG' and she followed up with another note on Sunday 20 September: 'LC finally told part of the truth'. The 'truth', according to Ainsley, was that he had been having an affair for about 12 months. Carroll moved out of Midshipman Court on 7 October and, soon after, Ainsley fired him from AGI. Carroll continued to feature in Ainsley's diary, and she recorded that while on the farm on 12 December, 'LC swore'.[14]

Two days after Ainsley had learnt of Carroll's affair, she received an unexpected phone call from her father. In a subsequent letter to him of 24 September she wrote that life was 'relatively bloody'. She had fallen deeply in love and had found 'the joy of finally feeling that I had found someone who actually liked me for myself, and allowed me to be myself'. (Unless there was someone else, she was not telling her father anything approaching the whole story.) Ainsley then supplied Sid with the details he requested about her financial situation and concluded by expressing sadness about his admission that he should never have divorced Lesley. It was probably not the occasion to mention that Lesley in fact divorced him, but it was fair to say his actions 'alienated your children from you . . . as you wanted things other than wife and family'. Ainsley wrote again on 2 November thanking her father for 'the wonderful gift' of $50,000.[15] The money rescued her from 'a desperate, immediate hole'; her bank was about to foreclose on its loan to AGI. She continued: Ric had put Eaton Square on the market; she does not have to see Carroll again because Ted Benson was now the point of contact with him; and a Gold Coast developer had lent her a weapon and showed her how to use it, and her two cattle dogs would also provide security and companionship.

Ainsley and Carroll agreed that she lease his half of the property and pay him a modest monthly rental. Carroll, however, wanted to retrieve his investment by subdividing the property and thereby, he believed, increasing its overall value. He sent a fax to Benson on 21 January 1991 telling him Ainsley was behind with the rent by two months. He also said that an application for a subdivision had been approved by the Albert Shire Council, subject to conditions which 'our surveyors' have asked Council to delete in some instances. Carroll wanted to know if Ainsley or Benson had reached any decisions on joint ownership. The past three months had been an 'emotional time' for Ainsley and himself, but they had time to reflect on their respective futures, and it was now time to decide. Carroll saw no great obstacles to subdivision and, as they both wanted to stay on the farm, it made sense to follow that path or, if not, for one owner to buy out the other or to sell the entire property. He was 'flexible' and open to any of the three options but was not prepared to continue without a plan for settling the issue.[16]

Carroll's fax infuriated Ainsley who, when riled, could take a stand regardless of the cost. She did not want to sub-divide the property, refused to contribute to the cost of the subdivision application, insisted that 'our surveyors' were 'his surveyors' and refused to sell her interest to Carroll. She also wanted Carroll to accept that she had provided more of the original capital and paid for most of the improvements and running costs. To fight, Ainsley needed money but had already borrowed up to the hilt and had no immediate financial resources. She telephoned Ric Mauran and wrote to him on 15 May 1991, some weeks after making the call. Ainsley began by apologising for being so upset on the phone: 'I was at my wit's end and seemed to be drowning in problems.' Some were not financial. Her father had been very ill in Canberra and her stepfather, James Nutting, was similarly afflicted. Ainsley had arranged to bring Sid to Bribie Island, and probably prolonged his life in doing so, but she had created a bizarre situation. Sid was now occupying Lesley's bedroom; James was in another bedroom in the same house; and Lesley had moved out to leave her current and her former husband in the care of their respective nurses.

After relating this story, Ainsley gave Mauran the details of her predicament. The relationship with Carroll 'has completely broken down'. He wanted to sub-divide the farm but she, for deeply personal reasons, wanted to retain it in its existing form. It was the only asset she had left, either for today or in the future, and she had rejected Carroll's preference for a sale of the whole or in two parts because this was a bad time to sell property. Ainsley simply wanted to buy Carroll's share but there were two obstacles in the way. First, she did not have the funds to do so. Ainsley had already increased her bank mortgage to buy out Archer and to run AGI. While her property would be 'extremely valuable' in the medium term she could not approach the bank for an additional loan. Secondly, even if she had the funds Carroll would almost certainly reject an offer of purchase bearing her name. Her plan, endorsed by Ted Benson, was to avoid an auction and to have someone make a written offer. Ainsley had a straightforward proposal and a complicated one. The preferred option was that Ric would take a mortgage of $US 140,000, enough to buy Carroll's half share as assessed by an independent valuer. That amount would be repayable in full in five years (1996) plus 10 per cent interest. Ainsley concluded: 'please see if you can find a way to help me, if not for sentiment's sake, then for monetary gain!'[17]

On 5 June Mauran faxed his agreement to the above terms, though he believed Ainsley should let Carroll have her half of the property 'and be done with it'. If, in 1996, Mauran decided not to buy the property, Ainsley would pay him 25 per cent (as he calculated, $US 87,471) on top of the original loan. That interest payment, he wrote, 'is to keep you honest'.[18]

There remained obstacles, in part created by Carroll's persistent belief that a sub-division would yield a higher return and by arguments over the terms of the lease arrangement which Carroll threatened to cancel in July 1991. Ainsley's solicitor sought advice of counsel on proceeding with a sale and received a Court Order on 16 October approving that course.[19] The property was to be held in trust until sold by public auction and, after settlement, Ainsley should receive $20,000 as compensation for her expenses, and the remainder should be divided equally between the parties. The Gotto-Mauran mortgage was registered on April 1992. By any calculation, and including out-of-pocket legal and accountant's fees, 'the unquestioning provider' of the Gotto-Carroll relationship received a poor return on her original investment and subsequent outlays. Ainsley might have been better off taking Mauran's unsentimental advice but her sentimental attachment to a piece of land and a determination to stand up to Carroll mattered more to her.

While the legal matters were being pursued, Ainsley thought of, and largely organised, a surprise 80th birthday dinner for John Gorton at Old Parliament House for 17 September 1991.[20] The cross-party official invitation was issued by Clyde Cameron, Tom Hughes and Doug Anthony. Ainsley arranged messages from Bill Hayden, the Governor-General, and a very warm one from Prime Minister Hawke. Ten former MPs and senators also sent messages. The evening began uncertainly. Ainsley collected Gorton from his Narrabundah home, ostensibly to have dinner with Ainsley and Clyde and Doris Cameron. Gorton was in no mood for going anywhere. His spirits lifted when he walked into the former Members' Dining Room to see tables set for 20 retired politicians and some wives. He was overwhelmed that so many people from nearly all the States had made the trip to Canberra.

It helped the mood that Don Chipp, who had led the Australian Democrats after quitting the Fraser-led Liberals, could remark, 'there isn't one bastard in the room'. Everyone agreed it was 'a memorable evening' honouring the man Doug McClelland, a former Labor senator, called 'a great Australian'. After receiving copies of photographs taken during the evening, Clyde Cameron wrote to Ainsley: 'That was your idea; and you have every reason to feel proud of the happiness you gave our dear mutual friend.'

Two days after leaving the dinner, Ainsley's Bonogin property and the properties of her neighbours were alight. Twenty-one volunteers fought the blaze over five days. Ainsley's tin shed and the generator survived but she lost the rest. Early in December floods cut three kilometres of dirt road leading to the property. Ainsley fled to London on Christmas Day, returned in February 1992 and her father died on 25 May. James Nutting had predeceased him by five months leaving Lesley and her two surviving daughters with substantial access to an estate with a net value of $2,285,887. Sid's funeral attracted 17 mourners, headed by Lesley Gotto Nutting, and including Ainsley, Ted Benson and Allan Pidgeon.

Robin and Odile Kerr wrote to Ainsley on 2 October 1991. They were having their own problems because their antique business was in a luxury market which was suffering from the world-wide economic downturn. Robin Kern told her that Robin Day had his picture in the papers during the recent Tory Party Conference. He had taken a girl out to dinner and caused a rumpus because she would not go back to his hotel afterwards. 'Doesn't change, does he?' After all her 'personal complications', Robin Kern could see why Ainsley preferred 'males of the four-legged variety' but asked her not to judge the species too harshly:

'I am certain there must be a Mr. Nice Guy for you somewhere in this world. You deserve happiness and peace of mind – you will get it one day . . . Keep your chin up (I know I need not say this as I have never known anyone with your courage) and keep that big smile on your lovely face.'[21] Aidan Crawley wrote to Ainsley in the following January after seeing her in London in the previous week. He wished she would come to England more often and hoped that she would have 'a vastly better and happier year than the last one which should be quietly erased from the record book'.

[1] I contacted Lee Carroll by telephone and email in 2017 and left it to him to contact me if he was prepared to be interviewed. He did not reply to my email.

[2] General Correspondence 1984-1985, Gotto Papers, NLA, MS 9895/1/3.

[3] *Ibid.*

[4] Interview: AG, 2 May 2017.

[5] *Muse*, June and *Prime Time*, October 1986.

[6] Interview: AG, 2 May and 26 November 2017.

[7] *Courier-Mail*, 6 March 1986.

[8] *Prime Time*, October 1986.

[9] Valuation Report of Rural Property, 6 March 1991, L. Carroll/Farm 4, Gotto Papers, MS Acc 07/127, Box 11.

[10] Interview: Pidgeon, 4 March 2018. Pidgeon is currently a Federal Vice-President of the Liberal Party.

[11] *Gold Coast Bulletin*, 22 July 1988. In 1996-2000 John Moore was a senior minister in the Howard Government.

[12] Interview: Glen-Marie Frost, 10 April 2018.

[13] For these and other letters, see Gotto Papers, MS Acc07/127, Box 11. Interview: AG, 17 December 2017.

[14] Diary, 1990, Gotto Papers, MS Acc15.126, Box 33.

[15] Personal, Gotto Papers, MS Acc07/127, Box 3. Lesley demanded that Sid also help Kerrie who needed money for school fees, and he gave her $25,000.

[16] For the early exchanges see, L Carroll/Farm 4, MS Acc07/127, Box 11.

[17] *Ibid.*

[18] Benson/Mauran/LC, Gotto Papers, *ibid.*

[19]   L. Carroll/Farm 4, Gotto Papers, *ibid.*

[20]   For Gorton's 80th birthday, see Gorton Papers, Acc03/185, Box 1.

[21]   Gotto Papers, MS 9895/1/5.

16

A Marriage, a Celebration
and a Funeral

Early in 1993, according to Ainsley, Wendy Miller, a veterinarian then married to Harry M. Miller, introduced her to Nicholas ('Nick') Carson at a party in Sydney. Before the end of the evening Nick told Ainsley he was taking her to lunch the next day.[1]

Carson had been admitted to practice as a solicitor in 1964 and in 1968 became a partner and then a senior partner in the large firm of Blake Dawson Waldron. Principally a commercial lawyer, Carson had a longstanding personal and professional association with Tom Hughes, an Ainsley friend since the Gorton years. At the time he met Ainsley, Nick was divorced, not by his choice, had a daughter and son still at school and was in the middle of two related and complicated legal cases. In one he was the plaintiff in a defamation suit; in the other he had been accused of malpractice. Both cases were an offshoot of a long running legal battle between Tectran Corporation Pty Ltd and Dr Leszek Rajski over the delivery of a computer software system. Some of Rajski's allegations were published in the *SMH* in 1987 and 1988. Represented by Hughes, QC, Carson was awarded $600,000 in damages against Fairfax and one of its senior journalists. A majority decision on the NSW Court of Appeal set aside the verdict as excessive and Carson counter-appealed to the High Court and there the matter rested, along with Rajski's legal actions, at the time Carson took Ainsley to lunch at the Quay Restaurant in The Rocks.

After this first date, Nick made several trips to Ainsley's property in Queensland and in a short time they decided to marry. Ainsley believed that she became Nick's 'trophy wife' whose connections and social skills, along with the house he thought she owned in the best part of London, made her an attractive acquisition. Ainsley herself might have been looking for a safe roof over her head and an Eastern Suburbs lifestyle: black-tie dinners with the legal fraternity and parties at the Royal Sydney Golf Club; trips to rural properties and race tracks; visits to art galleries, concerts and the theatre; and travel to the UK, Europe and the United States. Yet the cynicism expressed by both sides later in the marriage should not colour the whole of the Carson-Gotto relationship. Ainsley, on her own reckoning, was seriously attached to her husband. Ric Mauran might have remained the great love, but Nick Carson, initially, meant much to her.

The couple were formally married at a London registry office on 21 July 1993. Ainsley was then aged 47 and Nick was 51. Their marriage was blessed at Wykeham Abbey on 18 August 1993 by the Rev. Canon Eric Richards in the presence of two witnesses – Viscount and Viscountess Downe – according to the rites and ceremonies of the Church of England.[2]

After the couple returned to Australia, Ainsley made several trips to Queensland before settling permanently in Sydney. Nick had already acquired a house in Darling Point with a view of Elizabeth Bay and of the properties on the water belonging to the very rich and to those merely very well-off. Extensive and expensive renovations, and the addition of exquisite artefacts and fine paintings, including the Mendoza portrait of Ainsley, turned 62 New Beach Road into a stunning and tasteful place to visit and enjoy. Nick and Ainsley entertained often, and Nick's substantial cellar and Ainsley's flair and organisation ensured they did it with style. The Carson-Gotto Christmas drinks became an annual event and many A-listers from the Eastern Suburbs and the North Shore were regular guests. Between 1994 and 2006 Nick and Ainsley, together or separately, hosted 861 lunches, drinks or dinners at home and jointly or separately attended 852 functions elsewhere.[3]

Ainsley had many special memories of the early days of the marriage. One was her 50th birthday in 1996, the highlight of which was the surprise dinner Nick had organised in a private room at the Royal Sydney Golf Club followed by a party at home which wound down around 3.00 am. The year 1996 was a good one in another respect. Blake Dawson Waldron rewarded Nick for his years of service with an overseas trip and he and Ainsley left in the last week of June and travelled to the United States, France and England before returning to Australia early in October.

So why did the marriage fail? Nick died on 20 September 2016 before research for this book was under way and Ainsley never wanted to talk about the subject except to criticise her former husband. The starting point might be to ask another question. Did the marriage have any prospect of success? Tom Hughes, who knew them both well, believed they should never have married: 'the odds were against two very strong-willed people lasting the distance. They were destined not to get on.' Tom admired Nick as a professional and thought he had many good qualities but knew him to be 'arrogant' and 'difficult', just as Nick's father was 'difficult' because of his failure to progress to silk at the Sydney Bar and having to settle with being a successful solicitor in Kalgoorlie. As for Ainsley, Tom felt that her 'strong character' militated against forming enduring relationships.[4]

There were immediate issues. Nick, a non-smoker, found smoking distasteful. Ainsley had given up trying to give up. She adored her two dogs, but Nick refused to let them into his home in Sydney. Harboured resentment existed on both sides, but the couple survived in the same house by pursuing separate lives. Ainsley found much to occupy her. John Howard acknowledged that she was 'a great networker',[5] a talent she applied within the Liberal Party to the benefit of aspiring politicians eager for advice and support. Ainsley threw herself into a campaign to celebrate John Gorton's life and to rehabilitate his reputation. She rose to prominence in the Queensland and NSW Divisions of the Women Chiefs of Enterprise and became President of the national body and a vice-president of the international organisation. In 2002 Ainsley was very active in promoting Dyson Heydon's appointment to the High Court to succeed Mary Gaudron.[6] She was always trying for jobs herself on government boards or councils. Ainsley had excellent contacts and well-placed referees. In 2003 she sent her *CV* to four federal government ministers with an opening statement: 'Ainsley Gotto is a vastly experienced Administrator, Political Adviser and Troubleshooter, with additional experience and interest in the Arts. She is also an outstanding corporate fundraiser.[7] It was no consolation to be told that her unique qualifications made it difficult to find her an appropriate job.

Nick, meanwhile, continued his work as a senior partner of Blake Dawson Waldron and had his own social life. After a jury awarded him $1.3m in damages in the retrial of the defamation case, he settled the matter on Hughes' advice by accepting a payment of $810,000. Ainsley attended the hearings and supported her husband throughout the drawn-out Rajski case, (the extent of that support was a disputed item in the divorce case). Importantly, Nick became progressively dismissive of Ainsley's activities and ultimately 'lost all respect' for her. This decline of respect possibly had its origins in Nick's observations of Ainsley's approach to her rural retreat in Queensland.

He recognised that after AGI disappeared behind a mountain of debt the property was Ainsley's one substantial asset and Nick initially supported its retention. With Ted Benson, he worked out a plan to protect Ainsley in the event of his death. As his children would have a claim on his estate for two-three years until they reached adulthood, Nick wanted to acquire Mauran's interest, and thereby give Ainsley ownership of an unencumbered property. Mauran accepted the plan and his entitlement to a return of $US186,340-06, thus securing a decent profit of $US46,340 on his investment.

The problem with the farm was that it brought no financial benefit until it was sold, and in the meantime was leaking money. In 1992 Ainsley had thought of putting beef cattle on a small cleared section of the property. She consulted Wendy Miller and Michael Brown, a Gold Coast developer, who reported that, after purchasing 30 steers and paying development costs of about

$6000 for gates and fencing, Ainsley was looking at a net profit of about $3000 pa.[8] In the following year, Ainsley installed tenants on the property who agreed to look after the two dogs, pay any phone bills and maintain the property and its equipment to 'an acceptable standard'. After visiting the property in mid-1996 Ainsley found that, while everything had been satisfactory for the first 18 months, the current level of maintenance was clearly inadequate and there had been no proper care of her dogs. She had to remind the tenant that his nominal rent did not meet the annual rates bill of more than $1000 by the late 1990s.

Ainsley always fought when convinced she was in the right. On 17 May 1995 the Queensland Office of State Revenue sent a letter claiming that she owed over $3000 in unpaid land tax for 1992-4 as well as a penalty for late payment. Her property did not appear to be her Principal Place of Residence where she was continuously resident in the six months prior to 30 June 1994. She was not, therefore, entitled to a concession. The Land Commissioner noted that her address for the service of notices and for local authority records was in Sydney and she was not registered on the Queensland electoral roll. Ainsley replied that she had never been on the Queensland electoral roll and had never received any land tax assessments for 1992-4. In fact, had the land tax assessments reached her earlier she would have sought the concession for a Principal Place of Residence because she had as many statutory declarations as might be required to prove that she was 'continuously in residence' at Mudgeeraba in 1992-4.[9] She had married in 1993 but did not move to Sydney on a permanent basis until after 30 June 1994. The Office of State Revenue removed the penalty for 1992-4, and land tax was paid after that date.

Nick Carson decided to end one of her battles. During 1994-5 Ainsley opposed a neighbour's application to the Albert Shire Council to approve a limited access rifle range. She argued that the guns and shooters' cars would disturb the quiet of a 'rural backwater' enjoyed by four families and disrupt a wildlife sanctuary of koalas and many forms of birdlife.[10] Council approved the rifle range application with many minor conditions, whereupon Ainsley appealed to the Planning and Environment Court to override the decision. Legal costs in 1994 amounted to $1288, and Nick, the effective breadwinner, pulled the plug when told that outlays for the appeal would be $8200 with an immediate payment of $800.

Ainsley's 265 acres had certainly appreciated in notional value. There was just one hitch. Ainsley was not prepared to sell her property to developers. Late in the 1990s she turned down an offer of $750,000 because the potential buyer intended to carve up the property into residential and commercial blocks. At the same time, she turned down a proposal from Telstra to establish a facility on her land; the proffered rental of $4000 pa was insufficient. In any case Ainsley wanted to preserve her privacy,[11] although she was hardly ever there. Ainsley remained, however, open to offers but considered it realistic to place a reserve price of $1m on what she wanted to retain as 'a rural backwater'.

Plainly, Nick had had enough. The Valuer-General had assessed the property to be worth $400,000 and, despite agreeing to Ainsley's reserve price and to her refusal to hold an auction, Nick was looking to take up anything on offer. Interest in the property was minimal. The best initial offer of $480,000 was eventually displaced by one amounting to $519,000 from the Gold Coast Shire Council which wanted to use the tin shed as accommodation for its rangers. While Ainsley was abroad, Nick signed the necessary papers for the sale of the property and of its attachments. Colin Greatorex, Ainsley's Gold Coast lawyer and a close friend of Lee Carroll, cleared all the legal obstacles. Greatorex reported to Ainsley on 30 May 2003. He explained that 'this complicated matter' had now been settled and the proceeds forwarded to Nick who had given his approval to sell the stove, firebox and generator for $1,100. Much of the rest amounted to junk and was not worth selling, while the cupboards were fixtures and taken over by the Council. Greatorex said he had avoided a law suit with the Council and had an embarrassing time settling with original bidders. He concluded with masterly understatement: 'this closes a rather interesting chapter in your life, no doubt with much relief, but also some sadness.'

Ainsley fired off a brief reply on 9 June. She wanted to know what happened to the Miele washing machine and dryer, the BBQ and other pieces. The cupboards were not fixtures. They were made by Ainsley's joiners and were brought from Midshipman Court. The Council should make an offer if it wanted to keep them. Greatorex in reply informed her that he had heard nothing about the washing machine or the dryer, the BBQ was not working, the fridge was dirty, rusted and broken and the rest of the furniture was old, weathered, broken, rotten or unusable. Further, he had discussed everything with Nick who had instructed Greatorex to settle 'and get the proceeds to him ASAP'. Greatorex concluded: 'No doubt you have discussed this with Nick.'[12]

Ainsley did not recall any discussion with Nick but had a clear memory of Nick selling her property against her wishes. As she explained to her divorce lawyer, it was Nick's decision to sell and he handled all the arrangements.[13] She saw his behaviour over the matter as typical of his bullying. It was also the behaviour of someone who for years had watched a little-used retreat, involving directly or indirectly two of Ainsley's ex-boy-friends, incur costs to himself, all to sustain what he evidently dismissed as a romantic fantasy.

For nearly four years Ainsley pursued a cause of greater importance than her farm, and one for which Nick, from his place on the sidelines, had some sympathy. From 1999 to 2003 Ainsley set about honouring John Gorton, the man she continued to regard as a great Australian. Her overriding concern was to rescue his name and achievements which had been either airbrushed out of history or remembered only because his time in office coincided with the Vietnam War. Worse, perhaps, by winning the 1969 election Gorton had delayed the arrival of the Whitlam Government.

In May 1999, Ainsley and John Hewson, the former Liberal Leader, had dinner with Gorton where they discussed the idea of publishing a book about his life and achievements. Originally, Hewson was to write the book supported by a research assistant. Eventually, it was decided to commission the present author to undertake a full biography and, with John Howard's agreement, I was appointed to John Gorton's staff under rules then applying to the entitlements of former Prime Ministers.[14] Ainsley Gotto was also appointed to Gorton's staff as a Senior Adviser. She worked with Fiona Inglis of Curtis Brown as the literary agent, played a central role in the search for a publisher and, on Gorton's behalf, conducted the contractual arrangements with Hodder. Throughout these dealings, she took advice from Jaqui Lane of

Focus Publishing whom she had come to know through their association in Women Chiefs.

While these preparations were underway, Ainsley agreed to talk to the media at the National Archives about the year 1969 as part of the embargoed briefing for the public release of Cabinet records on 1 January 2000. Ironically, Peter Bailey, her predecessor as PPS, preceded her in providing the assembled journalists something of the inside story of government in the year for which the records would be made available. Ainsley worked long and hard on her speech and it was the only one of the ten release years of 1965-74 which received a spontaneous round of applause from a room full of journalists, many of whom had been reporting politics in 1969.

The brief for writing the Gorton biography was that it had to be completed within two years because Gorton was becoming frail and the book had to be published in his lifetime. Other arrangements were unusual. Ainsley became my supervisor to meet Public Service requirements; she undertook considerable research on my behalf in the National Library; she was an essential source for the Gorton years in government; and was on hand to edit and to criticise. She prepared lists and addresses of some 80 people I should interview and wrote the letters asking them to see me. Gorton was hesitant about signing letters to Fraser, Howson and Sir Charles Court but Ainsley prevailed upon him to comply. Throughout the whole process, I saw at first hand examples of her dedication and loyalty to John Gorton. We had many sharp disagreements, but I learnt that what she called 'factual argument' could persuade her.

On 7 September 2001 some 258 people had gathered in the Heritage Ballroom of the Westin Hotel, Sydney, to mark John

Gorton's 90th birthday, two days in advance of the actual date. Ainsley, virtually on her own, had organised the 80th birthday party in Old Parliament House. On this occasion, she played a central role in initiating, organising and designing the event.[15] Ainsley experienced no difficulty in persuading Clyde Cameron, Tom Hughes and Doug Anthony to form the Friends of Gorton Committee and to sign the invitations. The guest list of the earlier birthday celebration of 1991 was limited to former MPs and senators, and their wives, and Ainsley was the one 'outside' guest. For this event, Ainsley, with the second Lady Gorton's assistance, had by mid-2001 composed a list of more than 400 invitees. They included Gorton's extended family, friends he had known almost all his life, politicians, lawyers, business figures, journalists, publishers, retired public servants, all as appropriate accompanied by wives, husbands or partners.

One of the many tasks involved using Ainsley's contacts, or contacts who had the right contacts, to invite prominent people overseas to send messages to be shown or read out on the night. The indirect contacts persuaded the Queen, Lord Carrington, Edward Heath and Denis Healey to send messages. Henry Kissinger, a Gotto admirer since Gorton's visit to President Nixon in 1969, responded warmly to Ainsley's personal request. Initially, Ainsley received a favourable response in April from her old friend Athol Guy that *The Seekers* would come to Sydney but in mid-May Guy said nothing could be arranged. Ainsley was more fortunate with Alan Jones, who happily acted as master of ceremonies. She directed Jones' attention to Gorton's speech in 1946 where the returned airman urged a packed hall in Mystic Park to guard the freedom bought by those who had lost their lives, and to build a world where 'meanness and poverty, tyranny and hate, have no existence.' Jones read out part of the speech at the birthday celebrations which so moved the audience that Ainsley posted a copy to everyone who attended.[16]

Many were involved in organising the night, but no one worked harder than Ainsley and no one was more personally committed to its success. She was involved in everything from seating plans, menus and table settings to printing, timing, sound systems, flags and portraits. She made sure that the occasion was not seen as a Liberal Party dinner, let alone a Liberal Party fundraiser. Jim Spigelman, Chief Justice of NSW and a former Whitlam staffer, and Race Mathews both said they would accept an invitation. Lionel Murphy's widow, Ingrid, and Margaret Whitlam (Gough Whitlam had another obligation) were also present. Ainsley wrote Gorton's speech for the occasion and he sometimes kept to the text.

Ainsley did much of the contact work for the biography with Matthew Kelly, a thoroughly professional publisher with Hodder. She was present at every stage leading up to the launch in March 2002. Alan Jones was again master of ceremonies. Ainsley wrote him the letter of thanks and arranged for a declining Gorton to sign, describing it as 'a very special and emotional day for me made all the more special because of your warmth and professionalism'. In reply, Jones spoke of 'the wonderful reunion which masqueraded as the launch of your biography'. Jones, who had worked for Fraser, thanked Gorton for his 'selfless efforts on behalf of your country and your people' and said he 'was immensely gratified by the decency and dignity of your note.' Ainsley sent a personal letter to Lady Susan Hussey at Buckingham Palace on 29 March 2002 enclosing a copy of Gorton's authorised biography and his personal message to the Queen. Lady Pagan had passed on Lady Hussey's message that Her Majesty might be interested in having a copy of the book.[17]

John Gorton died on Sunday 19 May 2002.[18] Aware he was failing, Ainsley had drafted a press statement as early as May 2001 and arranged for background notes to be available. She drew up plans for the 'old Church of England service' she expected would take place in St Andrew's Anglican Cathedral, Sydney. Ainsley had already thought about possible readings and readers, the special guests, the 'oration' and the wake.

There was some confusion at first over whether Gorton would have a State Funeral or a State Memorial Service. The family opted for a private cremation, after originally accepting the Prime Minister's offer of a State Funeral. There would be a Memorial Service at St Andrew's Cathedral on 31 May. Ainsley told a journalist she would be very upset if he claimed, falsely, that there had been a 'rift' between Gorton's extended family and the Prime Minister's office. There had simply been a change of mind. She explained that the cremation had been totally private for the family, except for Tom Hughes, Lady Pagan and herself being present at that service and at the wake held at 62 New Beach Road (she said there was no need to mention her husband's presence). Ainsley subsequently emailed Malcolm Hazell of the Prime Minister's office thanking him for helping to make the funeral and the wake very private. She thought the wake 'actually worked well getting the family together . . . when they basically don't speak to each other as an extended family'. Everyone there appreciated how much the Prime Minister and Hazell had done, and they would all attend the Memorial Service on 31 May. 'They are basically (the Gorton family anyway) just devastated. But thanks to your "privacy" – we managed to have a very private and v. special day (and night)!).'

There was no time for Ainsley to grieve immediately after Gorton's death, but others knew what it meant to her. Doug Anthony rang her the day after Gorton died because he knew Ainsley had just lost her 'best mate'. In the days following the cremation, Ainsley was heavily involved in liaising with the family, government and church officials and RAAF officers on matters ranging from invitations to VIP guests and transport and protocol issues to the Order of Service and contingency plans in the event of wet weather. The former 'mini-whip' did have some experience, given her role after Holt's death in 1967. Some of the issues were delicate and out of Ainsley's hands. Lady Gorton did not want Archbishop Peter Jensen to have any role in the Service which was a little tricky because, notionally, St Andrew's was *his* Cathedral. Her preference for Archbishop Carnley of Perth, the Anglican Primate, was even more awkward; a High Church Anglican would not have been welcome in the fortress of Evangelicalism. Archbishop Jensen survived the blackball, but Lady Gorton at least ensured that her offspring would sit alongside her in the front pew allocated for the family mourners. Gorton's three children sat in the second row.

On 27 May Ainsley joined some Gorton family members, Tom Hughes and Ian Hancock to hear members of the House of Representatives speak on the condolence motion. The Prime Minister hosted a lunch afterwards where there was a brief discussion on whether Malcolm Fraser should attend the Memorial Service. Sensibly, it was agreed to leave that matter to Fraser's judgment. There was also the question of his attendance at the post-Service reception to be held at the Town Hall courtesy of Sydney's Deputy Lord Mayor, Lucy Turnbull. Former politicians of all parties were the principal invitees. An officer from the Ceremonial and Hospitality Branch of the Department of the Prime Minister and Cabinet assured Ainsley that 'Malcolm Fraser has NOT been invited by us!'. Killen and Chipp told Ainsley they were 'totally horrified' at the thought of Fraser turning up. They 'promised to behave with dignity', notwithstanding Chipp's threat to 'deck' the 'tall bastard' if he showed up. All the former Gortonites who spoke to Ainsley beforehand agreed they would 'deck' Howson if he appeared. Neither Fraser nor Howson were present at the reception.

The Service proceeded without a hitch and was followed by a flypast of F/A-18 aircraft in 'missing man' formation. The talk afterwards focused on Tom Hughes' eulogy which Gorton had asked him to deliver.[19] Tom subsequently admitted to Ainsley that each draft was progressively stronger in excoriating Malcolm Fraser, sitting prominently with Whitlam in the Cathedral, for his role in Gorton's loss of the prime ministership. Ainsley attended the reception after the Service and then became immersed in dealing with the drawn-out aftermath of writing thank-you letters and replying to condolence messages. Ainsley wrote 76 letters for Lady Gorton to sign, and she had several of her own to write to people such as Margaret Guilfoyle, Dyson Heydon and Susan Renouf who were aware of her role in the Gorton story and of what Gorton meant to her. Ainsley also corresponded with the Lake Charm-Mystic Park Lions Club over a proposal to place a plaque outside Gorton's old property at Mystic Park. Ainsley did not want to be the 'ham in the middle of the sandwich' and suggested that the Club and Lady Gorton talk directly to each other. Nevertheless, she provided notes for a talk, suggested the Club invite Gorton's children and advised on the protocol for organising the trip and accommodation and who should meet the cost.

When it was almost all over, she wrote a private note acknowledging that her many tasks 'have all taken their toll'. Within a month Ainsley was pursuing another cause.

1   Interview: AG, 2 May 2017.

2   For the Order of Service, see Gotto Papers, MS Acc15.126, Box 8.

3   *Ibid.*, Box 19.

4   Interview: Hughes, 29 September 2017.

5   Interview: Howard, 17 April 2018.

6   For some of her efforts, see AG to Hughes, 24 June 2002, Gotto Papers, MS 9895/5/2. For Heydon's appreciation; see Heydon to AG, Gotto Papers, MS Acc07/127, Box 1.

7   AG CV – 2003, Gotto Papers, MS Acc07/127, Box 6.

8   Wendy Miller to AG, 16 April 1992, Farm-General, Gotto Papers, MS Acc07/127, Box 11.

9   See Kathy O'Connor for Land Tax Commissioner to AG, 17 May and AG to Commissioner of Land Tax, 15 June 1995, E. P. Benson: General, Gotto Papers, MS Acc07/127, Box 10.

10   AG to Shire Clerk, Albert Shire Council, 1 February 1994, Farm - Rifle Range Appeal, Gotto Papers, MS Acc07/127, Box 11: see a further letter of 25/8/1994.

11   AG to S. Muller, 18 August 1998, Farm-General, *ibid.*

12   *Ibid.*

13   AG to Briggs and Associates, 11 September 2009, Gotto Papers, MS Acc15.126, Box 13.

14   For the process which led to this appointment, see Allan Pidgeon re JGG Book, Gorton Papers, NLA, Acc03/185, Box 5. See also *ibid.*, Boxes 3 and 5-6 and Gotto Papers, MS Acc07/127, Box 5 for more material on the book.

15   For material on the 90th birthday, see Gorton Papers, NLA, Acc03/185, Box 7.

16   For a copy, see Hancock, *Gorton*, Appendix.

[17] AG to Lady Susan Hussey, 29 March 2002, Gorton Book, Gotto Papers, MS Acc07/127, Box 5.

[18] The material used below relating to Gorton's death may be found in Gorton Papers, Acc03/185, Boxes 1, 4 and 5.

[19] For a discussion of the eulogy, see Hancock, *Hughes*, pp 334-6 and Fraser and Simons, *Fraser*, p. 225.

17

Women Chiefs[1]

In 1945 a French industrialist, Madame Yvonne Foinant, founded *Femmes Chefs d'Enterprises* which later morphed into *Femmes Chefs d'Enterprises Mondiales* (FCEM), a world-wide organisation with national branches and consisting of women entrepreneurs who supported and promoted women in business. The first Australian branch was formed in Victoria in 1985. By 2010 there were six State Divisions, as they were then designated, and one in the ACT of what in Australia became the Women Chiefs of Enterprises International (WCEI). Ainsley joined the Queensland Women Chiefs in 1988 and was a Vice-President by 1993. She transferred her membership to NSW after moving permanently to Sydney and served as President of the NSW Division before her election as National President for the customary two-year term, 2001-03.[2]

Membership of WCEI was by invitation only but the definition of 'entrepreneur' was broad, embracing business owners or partners and directors or senior women executives in the private and public sectors. Ainsley's interior design business in Queensland initially qualified her for membership and she remained qualified after becoming a director of J. B. Nutting Investments Pty Ltd. She learnt later that an invitation to join was delayed because some women thought she was so well known and too important to bother with such an organisation. When she did join Ainsley found herself among a 'very good bunch of women' who could talk about more than just clothes and families. Membership for her proved to be a very effective way of creating and expanding a network.

In 1993 Ainsley was appointed to the organising committee for the 42nd International Conference of FCEM set down for Brisbane on 21-24 October 1994, the first FCEM conference to be held in Australia. She became the program director and one of her responsibilities was to find keynote speakers and someone of stature to open the Conference. Ainsley's personal connections meant that she was better placed than other members of the committee. Two previous approaches to the Prime Minister's office to ask Paul Keating to open the Conference had received non-committal responses. Ainsley could write to 'Dear Paul' on 12 December 1993 to ask him to give the official welcome. Keating could not accept the invitation. She also faxed her friend Philip Lader, President Clinton's new Deputy Chief of Staff whom she knew when he was President and Vice-Chancellor of Bond University (1991-3). Prompted by Ainsley, Lader – unsuccessfully as it turned out – tried to arrange a Hillary Clinton visit. Ainsley had other speakers in mind, including Benazir Bhutto, the Prime Minister of Pakistan, Mother Teresa and Oprah Winfrey. Negotiations to lure Judge Ruth Ginzburg of the US Supreme Court led nowhere. Ainsley wrote to 'Dear Rupert' upon learning that the organisers' first preference, his wife Anna Murdoch, was unavailable: 'Although we haven't spoken for many years, I hope you will forgive this approach from "a blast from the past" – and view it favourably.' Ainsley concluded her letter by sending her best wishes to Anna. Rupert Murdoch did not accept the invitation. It transpired that Ainsley had the contacts but not the influence. Leneen Forde, the first woman to be Governor of Queensland, opened the Conference on 21 October 1994. She was a very appropriate choice as well as easier to secure.

Ainsley soon became a prominent figure in the NSW Division of WCEI, first nominating for President in 1997 but then withdrawing in favour of Kaye Dening, the former tennis prodigy who became the first female master builder in NSW and now controlled her late father's building company. Ainsley said it was unfair and unnecessary to ask the membership of about 40 to choose between two good women.[3] In the same year she was Co-Chair of the Co-ordinating Committee for the Division's Conference held at The Sheraton on the Park in Elizabeth Street on 7-9 November. Ainsley took on probably the major organising role and enlisted Frank Sartor, the Lord Mayor, to hold a reception and arranged for John Howard, as Prime Minister, to send a warm message to the Conference.

As President of the NSW Division in 1999, Ainsley was well placed to become president of the national body. Under its constitution, the National Council of WCEI elected a President and a President-elect, with the latter normally spending two years as a member of Council preparing her to take over for a two-year term. At the end of her term, the President stayed on Council for a year as Immediate Past President. Notionally, therefore, someone selected for the highest office would have five years at or near the top of the national organisation. In Ainsley's case she had already served on the National Council as a State President when, in 2000, she became President-elect destined to take over from Yvonne von Hartel. A Melbourne-born child of Austrian parents, the first woman to graduate with honours in Architecture at the University of Melbourne, von Hartel had an outstanding reputation as an architect and was always in demand to sit on boards and committees of various boards. She was so busy that it was agreed she would take the presidency for just one year. Ainsley considered her 'a fabulous woman': 'she was brilliant at handling people, which I am not.' There was another point of contrast. Ainsley recalled that 'Yvonne did not care how she looked – she wore the same clothes every day'.[4]

Elevated to National President, Ainsley inherited 'some very difficult people' on the National Council. She intended to be an activist President, wanting 'to grow' the organisation and be 'less discreet' than her predecessors in seeking a national profile. She took an early step in March 2002 by invite female politicians of all persuasions to a party in Canberra. Penny Wong, a senator-elect, attended principally, she said, to meet Ainsley Gotto.[5] Ainsley tried not to be too 'Gortonian' in pursuing her objective 'but I don't think total patience is my greatest virtue, particularly when something is the right thing to do'. It did not help that one of the State Presidents was 'incompetent' and should never have been in the position. Another was simply 'a nightmare'. Ainsley was told that the new Treasurer/Company Secretary would be 'the solution' for the organisation's chaotic finances: 'she wasn't.' Worse, the new appointment became part of the problem by assuming powers and responsibilities which were not hers under the WCEI constitution and Policy and Operations Manual.[6] Ainsley concluded that some women were 'difficult' because they were jealous of her. She had always believed that 'women couldn't and wouldn't be like that'.[7]

The 'difficult people' alleged that Ainsley failed to follow proper procedures in making and implementing her decisions and, more specifically, spent or committed WCEI funds without prior approval. These criticisms came to a head at a meeting of the National Council in Sydney on 2 May 2003.

As National President, Ainsley was required to visit every Division during her two-year term of office, her trips being funded by WECI and by the host Division. According to the Manual, she should be reimbursed for attending the annual International FCEM Congress and the meetings of the World Committee of FCEM comprising the Presidents of member countries. Ainsley felt she had an obligation to attend the FCEM Congress in Slovenia in May 2003. Three State Presidents insisted that the budget could not meet her costs, and one said that if the National President went to Slovenia it would be 'at her own choice (and at her own risk) and not at the Council's directions'. There was qualified support for Ainsley making the trip and receiving some funds, principally because Australia should have a presence at the Congress. The minutes concluded: 'A. Gotto drew the discussion to a close by saying that she would take all comments on board and let the Council know of her decision.'

A further criticism levelled at Ainsley related to the reception held for Cherie Blair, the wife of the British Prime Minister. Early in 2003 the Victorian Division of WCEI had learnt of Cherie Blair's planned private visit to Melbourne to attend an international law conference. The Division approached Downing Street with an invitation for Mrs Blair to attend a WCEI meeting, possibly in the form of a cocktail party. Downing Street knocked back the proposal. The National President stepped in. Ainsley knew the British High Commissioner to Australia, Sir Alastair Goodlad, and his wife Cecilia. Ainsley asked Sir Alastair if he might use his contacts with Downing Street to invite Mrs Blair to a special WCEI cocktail party on 15 April. At around 5.20 am on 11 April Downing Street contacted the High Commission to say that Cherie Blair was delighted to accept the invitation. Goodlad immediately passed on the message to Ainsley who arranged to send out an invitation at 9.00 am to all 283 members of WCEI (Australia). The party was to be held at Lady Renouf's house in Toorak. Ainsley appreciated there was very short notice but here was a great opportunity to 'increase our profile, and will provide an exciting occasion for members to meet a truly outstanding woman'. In the event, 77 members attended the function and paid $50 a head, and there was an overall deficit of about $300. One normally sceptical member later commented that everyone there 'had a ball'.

The Blair function was reviewed under 'any other business' at the May 2003 meeting of Council. Ainsley said that Cherie Blair was a leading figure at the English Bar, a mother of four, the wife of the British Prime Minister and was attending a Commonwealth Law Conference. She then observed: 'There seemed to be a suggestion that the meeting should not have happened.' Jan Taylor, the Queensland President, raised three questions: whether the National Council was happy to have such an event hosted in its name; whether in view of the parlous financial situation the Council should hold functions without prior Council approval; and whether all the costs had been included in assessing the financial outcome. Mandy Keillor, the South Australian President, said there was a procedure for State and National Presidents to follow and no one was entitled to act alone in respect of costs, even if the event was a great one for WECI. Katie Watkin, the Victorian President, stated the obvious: there would never have been a meeting had it not been for Ainsley Gotto. Watkin did not have the contacts or the standing to persuade Downing Street or Susan Renouf to co-operate. Another Council member asked whether Ainsley was supposed to tell Downing Street at 5.20 am to hang on until, say, 10.00 am, while approval was sought around Australia. Ainsley concluded the discussion by tabling a letter from Lady Goodlad complimenting the WCEI on the occasion and reporting that Cherie Blair was thrilled to have been there.[8]

Unable to attend the May Council meeting, a very supportive von Hartel sent an email two days later to all those who were there. Referring to the 'less than positive feedback' she had received, von Hartel said she hoped for 'an appropriate acknowledgement of Ainsley's achievements at National level'. She did not want to be 'alienating or disruptive' but would not enter into any correspondence on the subject.[9] The critics, however, persisted, prompted by Ainsley's decisions to go to Slovenia at the end of May and, with Jaqui Lane of the NSW Division, to set up an ACT Division of WCEI.

Keillor emailed all members of Council seeking an extraordinary meeting to be held by mid-August 2003. She wanted the meeting to address budgetary issues, the President's report on the Slovenia Congress, and the process of setting up a Canberra Division. Despite some clumsy wording, the message was clear enough. Keillor wanted to focus on 'tightening' the decision-making roles and responsibilities of the President and of Council 'to ensure future cohesiveness, good corporate governance and responsible financial management'. She wanted an open discussion on these issues 'which it seems are causing tension and disunity within the WCEI National Council'; 'resignations', she wrote, 'are being considered'.

Keillor's call for what became known as an 'emergency' meeting precipitated a veritable avalanche of emails. Ninety alone were devoted to Ainsley's travel expenses and many emails addressed to Ainsley were copied to all members of Council. Jan Taylor relayed four objections to Ainsley's leadership style and decision-making: she had overruled the majority by going to Slovenia; she wanted funding to attend a conference in Mauritius; she had not produced a national budget for 2003-04; and she had not disclosed the full costs and procedures for setting up the Canberra Division of WCEI. Ainsley replied formally to these charges in a letter sent to Taylor on 8 August. Calmly she corrected the 'mistakes' in the first two complaints and provided the information necessary to counter the other two. One statement especially annoyed her. Taylor had claimed that Ainsley had travelled to Slovenia in 'apparent complete disregard . . . of the expressed wishes of a majority of the board'. Ainsley referred to the minutes: there was no resolution or motion to approve or disapprove; she would take account of the views expressed around the table.[10] Ainsley was also angered by Taylor's use of global emails sent to all members of Council. She believed that the proper course was to approach the President first, and interpreted Taylor's actions as an attempt to build an opposition and undermine her authority.

Ainsley consulted Fiona Shand, a lawyer, and Jaqui Lane before sending her reply to Taylor. Perhaps their advice, or her own second thoughts, explain the excision from her draft of the following paragraphs:

> [your criticism is] inaccurate, time consuming, energy sapping and
> costly in terms of the health of all of us. It has also contributed to
> a sense of unease and unrest at National Council level . . .

> If any National Councillor wishes to resign from Council – please
> feel free to forward me your resignation.

> All of us are different – highly competitive, hard charging success-
> oriented women. Some of us have a management style that others
> do not like. I have always tried to be open, above-board, direct
> and frank in my dealings with the National Council and I would
> expect the same courtesies from the National Council members
> themselves . . .

> I trust this will clear the air and that we will have no more inaccurate
> statements or inflammatory language in our communication, and
> that the unprofessional manner of global emailing will cease.[11]

On 30 July, Keillor withdrew her request for an emergency
meeting because Ros King, the President-elect from Western
Australia, was unable to attend. She had not withdrawn her specific
concerns and still believed there was a lack of recognition about
the 'unrest' in the Council.

For all her protests, Ainsley clearly enjoyed the politics of the
presidency. Her final meeting in office was the annual conference
set down for Hobart in October 2003. Ros King was due to
replace her, but the conference had to choose a president-elect.
Mandy Keillor nominated for the post stressing her success as a
builder and designer and her discovery, on joining WCEI, that
for the first time in her professional life she 'had met a group of
women [whom] I would consider my equal'. Keillor's nomination
merely intensified Ainsley's determination to secure Katie Watkin's
election. Drawing on a long experience of working and counting
the numbers, Ainsley sent out an email on 10 October to known

Watkin supporters – among them, von Hartel, King, Lane and Jane Dawson (a sculptor) – who had previously agreed to 'get Katie Watkin up'. She did not regard Mandy as 'the best choice' for this time. As Katie could not be expected to canvass for herself it was 'up to us' and anyone 'you can "trust" in your own State Division, to get cracking and really work the phones to the membership'. Ainsley believed that one current and one former State President were collecting proxies. It was critical, therefore, to get every proxy from every State, and especially to work on the Tasmanians who could be expected to turn up in force. Katie Watkin left the Hobart meeting as the President-elect.

When Ainsley made her final presidential speech at Hobart, she sensed that the dissidents hated her even more. She said she came into the role 'believing that the mandate of the National President – as set out in Policy and Procedures Manual – is to lead the organisation in the spirit of team work and cooperation'. Moreover, the President has a hands-on role; 'nothing happens without strong leadership and a clear view of what WECI is and should be about'. Ainsley found it 'personally and professionally disappointing . . . that some State Presidents have seen fit to see their task as undermining the role of the National President with petty "bureaucratic-style" criticisms'. Further, these Presidents spent so much time criticising her, they failed in their own States to order their finances and fulfil their commitment as directors of the Company. Ainsley expressed her gratitude for the support of many in the organisation and said that, 'while the path was not always smooth, as many of you know, I am not one to undertake a commitment such as leadership of this organisation lightly.' She concluded with the observation that WCEI-Australia and FCEM 'are extremely important for the advancement of women in our society . . . We are not simply a "lunch club", but an organisation whose aim is to make visible the worth of women as entrepreneurs – as "Alone we are invisible . . . together we are invincible".'

Ainsley could look back with some pride on her achievements as National President.

She could claim that the Canberra meeting of March 2002 and the Blair function of the following April were critical in helping to secure 'WCEI's place on the map in business and government circles'. She could also point to what the *Australian Financial Review* of 18 July 2002 called 'a heavyweight lunch' held at Blake Dawson Waldron in Sydney with a guest list of over 60 leading business and media figures. Ainsley was an arresting public speaker, explaining that the qualification for joining WCEI was that 'we – to use a male term – put our balls on the line'. The Women Chiefs were like the Young President Organisation except there was no retirement age and 'and, overall, we're – frankly – better looking'.

While actively promoting WCEI Ainsley worked hard administering the organisation. Her work ethic was as strong as ever. She spent an average of two days a week on WCEI business, not including Saturdays where she worked alongside Cynthia Copock, a secretary recommended by Watkin. Ainsley never had any real spousal support. On Saturdays, Nick would arrive home from a game of tennis and ask, 'Where's lunch?' He regarded Women Chiefs as the equivalent of basket-weaving in Balmain. From his perspective the saving grace was probably that Ainsley was very preoccupied; it is equally probable he resented any subsidising of her involvement. Nick, nevertheless, accompanied his wife on what became an expensive 'grand tour' with the FCEM congress in St Petersburg in mid-September 2002 as the focal point. The pair stopped over in London and Yorkshire before the event and in the medieval French village of Tourettes-sur Loupe, New York, Chicago and San Francisco on the way home.

Her work done in the national body Ainsley turned her attention to the international organisation. Under Leyla Khaliat of Tunisia, who had been World President since 1998, Ainsley became a vice-president for the Asia-Pacific region.[12] She went to Fiji in February-March 2005 and helped in the formation of a Fijian version of Women Chiefs and earned the gratitude of the first National President: 'Never have feet so small as yours left such an imprint on our shores!' She was thanked for her 'smiles, professionalism, attitude, style, dynamism and everything else'.[13]

Leyla Khaliat planned to retire when the Council met in Fez, Morocco, in April 2005. It was important to ensure there was an ordered process for electing her replacement. Khaliat appointed Ainsley to work with Eugenie Burgholte-Kellermann, a former Vice-President from Germany and head of the FCEM's Task Force for Statutes and Internal Rules, to prepare a set of procedures for electing the next President. Ainsley presented the recommendations of the Task Force to the FCEM Steering Committee in Glasgow in October 2004 which approved the proposals. By this time Ainsley had established a close friendship with Arlene Woutersz of the British Association of Women Entrepreneurs. Woutersz and other FCEM members from Europe and North America had decided it was time to address the language and cultural differences which were hindering cooperation in FCEM. They organised a 'ticket' whereby Woutersz would nominate for the presidency and, after three years, make way for Christine Chauvet of France. Ainsley strongly supported the move and corresponded regularly with Arlene by email from early 2005. There proved to be constitutional problems with the ticket so that Woutersz alone, backed by Chauvet, nominated for the presidency. So did Marta Turk of Slovenia but no one outside her country expected her to win.

Françoise Foning of the Cameroon was a different proposition. Starting with very little, Foning had placed her hands in and over many substantial businesses in Cameroon, and there was plenty of evidence to suggest those hands were not always clean. Foning became a wealthy, generous and strong-willed 'heavyweight' (one of her nicknames) who was accustomed to getting her own way. It helped that she fawned over Paul Biya, Prime Minister and then President of Cameroon since 1975, who miraculously won elections at a time when he was almost universally unpopular. Arlene and Ainsley feared that Foning would bring the stench of corruption with her. Moreover, a Foning victory would probably mean that the African members who voted for her would expect financial support from FCEM in return. There was also a question of principle. It was an article of faith that the national and international Women's Chiefs should remain separate from government and politics.

It was soon apparent that Etta Carignani, the FCEM Secretary-General from Trieste, regarded the approved election procedures as no more than a preliminary guide. Carignani had clashed several times with Ainsley when she was National President, and most notably over what Ainsley saw as an improper process which had earlier given Khaliat a renewed term as World President. Ainsley, a stickler for due process, went into battle but it was hard to make an impression with emails sent from Australia. What outraged her most was that Carignani wanted non-voting members of FCEM to be present in the same room as the valid electors. The concern for Arlene and Ainsley was that the result could be manipulated with the Secretary-General, backed by the retiring World President, making up election rules as it pleased them, but principally to make a show of the event in line with Foning's preference for grandstanding. In an email to Ainsley, Arlene visualised Foning's arrival in Fez:

> Foning will start performing as soon as she enters Moroccan airspace and will have TV, Media and a large crowd of body slaves and supporters running in front and behind, while she eats, burps, farts and talks on her mobile phone.

Foning won 18 of the 28 votes in the final ballot and remained in office for six years.[14] In May 2006 the national organisations of Australia, Canada, France, Germany, Mauritania, Morocco, the Netherlands, South Africa, the United Kingdom and the United States formally launched a new organisation in Amsterdam: Network of Entrepreneurial Women Worldwide (NEWW). Christine Chauvet became the first President. Australia remained attached to both bodies but, initially, Ainsley focused her attention on NEWW. For her, the important feature of the new organisation was that it was not a network for government or semi-government activities. Ainsley worked with others in framing a constitution and rules of procedure while fearing that NEWW was not making its intended mark. She continued to attend meetings of the NSW division of WCEI and, as an honorary life member, had to remind the secretary that it was not appropriate to send her a letter requesting payment of the annual membership fee.

Ainsley put a lot of time and industry into working for the Women Chiefs. Was it all worthwhile? The short answer, in terms of personal satisfaction, is 'Yes'. Ainsley met and worked with women she liked and admired, while she enjoyed applying the political, social and organisational skills she had acquired over four decades. Ainsley also entered new territory. The young woman who had never seen herself as a role model when she was John Gorton's PPS, and who rejected what she saw as the objectives of the Women's Liberation Movement, committed herself, 40 years later, as a leading member of WCEI (Australia) and FCEM to the promotion of women in business and to raising the profile of women in the world at large. In November 2002 she aligned WCEI (Australia) – albeit unsuccessfully – behind the nomination of three female (Australian) lawyers as judges or prosecutors on the new International Criminal Court. Ainsley, however, never saw herself as a feminist; she never deviated from her perception of herself as a woman 'second' in whatever career she undertook.

By 2007 Ainsley had other priorities: to win a satisfactory divorce settlement and to secure paid employment.

[1]   Boxes 12-21 of Gotto Papers, MS Acc07/127 contain relevant material and the author is currently in possession of Ainsley's email records.

[2]   Interview: AG, 8 June 2017.

[3]   AG to Anne McDonald, 24 November 1997, WCEI NSW Membership, Gotto Papers, MS Acc07/127, Box 13.

[4]   Interview: AG, 8 June 2017.

[5]   *Ibid.*

[6]   See the email exchanges of March 2003 in National Council – May 03, Gotto Papers, MS Acc07/127, Box 17.

[7]   Interview: AG, 8 June 2017.

[8]   Blair Function, Gotto Papers, MS Acc07/127, Box 15.

[9]   National Council – May 03, *ibid*, Box 17.

[10] WCEI National Council 22-23/10/03, *ibid.*, Box 14.

[11] *Ibid.*

[12] During her presidency Ainsley lobbied Khaliat to remove Noelle Tolley of South Australia as Regional Commissioner for that area.

13 Bernadette Ganilau to AG, 7 March 2005, Women Entrepreneurs Fiji, Gotto Papers, MS Acc07/127, Box 12.

14 Foning died following a car accident in Cameroon in 2015.

18

Divorce

Ainsley's marriage was clearly in trouble around the turn of the century. There were occasions when she and Nick spoke harshly to each other in front of friends and Nick could be brutal in her absence, once remarking at a dinner party as Ainsley left the room, 'there goes a child in a woman's body'.[1] She recalled that Nick 'would discount what I said and publicly put me down or dismiss me'. When Ainsley expressed an opinion, he would ask whether she had picked it up in the *Daily Telegraph*. Throughout the marriage, Nick always referred to 62 New Beach Road as 'my' and not 'our' house. There was a serious concern of another kind, one which echoed Ainsley's experience during her relationship with Lee Carroll: 'I felt as though I was losing myself as a woman – no warmth or tenderness. Any attempt by me would be refused.'[2] When, as she saw it, Ainsley tried to retrieve the situation, and had expensive cosmetic surgery during one of Nick's trips to France, her husband either did not notice the change or chose not to comment.

Nick Carson left his wife a curt note on 7 October 2005. Addressed to 'Ainsley', it began: 'Cheque attached.' The cheque was probably made out for $2500, representing the agreed month's housekeeping. Ainsley deeply resented Nick's refusal to arrange an automatic bank transfer; she often had to ask him for the cheque. On housekeeping, he told Ainsley she 'should do more than say to Felicia [their cleaner] "Clean the fridge". You should monitor what is there & use food while it is fresh. And, I do not see why you cannot play some part in watering the plants. Please think about these matters.' Ainsley replied that she would not respond in the same 'rude manner'; people only wrote that way to an employee or to a servant. After refuting the specific charges and insinuations, she declared she would not 'be bullied either verbally or emotionally any more . . . If you are seeking to get me to leave, then you are going about it the wrong way.' Nor would she continue to live with someone she considered an alcoholic whose basic good nature changed after drinking. Her husband 'became an aggressive, rude, overbearing and pompous person' and was not the man she had fallen in love with and had married. 'And while you hurt me immensely, you demean yourself.' In her final thrust Ainsley asked him to cease discussing their marriage outside the family. 'If you have any points . . . to make please have the guts to make them to me yourself.'[3]

Ainsley soon had to adjust to another family situation. Her sister Kerrie died of cancer in Venice on 29 December 2005. Susan Renouf was among the friends who sent condolence letters to Ainsley. A couple who knew of Ainsley's 'difficult relationship' with Kerrie nonetheless ventured that it must have been hard for 'a caring, generous & warm person' not to be able to support her sister at this time. What Ainsley could do was contribute suggestions from Lesley and herself about readings and prayers – 'not too religious . . . more spiritual' – for the order of the funeral service to take place in Venice on 5 January 2006. Just two of the several suggestions were accepted by Kerrie's children: the hymn, 'All Things Bright and Beautiful', and the biblical reading from St John's Gospel used at the Gorton Memorial Service, 'Let not your heart be troubled'. Charles Gotto, the son of the Gottos Ainsley first met in London in 1969, gave what Ainsley called a 'not particularly accurate' account of Kerrie's life.[4] She bridled at descriptions of her sister as highly principled and possessed of a strict moral code.

The industry Ainsley exercised in assembling suggestions for the funeral may have reflected a sense of guilt about her antipathy towards her sister. The two sisters had never been on amicable terms since the 1960s. In 1992 Kerrie's son, Ben, described the widening gulf between them as a 'huge chasm'.[5] Ainsley had long disapproved of Kerrie's behaviour towards her first husband and of her subsequent relationships.[6] Several times during 2017 she liked to quote Ric Mauran's comment: 'you must understand Ainsley that Kerrie is a taker not a giver.' Kerrie resented the fact that Ainsley received preferential financial treatment from Sid prior to his death in 1992 and believed that Ainsley had joined their mother and Ted Benson in making self-serving decisions in dealing with Sid's estate. In a letter complaining to the Institute of Chartered Accountants about Benson's actions, Kerrie noted that Sid divided his estate equally between Kerrie and her 'unmarried, childless sister, Miss Ainsley Gotto' because he had 'grave doubts about her financial capabilities', his exact words being 'she's hopeless with money'. There was little subtlety about another passage from the same letter. Despite Ainsley having 'no training, qualifications or experience in interior decorating nor in running a business', Lesley had arranged financial support to buy the business on the Gold Coast so she could have one daughter living in Australia;

'a decorating business was seen as a suitable project for my somewhat high profile sister'.[7]

Four months after leaving his message of October 2005, Nick hosted a 60th birthday party for his wife, a black-tie dinner held at the Royal Sydney Golf Club on 14 February 2006. Ainsley wanted a party for those who were important in her life. Kerrie's death meant that her mother was the other surviving member of Ainsley's immediate family, but a last minute health problem prevented Lesley from flying to Sydney. Ainsley and Glen-Marie Frost did most of the organising for the event, and Ben handled the technical side of Glen-Marie's picture show. Nick, as master of ceremonies and under pressure from Glen-Marie to declare his love for Ainsley, managed a perfunctory reference to 'my darling wife' and left it to Race Mathews and Glen-Marie to talk about her. They both provoked much laughter while making serious points along the way, and Mathews proposed the toast – 'Ainsley, the best is yet to come'. In fact, the worst of times were already within sight.

For Ainsley it was a very happy and teary evening, soured slightly when she got home well after midnight. She had received two phone messages from an angry Susan Renouf, who complained that Andrew Peacock and his third wife were seated at the main table and she was not.[8] Susan interpreted the seating arrangements as Ainsley's commentary on the status of their friendship.

It will be recalled that, in one of the *Woman's Day* articles of 1971, Ainsley was ambivalent in her feelings about Susan Peacock. Despite speaking against him in 1968 when Gorton was thinking of promoting Peacock to the ministry, she retained her warm feelings and high regard for him over the next four decades. Yet she saw much less of Peacock in those years than she did of his first wife. Ainsley and Susan were seen together on Melbourne Cup Day or at charity functions, and Susan sometimes stayed at one of the residences Ainsley occupied in London. Ainsley supported Susan in the aftermath of her minor accident on 24 February 1995 when she drove her black BMW into the back of another car after leaving a lunch at the Catalina restaurant in Rose Bay. In turn, as described in the previous chapter, Susan made her house available to WCEI to entertain Cherie Blair and she was there for Ainsley after Kerrie died.

Given their closeness over the preceding decade it is understandable that Susan Renouf expected to be placed near her friend on the special night, particularly given the prominence assigned to her former husband. Ainsley's anger at the late-night phone calls is also understandable. It seemed to her that 'Susie' had forgotten that it was supposed to be *Ainsley's* night. Yet, for someone so sensitive and smart when it came to seating arrangements, it is surprising that Ainsley did not foresee the hurt of a long-term friend. When Ainsley wrote to 'Dear Susie' in 2013, after hearing from Glen-Marie that Renouf had been diagnosed with cancer, she began by acknowledging they had not spoken for 'some years'. Ainsley was by that time winning her own battle against cancer and felt able to identify with Susan Renouf's circumstances. She offered the warmest words of encouragement, and concluded: 'You will get through this, and you are in in my thoughts and prayers.' [9] There is no record of a reply in Ainsley's papers.

On 19 February 2007 – a year and five days after the 60th birthday party – Ainsley consulted Stuart Fowler, an experienced family lawyer who would act for her until his appointment to the Family Court later that year. Nick went to Europe on 12 March, by which time Ainsley was working in support of what became Pru Goward's successful campaign to win the seat of Goulburn for the Liberals in the State election of 24 March.[10] Nick returned on 23 April. In an affidavit Ainsley recounted a conversation which probably took place on Anzac Day. She asked: 'Did you think about our marriage as we discussed? I think providing that there is a bit of respect we can continue'. He replied: 'I don't respect you at all.' Ainsley: 'Well I don't think there is any basis for our marriage then.' Nick responded: 'That's right.'[11] While the marriage ended at that point, Nick and Ainsley continued to cohabit until she moved out on the following 28 November. At least Ainsley was able to use Nick's desire to remove her from New Beach Road – he was keen to sell – to receive $1.5m as an advance on the financial settlement. This sum enabled her to buy a basement apartment in Edgecliff which she furnished with the expected good taste and style.

Their divorce became absolute on 22 May 2009. For Ainsley, it represented another relationship failure. Blaming Nick eased the hurt and helped to maintain her sense of self-worth. For further protection, Ainsley did not make the separation public until she moved into her apartment. A few friends were aware of what had happened. The irrepressible Roderick ('Roddy') Meagher, a former Judge of Appeal of the Supreme Court of NSW and a regular guest, wrote to her after a dinner at New Beach Road to say that rarely had lamb chops 'tasted so delicious', and the 'politico-legal gossip . . . was as stimulating as ever'. But there was something 'slightly melancholic' about the entire evening because it 'would probably be the last time you will entertain me in that lovely house'.[12] The more dismal truth was that Ainsley and Nick would fight each other for five years over a financial settlement.

There were two broad issues: the size of the asset pot and who was entitled to what. The lawyers began exchanging claims and counter-claims in mid-2007 and Nick made an offer which perhaps ought to have been accepted, given that the judicial settlement of 2010 was roughly of the same order. Early in 2008 Ainsley's replacement lawyer thought that, despite a breakdown in a mediation, a settlement was still possible. Yet the parties continued the war and simply transferred their contest to one over costs after the 2010 settlement. There were substantive issues such as the condition of Nick's New Beach Road property at the commencement of co-habitation and Ainsley's contribution to its transformation. Another was the status of the US$350,000 given to Nick by an American investor: was it just a 'gift' or payment for legal services and should it be included in the asset pot? There was a long running dispute over Lesley's testamentary capacity and Ainsley's entitlement through her mother's Will to one-sixth of J. B. Nutting Investments Pty Ltd. Price Waterhouse calculated in 2005 that Ainsley's share would be worth between $447,000 and $600,000. Alongside these issues several others were fought with unrelenting endeavour over matters which appear relatively trivial. For example, the parties could not agree about who did or did not water the outdoor plants at 62 New Beach Road and who did what cooking and when and for how many. Ainsley's senior counsel, conscious that 'an enormous amount of money [had been] expended on legal costs', observed in July 2011 that this expenditure was 'an inevitable by-product of what has become the bitterness of the dispute resulting in every issue being examined in detail seldom seen.'[13]

It is not hard to explain why the parties were unrelenting. Ainsley was at a disadvantage from the start. As Nick's solicitor pointed out, her initial capital contribution amounted to just 7.7 per cent of the net asset pot. There were no children of the marriage requiring upbringing and Nick's offspring were now adults. Ainsley, therefore, had to demonstrate a material and emotional contribution to the marriage and that required her to propose and defend anything and everything that could enhance her input. As ever, when believing in the justice of her case, she saw everything in black and white and fought accordingly, driven by her conviction that Nick was hiding some of his assets in France. For his part, Nick refused to accept that Ainsley had made any substantial or sustained contribution to the marriage and refused to give away more than the barest legal requirement to someone for whom he had no regard. Very simply, they needed to fight: Nick had too much to lose and Ainsley had everything to gain.

Inevitably, there was collateral damage. Ainsley was very fond of Nick's children, Catherine ('Kate') and Simon, and believed she had a very good relationship with them. That view appeared confirmed when Kate sent an email to Ainsley for her birthday in 2008; that is, ten months after the separation. She signed off, 'LOL on your special day', and promised to send pictures of her children looking 'divine and cosy' in the jumpsuits Ainsley had sent them for Christmas.[14] Ainsley was shocked and hurt when Kate and Simon signed affidavits bearing out their father's version of events. Both children insisted that they did not need Ainsley's assistance to get close to their father, and Kate said that sometimes she got on well with Ainsley but sometimes she did not. Kate had to wait a year before her stepmother would give her a key to the renovated house at 62 New Beach Road. Ainsley did have a case: Kate and Simon tended to walk into the house and arrive unannounced in the main bedroom.

The Carson-Gotto war was marked by long pauses between frenetic exchanges. Ainsley found every hiatus frustrating, seeing

Nick's long and frequent stints in France as contrivances to wear her down in the face of rising legal bills. Yet Ainsley also contributed to the delays. She needed paid employment to pay the bills and to maintain something of her preferred lifestyle. At the end of 2009 both parties rested on medical grounds. Ainsley underwent a partial mastectomy followed by intensive radiation and daily medication. Her oncologist reported in March 2010 that the risk of relapse for someone of Ainsley's age and with similar tumour characteristics was not high.[15] Nick Carson had a radical prostatectomy in 2009 and the cancer had spread beyond the margins of the excision. He also had shoulder surgery and was restricted in movement because of his knees. Neither party, however, was prepared to change long-held habits. Ainsley continued to avoid exercise and a healthy diet and continued smoking, while both continued to drink as they had done before.

Throughout the proceedings Ainsley was at war on another front. After Fowler departed, Helen Coonan recommended a former colleague, Marcia Briggs, to replace him, and Briggs served in that role for four years. It was inherently unlikely that Ainsley – indeed, anyone – would have had a consistently happy relationship with a solicitor over such a long haul through bitter disputation. Ainsley, however, was a particularly difficult client. She moved at a faster pace than the law and the lawyers. She kept having brainstorms and became angry or frustrated when Briggs' responses were delayed or deemed inadequate. In December 2009 she asked Coonan to intervene after Briggs had ignored her proposal to use her cancer strategically 'to get this [whole matter] concluded'. Ainsley now expected to get another bill from her barrister and her solicitor for attending a hearing where nothing would be done to resolve anything. 'I just can't deal with this lack of management of my case.' Ainsley became especially worked up in September 2011 when costs were being contested. She complained that advice was not delivered to her except at the last minute or arrived in poor shape, and that Briggs had failed to do what she had been asked to do. On this occasion, Marcia Briggs responded immediately pointing out that Ainsley had failed to attend scheduled conferences and had failed to provide proper instructions or important information when asked to do so.[16]

Justice Loughnan of the Family Court handed down his orders on 19 August 2010.[17] He identified 17 areas of disputed facts between the parties. He awarded Ainsley 34.36 per cent ($2.8m) of the asset pot of $8m, of which she had already received $1.5m. As she often did during the case, Ainsley jumped in without properly examining the figures and concluded that she would only receive $750,000 and Nick would get $6m. Towards the end of his 69-page statement of reasons for his judgment, Loughnan described Ainsley as 'a person of obvious intelligence and experience' but observed that she was less effective than the husband as a witness. She was obliged to concede that several elements of her written testimony were wrong. There were many occasions where her recall of events and of documents proved to be faulty, even in the case of documents she had recently read. Unlike Nick, however, who was the better witness on matters of fact, she was more generous when making concessions.

Amid the legal proceedings Ainsley threw herself into three separate and time-consuming jobs. She applied to work for the Task Force preparing for the Asia-Pacific Economic Cooperation (APEC) meeting held in Sydney between 2 and 9 September 2007. Ainsley approached Max Moore-Wilton, the former head of the Commonwealth Department of the Prime Minister & Cabinet (PM&C), asking him to intercede on her behalf with Alan Henderson of PM&C, the head of the Task Force. She did secure an interview with Henderson and Ainsley thanked Moore-Wilton for his 'intervention'. Henderson, she wrote, was 'delightfully honest' in saying 'there was nothing he could offer me that would suit my ability and seniority, and he therefore wouldn't insult my intelligence by pretending otherwise'. Henderson did not disclose another fleeting thought: he wanted to remain in charge![18] Ainsley had thanked Henderson for his 'courtesy and honesty' and told him she would love to be involved if things changed. 'Finally – some straight talking – for which I thank you [Max] enormously.'[19]

Nearer the event some areas needed sorting out and one of Henderson's senior staff approached Ainsley who gladly accepted an invitation to work in hospitality and personnel. In her words, she encountered 'a shambles' on her arrival on 15 August 2007. Alan Henderson knew beforehand about 'her competence at the highest level' and about 'her charm and personal skills'. Ainsley not only brought those qualities to bear, 'she worked around the clock like a navvy' organising invitation cards, placing people where they should be and preparing name plates. Meeting and greeting arrivals at the Opera House was 'bread and butter' to her as she chatted easily with heads of government. There was no pecking order among the staff. Ainsley saw herself as part of the team, even on the few occasions when she felt obliged to assume control because younger and inexperienced staff got into difficulties. Henderson's own job was never under threat.[20]

Ainsley secured further paid employment at the end of 2007 when she worked for Malcolm Turnbull, the Minister for the Environment and Water Resources in the Howard Government, who was recontesting his seat of Wentworth. She worked hard and for long hours. Although the Coalition lost office, Turnbull easily retained the seat and just failed to win the Liberal Party leadership afterwards. Ainsley sought a position as his electorate officer and, on paper, looked unbeatable.[21] She ticked every conceivable box, and the unspoken ones of loyalty and total commitment. The job went to someone else. At a loss to explain her rejection, Ainsley recalled an earlier assessment she had received from an employment agency: in addition to the age factor she had 'unique qualifications' which disqualified her. Perhaps, however, her main problem was her reputation for being abrupt. Ainsley tended to be critical of incompetent or lazy fellow workers but would have been excellent in dealing with the public.

Ainsley found herself in serious financial difficulties in mid-2008. Nick ceased paying her $2500 a month in August of that year, her legal bills were mounting and applications for employment never reached the interview stage. Fortunately, Helen Coonan stepped in. Senator Coonan had served in the Howard Cabinet as Minister for Communications, Information Technology and the Arts (2004-07). After the Coalition lost office, she became Shadow Minister for Human Affairs and Manager of Opposition Business in the Senate and represented Malcolm Turnbull, the Shadow Treasurer, in the Senate. Coonan had a vacant position in her private office after Peta Credlin, her Chief of Staff, joined Brendan Nelson's office when he became Leader of the Opposition. Coonan offered the job to Ainsley who accepted it immediately.

At the age of 62, and 40 years after taking an appointment as Gorton's PPS, Ainsley became Coonan's Chief of Staff. Described by Michelle Grattan as 'once a cover girl of national politics' and 'to put it bluntly, media unfriendly',[22] Ainsley returned to a very different Parliament from the one she had left in 1972. If, for Ainsley, it was like 'stepping into an old pair of slippers',[23] she stood out and apart from most staffers as one of the oldest advisers. Ainsley also had to adjust to different portfolios and inform herself on unrelated areas. When Turnbull ousted Nelson from the Party leadership in September 2008, he moved Coonan to Foreign Affairs but then, with the need to shift the misfiring Julie Bishop out of the shadow Treasury portfolio, Coonan vacated Foreign Affairs and took over Finance, Competition Policy and Deregulation.

Very few politicians and staffers knew who Ainsley was or knew her history. Ainsley could not, therefore, expect deference. More importantly, she had entered a world where her imperious and brusque manner of the Gorton years was simply unwelcome and not tolerated. Ainsley had many run-ins with Coonan's other staff. One had to be persuaded not to pursue a harassment case, others simply preferred not to be in the same room. Ainsley had high expectations of what staff could and should do and, while she could meet her own standards, many staff did not. Unfortunately, the young woman who did meet her standards and could be considered 'AG trained' left for another career. Ainsley did not hold back when in attack mode. She made notes of a meeting with her boss in October 2008 after Coonan had taken over the Foreign Affairs portfolio. It is easy to detect Ainsley's contribution to the decisions taken. One staff member was to stop 'whingeing and whining', another needed 'a reality check' on both a capability and personal level and all staff needed to understand that things will now be 'DIFFERENT'. If they did not apply themselves, accept the authority of the Chief of Staff and meet deadlines, 'they will be out'.[24] Yet Ainsley could still charm staffers working in other offices. Nathan Winn was a clerk in the office of the Chief Opposition Whip. He wrote to Ainsley on 29 August 2011 confessing that he felt both excited and nervous at the prospect of meeting 'an icon of the party'. Winn said it was 'a privilege' to have worked with her and thanked her for being 'a great colleague'.[25]

Helen Coonan had a high regard for Ainsley. Like John Gorton, she appreciated her total commitment, efficiency and loyalty. Ainsley was prepared to work crippling hours without complaint and endure the return travel between Sydney and Canberra and a life in rental accommodation in the national capital. While Ainsley's oncologist thought in March 2010 that the risk of a relapse was not high, she had warned her to avoid stressful jobs, and especially those involving long hours.[26] Ainsley continued working long hours in a stressful occupation. It was more than just loyalty to a job and to a friend. Coonan recognised that Ainsley 'was entranced by ideas, loved politics, bled "Blue" . . . and to her dying day was interested in the political space'.

Ainsley, in turn, held Helen in the highest regard but, if she felt her shadow minister needed correction, said so. In August 2009 Ainsley told her boss 'it was not a good look' for the Shadow Minister of Finance to be seen on television leaving the Chamber before another Liberal Senator tabled a statement on her behalf. Nor could Ainsley understand why Helen did not attend the Joint Party Senate meeting at 6.30 pm or inform the Whips' office she was departing for the evening at 7.00 pm.[27] Ainsley was forever coming up with suggestions, some edged with criticism directed at the wider front bench. For example, early in 2009 she prepared a ten-point plan for improving collaboration between the three principal Coalition shadows handling economic policy, partly to ensure 'we . . . stop doing things several times over, and do them only once, and well'.[28]

She knew when taking the job with Coonan that it would not

last. Helen had been re-elected to the Senate in 2007 with the No 1 spot on the Coalition ticket for NSW but did not want to sit on the Opposition benches for six years. It would be unconscionable to resign immediately upon moving into Opposition. Her opportunity to ease into an honourable departure arrived when Abbot replaced Turnbull in December 2009. She could begin by leaving the Front Bench and eventually resigned in August 2011, nearly two-thirds of the way into her elected term. Ainsley was able to stay on salary until the following November when Arthur Sinodinos filled the casual vacancy created by Coonan's retirement. Ainsley kept applying for other jobs, looking particularly for employment with the newly-elected Liberal Government of NSW. She was always rejected without securing an interview.

In 2011 Ainsley was still engaged in a legal battle over costs. She had already spent nearly half a million dollars one way or another in pursuit of what she viewed as justice and her entitlement. Yet, as she believed Nick's actions and inaction had increased the costs of litigation, so Nick was convinced that his more substantial costs had escalated because of her obstinacy and failures to act reasonably and quickly. He came up with an idea to bring everything to a close. If Ainsley would agree that they each should pay their own costs, and she made a provision in her Will to provide Kate and Simon with equal parts of $100,000, he would agree to a settlement. Ainsley had no intention of agreeing to anything which directly benefitted Nick's children. She remained hurt by their support for Nick. The details of the final settlement are not available, but Ainsley continued to express dissatisfaction.

At least, with the help of her astute accountant, Sabina Donnelly, her financial situation was reasonably secure. Divorced and having beaten cancer, Ainsley could look forward to happier years ahead.

[1]   Private information.

[2]   Interview: AG, 7 June 2017.

[3]   Gotto Papers, MS Acc15.126, Box 19.

[4]   AG to Diana Downe, 27 January 2006, Kerrie Gotto Elsaesser, Gotto Papers, MS Acc07/127, Box 2.

[5]   Ben Gotto Smith to AG, 9 September 1992, Gotto Papers, MS 9895/1/7.

[6]   See Sid Gotto to Lesley Gotto Nutting, 29 September 1983 for Ainsley's disapproval of her sister, LGN Correspondence 1980s, Gotto Papers, MS Acc15.126, Box 9.

[7]   Kerrie Elsaesser Gotto to Brook Broughton, 20 May 1999, Gotto Papers, Acc07.127, Box 2.

[8]   AG: personal communication, February 2006.

[9]   AG to Susan Renouf, 4 February 2013, Gotto Papers, MS Acc13.206, Box 5.

[10] The pair had first met when Goward was working on the TV series, *The Liberals*, in 1994. Ainsley agreed to co-operate to ensure an 'accurate recording' of Gorton's prime ministership, which meant alerting Goward to Fraser's tendency 'to deal lightly with the truth'. See AG to Tom Hughes, 18 April 1994, Gotto Papers, MS 9895/5/5.

[11] Gotto Papers, MS Acc15.126, Box 14. There is a slightly different version in Box 16, *ibid.*

[12] 2007, Gotto Papers, MS Acc10/050, Box 1. Meagher, a Judge of Appeal of the NSW Supreme Court, had been a regular guest, loved for his conversation and political incorrectness. For Meagher, see Dyson Heydon's obituary in *Bar News*, Winter 2011, pp. 136-41.

[13] C. M. Simpson SC in Gotto Papers, MS Acc15.126, Box 16.

[14] *Ibid.*, Box 19.

[15] See the affidavit dated 10 March 2010, *ibid.*, Box 16.

[16] This correspondence will be found in *ibid.*, Box 18.

[17] *Ibid.*, Box 17.

[18] Interview: Henderson, 18 December 2017.

[19] 2007 File, Gotto Papers, MS Acc10/050, Box 1.

[20] The above two paragraphs draw on *ibid.*; interviews: AG, 12 November 2017 and Henderson, 18 December 2017.

[21] Copy in the author's possession.

[22] *Age*, 29 May 2008.

[23] Interview: Helen Coonan, 10 May 2018.

[24] Notes of Discussion HLC/AG, 3 October 2008, 2008 file, Gotto Papers, MS Acc13.206, Box 2.

25 Nathan Winn to Ainsley Gotto, 29 August 2011, 2011 file, *ibid.*, Box 3.

26 See the affidavit dated 10 March 2010, Gotto Papers, MS Acc15.126, Box 16.

27 Memo from Ainsley Gotto to Senator Coonan, 11 August 2009, 2009 file, Gotto Papers, MS Acc13.206, Box 2.

28 Memo from AG to Senator Coonan, 23 February 2009, *ibid.*

Conclusion

'we are – ultimately – alone.
Whether we like it or not.'

In 2011 Ainsley reinstated her half of what she labelled 'the traditional Gotto-Carson Christmas drinks' and impressed guests in her new apartment with the innovation of singing carols. Ainsley continued her lifetime habit of living well and close to the edge of her financial resources. Her diaries record travel abroad, lunches and dinners at good restaurants and at home, visits to country races, attendance at weddings, a dinner at Government House in Sydney and visits to the theatre, galleries and the Opera House. Ainsley continued to work for Pru Goward and Malcolm Turnbull and was very active in supporting Liberal candidates in local government, and especially Mary-Lou Jarvis who won a seat on the Woollahra Council and the presidency of the Women's Council of the Liberal Party's NSW Division. Ainsley's telephone rang during almost every one of my interviews with her in 2017 with callers requesting advice on Liberal Party matters, further evidence of what John Howard called 'a great networker' in action.[1]

Ainsley continued to nurse a grievance against Nick, inspired by her conviction that he had cheated her over the size of the asset pool, a conviction reinforced when told he was boasting about hiding some of his funds abroad. Friends were dumbfounded when Ainsley visited Nick in hospital in 2016 and took such a close interest in advising and helping him through his dying months. Was this evidence of the kind of guilt which drove her to frenetic activity in producing an order of service for Kerrie's funeral? Ainsley spent time and money trying to prove against all the evidence that the authorities caused Debbie's death in 1972 by allowing a tree to fall across the Hume Highway. Each of these events, like the death of her father in 1992, left her feeling the need to compensate for things done or not done in the past.

Ainsley never could understand her mother's commitment to Christian Science and shrugged her shoulders on receiving written homilies and advice to read tracts about 'Life'. Ainsley was also very critical of what she believed was her mother's neglect of James Nutting in his final years. Nevertheless, she made trips to Queensland during and after her legal battles with Nick to make sure that 'Mummy' was properly looked after in care. Lesley died on 5 October 2017 and Ainsley, though weakened by her illness, went to Brisbane for the funeral.[2]

Ainsley started to experience back pains in 2015 which became more acute in the following year. In July 2016 she was found to have an unrelated form of lung cancer, but the return of her more serious breast cancer was undiagnosed for some months. Ainsley was told early in 2017 that she had between three and six months to live but, with the help of chemotherapy, an improvement in her pain management – thanks to Helen Coonan's intervention – and a characteristic refusal to accept defeat, she survived into the following year. Ainsley was admitted to the Sacred Heart Health Service and St Vincent's private hospital but was much happier when Coonan secured her admission to the Wolper Jewish Hospital, Woollahra, located two blocks away from Ainsley's apartment in Edgecliff Road. The few who knew of Ainsley's illness ensured that her room was regularly re-stocked with flowers of the finest beauty and fragrance.

Pain-free, Ainsley drifted into an unconscious state where she remained for more than a week before her death on Sunday 25 February 2018, eleven days after her 72nd birthday. Kerrie's three children and selected close friends attended a private cremation on the morning of 5 March. In the afternoon, John Howard and Tom Hughes delivered eulogies at the memorial service in All Saints' Anglican Church, Woollahra. Many of the mourners went to the wake which was held in the Royal Sydney Golf Club where Ainsley had celebrated her 50th and 60th birthdays. On the instructions of the executors of the estate – Helen Coonan and Nicholas Eddy, a Sydney solicitor – Ainsley's belongings were divided into 262 lots, which included the June Mendoza portrait, a wardrobe of furs, hats and Yves Saint Laurent handbags and six very good bottles of shiraz, all auctioned online. Ainsley's apartment was sold in July 2018 for $1.587m. Roman, Ben's son, was a principal beneficiary of the Will.

A few who attended the memorial service had direct contact with Ainsley at the time she was John Gorton's PPS. Two flew in from Melbourne: Robin Gorton, the youngest of the Gorton children, and Race Mathews who, of all the men in Ainsley's life, remained the truest of friends and the closest of confidants. Looking around the assembled congregation it seemed that most had not known the Ainsley of the Gorton years in government.

Therein lay a sad part of her life. She had climbed the highest whilst very young. So many who mourned her death did not know her at the time when she 'made a difference'.

What kind of difference did she make? Speaking at her 60th birthday celebrations, Race Mathews said that Ainsley 'punctured, albeit sadly failed to shatter, the glass ceiling of the day'.[3] She should certainly be remembered for piercing the ceiling long before its survival was challenged but she did so whilst remaining almost wilfully oblivious of its existence. Her rejection of Women's Liberation probably disqualifies Ainsley for recognition as a feminist icon, especially given her explicit disavowal of any role as a trail-blazer. The fact remains that she registered two firsts in what had been, and remained for some time, an exclusive male world: she was the first female PPS and the first female political staffer of an Australian Prime Minister.

She confronted two prejudices in 1968 – age and gender – and Dudley Erwin found one word to fuse them: Ainsley was a 'girl', too young to be given responsibilities and, as a female, she would and should marry, have children and be out of the paid work force before she turned 30. Erwin focused on what a 'girl' could not and should not do. Peter Howson's complained that this 'girl' was doing what she should not do and, worse still, was doing it effectively. Ainsley had not only registered two firsts; she advanced the transformation of the position of PPS into one more akin to that of a chief of staff, and she demonstrated that a young woman with the right attitudes and the willingness to work could do the job. Germaine Greer was right: Ainsley was 'liberated' solely because of her appointment and because her boss who made the appointment had a progressive instinct.

Ainsley was not wrong: her 'performance' in the job, not a law requiring equality or diversity, established and confirmed her right to be there. Unfortunately, Ainsley was seduced into thinking that what she did and what she gained between 1968 and 1971 gave her an unbeatable reference; she needed to acquire some solid and unbeatable qualifications and was never prepared to do so.

Ainsley was no Peta Credlin. Tony Eggleton concluded that 'Credlin's role as chief of staff, and the extent of her influence, put Ainsley Gotto in the shade'.[4] Ainsley agreed with this assessment. In any case, she did not care for Credlin's approach, demeanour or behaviour, even though at times Ainsley had seemed to be heading in that direction. It suited her obsession with privacy to be *in* the shade as well as being shaded. It also suited her to work for and with a Prime Minister who did not allow himself to be mothered. No one joked about her being 'the real Prime Minister' or seriously considered her a factor in Gorton's loss of office. What she could claim was that for three years she occupied, as Rosemary Munday put it and this time without exaggeration, 'the front seat of the nation's most strategic administrative post'.[5] In this role Ainsley was indispensable, contributing to the day-to-day and overall management of government by keeping Gorton focused, by protecting him from intrusions and distractions and by being a frank and loyal confidant in an atmosphere where disloyalty and duplicity had become commonplace.

For all that many things went wrong during her 'after-life', Ainsley would not have agreed with John Howard and Tom Hughes who told me that she seemed to have led an unhappy life. There was so much she enjoyed: entertaining guests at lunch and dinner, listening to music, reading fine literature, travelling, collecting beautiful *objects-d'art*, re-designing her living space, following cricket, every football code and especially the Swans in the Australian Football League, playing with the children of her friends, being part of a lively conversation with people who had done something special with their lives, introducing friends to friends and subsequently attending their weddings and giving thoughtful and very welcome gifts to those she loved and cared about. There were so many moments of satisfaction and reassurance, like reading the letter from the adored Roddy Meagher in 1995 recounting his first meeting with John Gorton over lunch at 62 New Beach Road: 'How different from the caricatures the newspapers depict! Intelligent, sympathetic, gentle, charming. It was a great honour to be there.'

Ainsley courted disappointment. As a friend she gave a lot to others but could test friendship as an unrestrained critic of things she saw or felt were not quite right. Women were more likely to experience this side of Ainsley, and some blamed alcohol and illness for a latter-day excess of forthrightness and forgetfulness. Ainsley was easy to like but perhaps made herself harder to be loved over the long haul. Race Mathews discovered in 1970 that she 'had never been wrapped in love'. Her upbringing, her determined privacy and what many found to be a surprising shyness made it difficult to get close to her, and may explain why, as relationships failed and some friendships fractured, Ainsley could once advise her father that 'we are – ultimately – alone. Whether we like it or not.'[6]

Ainsley remained a fighter and within days of being floored by a setback would rise and attempt something different, just as she never allowed a long final illness to conquer her will to live.

[1]   Interview: Howard, 17 April 2018.

[2]   For Lesley's obituary, see *Courier Mail*, 31 October 2017.

[3]   Copy in the author's possession.

[4]   Savva, *Road to Ruin*, p. 320.

[5]   Melbourne *Herald*, 26 September 1970.

[6]   AG to Sid Gotto. 2 November 1990, Personal, Gotto Papers, MS Acc07/127, Box 3.

Select Bibliography

Manuscripts

Personal Papers held in the NLA
Erwin, Dudley
Cramer, Sir John
Gorton, Sir John
Gotto, Ainsley
Howson, Peter
Hughes, Tom
Reid, Alan
St John, Edward
Wheeler, Sir Frederick

Personal Papers held in the NAA
Bunting, Sir John
Eggleton, Tony
Gorton, Sir John
Wheeler, Sir Frederick

Interviews: NLA
Bailey, Peter
Cameron, Clyde and Gorton, Sir John
Erwin, Dudley
Fairbairn, Sir David
Fitchett, Ian
Jessop, Don
McLeay, John
Whitrod, Raymond

Magazines and Newspapers
Age
Australian
Australian Financial Review
Business Queensland
Business Review
Canberra Times
Courier-Mail (Brisbane)
Daily Express (UK)
Daily Mail (UK)
Daily Mirror
Daily Telegraph (Sydney)
Daily Telegraph (UK)
Gold Coast Bulletin

Herald (Melbourne)
Independent Business Queensland
Muse
National Times
Pix/People
Prime Time
Private Eye (UK)
Sun (Melbourne)
Sun (Sydney)
Sunday Australian
Sunday Mirror
Sunday Telegraph
Sun-Herald
Sydney Morning Herald
Times (London)
Truth (Melbourne)
Woman's Day
Women's Weekly

Political Memoirs and Diaries

Brown, Neil, *On the Other Hand . . .: Sketches and Reflections from Politica Life*, Poplar Press, Woden, 1993.

Cameron, Clyde, *The Cameron Diaries*, Allen & Unwin, North Sydney, 1990.

Chipp, Don and Larkin, John, *Don Chipp: The Third Man*, Rigby Limited, Adelaide,1978.

Cramer, Sir John, *Pioneers, Politics and People: A Political Memoir*, Allen & Unwin, North Sydney, 1989.

Downer, Alexander, *Six Prime Ministers*, Hill of Content, Melbourne, 1982.

Fraser, Malcolm and Simons, Margaret, *Malcolm Fraser: The Political Memoirs*, Miegunyah Press, Carlton, 2010.

Hasluck, Paul, *Light that Time has Made*, National Library of Australia, Canberra, 1995.

Hasluck, Paul, *The Chance of Politics*, ed. by Nicholas Hasluck, Text Publishing, Melbourne, 1997.

Howson, Peter, *The Life of Politics*, ed. by Don Aitkin, Viking Press, Ringwood, 1984.

Killen, Sir James, *Killen: Inside Australian Politics*, Mandarin, Port Melbourne, 1989.

Snedden, Billy Mackie and Schedvin, M. Bernie, *Billy Snedden: An Unlikely Liberal*, Macmillan, South Melbourne, 1990.

St John, Edward, *A Time To Speak*, Sun Books, Melbourne, 1969.

Other Books

Ayres, Philip, *Malcolm Fraser: A Biography*, William Heinemann Australia, Richmond, 1987.

Curran, James, *Unholy Fury: Whitlam and Nixon at War*, Melbourne University Press, Carlton, 2015.

Duthie, Gil, *I had 50,000 Bosses: Memoirs of a Labor Backbencher 1946-1975*, Angus & Robertson, Sydney, 1984.

Edgeworth, Anne, *The Cost of Jazz Garters: A history of the Canberra Repertory Society 1932-1982*, Canberra Repertory Society, Kingston, 1992.

Fewster, Alan, *Three duties & Talleyrand's dictum: portrait of a working diplomat*, Australian Scholarly Publishing, North Melbourne, 2018.

Fitzgerald, Ross and Holt, Stephen, *Alan "The Red Fox" Reid: Pressman Par Excellence*, New South, Sydney, 2010.

Freudenberg, Graham, *A Certain Grandeur: Gough Whitlam in Politics*, Macmillan, South Melbourne, 1977.

Gotto, Brian, *Renfrew: A Short Biography of Captain Renfrew Gotto CBE DSO*, privately published, Haslingfield, 2009.

Grattan, Michelle, *Australian Prime Ministers*, New Holland Publishers, Sydney, 2000.

Hancock, Ian, *John Gorton: He Did It His Way*, Hodder, Sydney, 2002.

Hocking, Jenny, *Gough Whitlam: A Moment in History*, vol 1, The Miegunyah Press, Carlton, 2008.

Horne, Donald, *Time of Hope: Australia 1966-72*, Angus & Robertson, Sydney, 1980.

Hughes, Colin A., *A Handbook of Australian Government and Politics 1964-1974*, Australian National University Press, Canberra, 1977.

Larkin, John (ed.), *Chipp*, Methuen Hayes, North Ryde, 1987.

Moore, Leslie, *Not Like Ghosts at Cockrow: An Australian Family Story 1849-1998*, privately published, Canberra, 1998.

Mullins, Patrick, *Tiberius with a Telephone: The life and stories of William McMahon*, Scribe, Melbourne, 2018.

Parker, Pauline, *The Making of Women: A History of Mac. Robertson Girls' High School*, Australian Scholarly Publishing, North Melbourne, 2006.

Purcell, Frank *The Prison on the Bay: The Story of the Victorian Training Ship John Murray*, Frank Purcell, Frankston, 1997.

Reid, Alan, *The Power Struggle*, Shakespeare Head, Sydney, 1969.

------- *The Gorton Experiment*, Shakespeare Head, Sydney, 1971.

Savva, Niki, *The Road to Ruin*, Scribe, Melbourne, 2017.

Teese, Richard, *For the Common Weal: the Public High Schools in Victoria, 1910-2010*, Australian Scholarly Publishing Ltd, North Melbourne, 2014.

Woolcott, Richard, *The Hot Seat: Reflections on Diplomacy from Stalin's Death to the Bali Bombings*, HarperCollins, Sydney, 2003.

Reference Works

ABC TV Series: The Liberals, 1994

Australian Dictionary of Biography

Australian Journal of Politics and History

Individual Service Records: NAA

Reserve Bank of Australia Inflation Calculator

INDEX

www.ingramcontent.com/pod-product-compliance
Lightning Source LLC
Chambersburg PA
CBHW060837100426

42814CB00016B/408/J